IMPORT/EXPORT

Other Books by Carl Nelson

Nonfiction

Your Own Import-Export Business: Winning the Trade Game

Global Success: International Business Tactics of the 1990s

Managing Globally: A Complete Guide to Competing Worldwide

Protocol for Profit: A Manager's Guide to Competing Worldwide

International Business: A Manager's Guide to Strategy in the Age of Globalism

Exporting: A Manager's Guide to World Markets

Fiction

The Advisor (Cô-vân)   This Vietnam War thriller won the Southern California Writers Conference's award for best fiction.

Secret Players   A historical saga that won the San Diego Book Awards Association prize for best thriller of 2003.

Madam President and the Admiral   Finalist 2008 National Best Book Award and nominated for Pulitzer.

IMPORT/EXPORT

How to Take Your Business Across Borders

Fourth Edition

Dr. Carl A. Nelson

New York   Chicago   San Francisco   Lisbon
London   Madrid   Mexico City   Milan   New Delhi
San Juan   Seoul   Singapore   Sydney   Toronto

1 2 3 4 5 6 7 8 9 0   FGR/FGR   0 1 5 4 3 2 1 0 9 8

ISBN: 978-0-07-148255-4
MHID: 0-07-148255-5

This publication is designed to provide accurate and authoritative information in regard to the subject matter covered. It is sold with the understanding that neither the author nor the publisher is engaged in rendering legal, accounting, futures/securities trading, or other professional service. If legal advice or other expert assistance is required, the services of a competent professional person should be sought.

—*From a Declaration of Principles jointly adopted by a Committee of the American Bar Association and a Committee of Publishers*

McGraw-Hill books are available at special quantity discounts to use as premiums and sales promotions, or for use in corporate training programs. To contact a representative, please visit the Contact Us pages at www.mhprofessional.com.

This book is printed on acid-free paper.

This fourth edition is dedicated to my daughter Monica who helped me bring this book to birth way back in 1987 and watched as it took a life of its own and remained a bestseller for more than two decades.

CONTENTS

LIST OF TABLES

LIST OF FIGURES

FOREWORD

Welcome to the world of international commerce. It began in a big way with the Phoenicians over 3,000 years ago and has been a prime mover in the development of civilization ever since.

It is a long, continuous story of people trading products unique to their regions for the products unique to other regions. For the early traders, this was often arduous work involving long and treacherous sea voyages and overland passages. As trade volumes and competition grew, strong pressures developed to produce the best product at the best price, to market these products more effectively, and to deliver them more efficiently and expeditiously. There was also pressure to improve accounting and communication systems to facilitate trade. For example, it was the Phoenicians who were responsible for the alphabet we use today. To simplify their business transactions, they replaced the cuneiform alphabet's 550 characters with a 22-letter system, which was further altered by the Greeks and Romans.

Over the centuries, commercial goals have spurred advances in a wide range of human pursuits, including transportation, communication, information technology, manufacturing, research, medical care, insurance, and entertainment, among others. The same commercial goals have created a need to travel to distant lands, learn other languages, and deal with other cultures. While the business ambitions of individual nations or regions led to conflicts at times, the overall effect of global trade has been to promote business growth and prosperity. In fact, I believe strongly that the continuous expansion of world trade to include the impoverished regions of the world is the surest path to world peace. This is because constructive trade leads to economic development, understanding, and trust, which are essential ingredients for peace.

To be sure, the international trade landscape has changed dramatically since the early days, and this is especially true of the last decade. Pulitzer Prize-winner Thomas Friedman has famously said, "The world is flat." He, of course, refers to the ability of nations previously isolated by vast distances to now compete successfully with developed countries through improved and low-cost communications and other technologies.

But one thing has not changed—and it will never change. Success in world trade will go to those individuals who are best prepared for it, including having an understanding of products, services, markets, suppliers, distribution, documentation, regulations, financial tools, and other aspects of world trade too numerous to mention.

In reading this book, you have made a good start to acquire the knowledge you will need to be successful. I hope it will lead to a rewarding career for you, and I wish you every success in this and all your future endeavors.

Guy F. Tozzoli
President
World Trade Centers Association

ACKNOWLEDGMENTS

I will always be deeply indebted to my daughter Monica Askari who helped me in the earliest stages to develop this successful book. Then there are those who have given of their precious time to update the four editions. These include Julie Osman of the Export Assistance Center, U.S. Department of Commerce, San Diego, California, for her expert advice on the chapter about exporting from the United States.

I am grateful for the research Helen Guvichy provided to update this fourth edition as well as that of my wife Dr. Dolores Hansen Nelson, who kept me on track. Last but not least, I'm thankful to McGraw-Hill associate editor Melissa Bonventre's guidance in preparing this new edition.

INTRODUCTION

Advances in technology have brought a changing world, one that many casually refer to as globalization. For instance, in the mid-1800s it took about a year to sail around the world. Now we fly it in a day, send instant e-mails anywhere, and watch with billions of others, the final match of the World Cup. But globalization is not new. It's just that the revolutionary changes of the twentieth century, particularly in communications, have brought about a rapid economic interdependence of countries worldwide and increasing volumes and varieties of cross-border transactions in goods and services. This includes free international financial flows, as well as rapid and widespread diffusion of technology. Human capital also flows freely, that is, the work either goes to the labor or the labor goes to the work. New words like *integration*, *outsourcing*, and *insourcing* are part of our everyday vocabulary.

We trade German cars, Colombian coffee, Chinese clothing, Egyptian cotton, and Indian software. As a result, families can purchase a wide range of goods and services at very competitive prices.

Globalization has brought us the World Trade Organization (WTO), the euro, and North American Free Trade Agreement (NAFTA). Billions of dollars are exchanged daily around the globe by electronic means at virtually no cost.

Because globalization spreads everything, it has become market theory at its very best and has made passé the neoclassical economic models, which were based on the impeded flow of goods and services between economic jurisdictions. Theoretical ideas like "comparative advantage" and "general equilibrium" no longer apply.

During the course of the transition we have learned that countries engaged in globalization have prospered—goods, capital, and labor flow remarkably freely among nations, and inequality among them has fallen.

Since World War II, globalization has brought a need for new levels in trade negotiations. Originally under the auspices of General Agreement on Tariffs and Trade (GATT), and more recently by the World Trade Organization (WTO) and the World Customs Organization (WCO), rounds of mediating trade disputes and tariffs have made significant contributions to the movement of goods and services.

World exports of goods and services grew from less than $100 million shortly after World War II to well over $11 trillion today. Gross global product (GGP) will rise from less than $5 trillion in 1970 to as much as $100 trillion by the mid-21st century, and international trade could be as much as $40 trillion, both approaching previously unthinkable levels. Figure I.1 shows the indisputable evidence of world trade expansion.

The result of this expansion will spawn a century even more prosperous than the previous because free and open international trade is the proven engine of economic development, and everyone is going to be a part of it!

The purpose of this fourth edition of *Import/Export: How to Take Your Business Across Borders* is to open the mysteries of international trade to everyone so that you too can be part of the exciting changes brought about by globalization.

The success of this book, which has continued in popularity as the bestselling, most popular book for its purpose,* is because it continues to be vibrant and relevant. From its many printings over the 20-year period it has been in print, thousands of people have read it and put it to work.

We (McGraw-Hill and the author) have stayed with a practical book that explains the basics of the international trade transaction from A to Z in terms anyone can understand, yet with each edition we have brought the book to the cutting edge of the times.

---

*Based on Amazon.com and Barnes and Noble.com sales statistics.

Figure I.1 World Exports of Merchandise, Goods, and Services

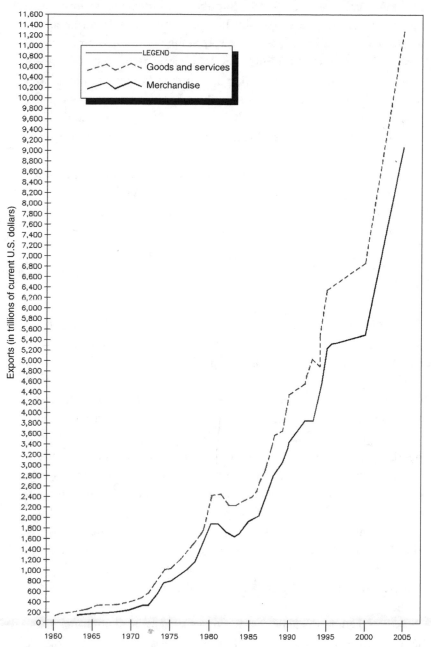

Source: World Bank

This new edition expands and updates the basic material and includes new information such as how to do online retailing, and what insourcing and outsourcing are all about. It explains how to take advantage of what's new on the Internet (Chapter 4: Selling with E-commerce) and how to do business in the integrated Americas (Chapter 10), as well as in the changed Europe (Chapter 11) and the growing opportunities in Africa (Chapter 12). Also you will find new chapters about doing business in China and India (Chapter 13), and the Middle East (Chapter 14). Each deals with the realities of the changing growth of these nations.

The book deals with every aspect of exporting and importing, citing helpful details, examples, and success stories. Its overall message is that doing business across national borders is not difficult and can be *very profitable*.

The Book's Approach

From the beginning, the approach was to write a professional how-to book that offers a small amount of theory with large portions of practical information in a tight, logical format that shows the details of the import/export *transaction*.

Unlike any previous book on international trade, this book presents the basics in terms of comparing and contrasting import and export. Other books on this subject separate importing from exporting, implying that the two are distinctly different. In fact, the mechanics of importing and exporting are basically the same. Importing is the mirror image (commonality) of exporting. For example, terminology and communication for exporting and for importing across borders are identical.

The commonalities of *import/export* are not country specific; that is, they work in any country and, therefore, the book has international appeal. Only two chapters (Chapters 7 and 8) are specific to the United States, and even those chapters are generic in the sense that the process is the same for all nations.

Nothing about the approach to international trade has changed, and its basic treatment is as applicable today as it was when the book was first written. The focus is on the profitable business, with the underlying concept that it is not enough to understand just exporting or importing. To be a successful trader, you must grasp your trading partner's problems. Therefore, you must understand both.

Who Is the Book For?

Import/Export: How to Take Your Business Across Borders is for the owner of a small manufacturing or service firm, the person in search of a second career, or the entrepreneur who wants to know how to get into this $11 trillion worldwide market. It is particularly important to women and minority-owned businesses, which have grown at higher rates than the national averages. The audience for this book will continue to be managers of firms who wish to expand internationally as well as students and entrepreneurs who see opportunity in the expanding global marketplace. It is especially valuable for the small- and medium-sized manufacturing and service firms that lack practical, hands-on experience and wish to learn the transaction mechanics of importing and exporting. A growing number of manufacturing and service companies worldwide are involved in international trade, yet as globalism sweeps across the land, to survive more must get into the game.

Because this book is written by an American does not mean that it is just for Americans. In every country of the world there are businesses that make things and sell them across borders. The process they use, except for a few differences in national rules and home country language, is exactly the same. This book describes that process and is a valuable tool for anyone in the world who wishes to profit from global trade.

Many people are intrigued by the thought and challenge of starting their own profitable business to market their own products, as well as those of others, across international borders. They see untapped markets and profits and want to know how to get into the growing business of international trade. An import/export business offers great opportunity to travel and enjoy the prestige of working with clients all over the world.

Many students (even those who have advanced degrees in business) who wish to enter and pursue a career in one or more phases of international trade read this book to learn the practical application of their theoretical work. Many teachers and professors have found it suitable as a classroom text that gives perspective and helps learners gain an appreciation of the total process and how their future fits into the big import/export picture.

Today there is more opportunity and freedom for women in world business than at any other time. In the United States there are more than 12 million women-owned businesses—30 percent of all smaller firms—grossing more than $950 billion in 2002, up by 22 percent since 1997. The rate of growth for women-owned businesses was 20 percent, while minority-owned businesses grew by 67 percent. As the total number has increased, so proportionately have those involved in international trade.

For new citizens of any country, many of the expected obstacles turn into advantages. For instance, when doing business in most of Africa it is an advantage to be a person of color. Most newcomers to any country have the advantage of speaking and understanding another language and culture. Getting off the ground in international trade is often easier because contacts are already in place.

What's in the Book?

This book is organized in an easy-to-understand anecdotal style that will appeal to everyone from an entrepreneur to a decision-making executive.

Import/Export: How to Take Your Business Across Borders does the following:

- Explains the import/export transaction in an entertaining way.
- Reveals the fundamentals of importing and exporting in terms of their similarities and differences.
- Shows through anecdotes and specific cases how to put these fundamentals to work to earn big untapped profits.

- Teaches readers how to use the Internet to increase sales.
- Explains how to shop the world for the lowest manufacturing costs.
- Shows readers how to do business in the globalized world.
- Explains the Homeland Security department's place in trade.

The Commonalities

This book cites sixteen concepts common to both import and export: six are presented in Chapter 3, six in Chapter 4, and four in Chapter 5.

Each fundamental concept is presented in this order to facilitate your understanding and because it is the order in which real-world transactions generally happen. Please don't mistakenly assume that the order represents a hierarchy of importance or that each concept can truly stand alone. Each fundamental is integrated with the other concepts in the process of international trade and each is equally necessary. Successful importers and/or exporters grasp the importance of the concepts and put them to work by setting up a firm as explained in Chapter 6.

The Differences

Some aspects of importing and exporting differ or are country specific. For example, "controls," except for import quotas, apply only to exporting, whereas tariffs (duties) relate only to importing. These distinguishing features of exporting and importing are offered in Chapters 6 and 7, respectively. This treatment should clarify any differences and enable you to understand them easily.

Doing Business

This edition has been organized with a new part, "Doing Business in the Globalized World," which explains how to conduct business in various nations and regions. For instance, Chapter 9 explains how to take advantage of world trade centers in most of the world's major cities. Because regionalism is a concept whose day has come, Chapter 10 is about doing business in integrated economies such as the Americas with their expanded NAFTA. Chapter 11 explains the basics of how to do business in the expanding single market of the European Union. And, of course, the book would be incomplete if it did not include a discussion of how to do business in Africa (Chapter 12), and China and India (Chapter 13).

What's New About This Edition?

This edition explains the import/export transaction process in many new ways and includes other new or improved information, such as:

- Extensive references to Internet sources and addresses
- An improved chapter about how to sell using E-commerce
- An improved part about doing business in the globalized world
- An updated chapter about world trade centers
- New information on product standards
- New information on integrated economies like NAFTA and the European Union
- Tricks of using letters of credit
- An updated chapter about how to do business in the nations of Africa
- An explanation of Homeland Security's place in international trade
- New guidance on how to use an online storefront

How to Use the Book

Whether you enter international trade through imports or through exports, you should understand the basics of both. Therefore, the best way to use this book is to first master the concepts presented in

Chapters 2 through 5. But it is unlikely that you will be ready to begin trading until you organize your business to do so. Therefore, Chapter 6 shows you how to set up and manage your company, and then put the fundamentals to work profitably in the import/export business setting. This is where the fun really begins.

The final chapter of this book (Chapter 16) offers 20 secrets to import/export success.

This book answers the following questions plus hundreds more; obey them and make big profits.

- How do I start my own import/export business?
- How do I choose a product for import or export?
- How does Homeland Security affect my business?
- How do I make overseas sourcing contacts?
- How do I make marketing contacts?
- How can I sell over the Internet?
- How do I get a Web site?
- How do I design a home page?
- How do I price a product for profit?
- How do I prepare a market plan?
- How do I negotiate a transaction?
- How do I protect patents and trademarks?
- What are the secrets of overseas travel?
- How do I finance an import or export transaction?
- What is outsourcing?
- What is a letter of credit?
- To whom do I go for an export license?
- How do I get through the customs maze?
- How do I use the harmonized tariff schedule?
- How do I figure import duties?
- How do I write a business plan for an import/export business?
- What are the benefits of NAFTA?
- How can I trade in Europe's single market?
- Where do I go for information on doing business in China and India?

Summary

This book offers a dynamic opportunity—the rewards are excitement, a touch of the exotic, and great profit potential. We hope it motivates you to travel to exotic places, meet interesting people, and make new international friends. Above all, we want you to earn great untapped *profits*.

Import/Export: How to Take Your Business Across Borders will change your life. Don't wait: the time to get into the import/export market is now!

PART I

THE COMMONALITIES

CHAPTER 1

WINNING THE TRADE GAME

International trade is the exchange of goods and services across national boundaries. *Exports* are the merchandise individuals or nations sell; *imports* are the goods individuals or nations purchase. By these methods, products valued at more than US$11 trillion worldwide are exchanged every year. When we as consumers enjoy fresh flowers from Latin America, tropical fruits in the middle of winter, or a foreign car, we are participants in, and beneficiaries of, international trade. International trade is not a zero-sum game of winners and losers; it is a game in which everyone wins.

Global Opportunities

Major changes that took place in the twentieth century have had a significant effect on international trade in the new century and have provided unprecedented opportunities.

The age of globalism has brought about worldwide distribution, the Internet, satellite communications, and speedy transportation systems. People all over the world seek the same luxuries and standards. They see things and, naturally, they want them.

Globalization is no longer a buzzword; it is a reality. National governments have a large stake in its outcome because this change affects their societies. As the process goes forward, the need for harmonizing interstate laws becomes more serious. Therefore international trade cannot be a static process, and businesses that make products and attempt to sell them across borders must constantly adjust.

U.S. Deficits and Surpluses

Figure 1.1 shows the history of American trade since the earliest days. You will note that it was not until about 1975 that trade began its chronic fall into significant deficits. Nevertheless, as Figures 1.2 and 1.3 show, the United States is at or near the top of the list in merchandise trade and commercial services. That is, America has the largest surpluses and deficits of any nation in the world, which means there is a lot of profitable merchandise moving around the world and you can have a part of that.

What Is an Import/Export Business?

The questions most frequently asked by interested parties are: "What is an import/export business?" and "What organizational methods do traders use?" The answers depend on whether you work for a manufacturer or are independent (for more detail see Chapter 6).

If you own or work for a manufacturer of an exportable product, your company can create and organize its own export department. Today, however, many manufacturers outsource their export function to import/export companies.

An independent import/export business is an individual or company that acts as an international middleman (a unisex term); that is, it sells foreign-made products (imports), sells domestic (home country) products in other countries (exports), or does both. See the Glossary at the back of book for an extensive list of the most commonly used trade terms.

Every manufacturer that is not already exporting can be a potential client for you; there are still many businesses all over the world that do

Figure 1.1 U.S. Balance of Trade: 1960–2004

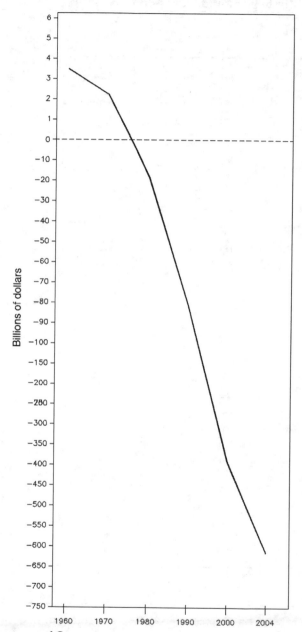

Source: U.S. Department of Commerce

Figure 1.2 Leading Exporters and Importers in World Merchandise Trade: 2004 (in billions of dollars and percents)

Rank	Exporters	Value	Share	Annual percentage change	Rank	Importers	Value	Share	Annual percentage change
1	Germany	912.3	10.0	21	1	United States	1525.5	16.1	17
2	United States	818.8	8.9	13	2	Germany	716.9	7.6	19
3	China	593.3	6.5	35	3	China	561.2	5.9	36
4	Japan	565.8	6.2	20	4	France	465.5	4.9	17
5	France	448.7	4.9	14	5	United Kingdom	463.5	4.9	18
6	Netherlands	358.2	3.9	21	6	Japan	454.5	4.8	19
7	Italy	349.2	3.8	17	7	Italy	351.0	3.7	18
8	United Kingdom	346.9	3.8	13	8	Netherlands	319.3	3.4	21
9	Canada	316.5	3.5	16	9	Belgium	285.5	3.0	22
10	Belgium	306.5	3.3	20	10	Canada	279.8	2.9	14
11	Hong Kong, China	265.5	2.9	16	11	Hong Kong, China	272.9	2.9	17
	domestic exports	20.0	0.2	2		retained imports a	27.3	0.3	13
	re-exports	245.6	2.7	17					
12	Korea, Republic of	253.8	2.8	31	12	Spain	249.3	2.6	20
13	Mexico	189.1	2.1	14	13	Korea, Republic of	224.5	2.4	26
14	Russian Federation	183.5	2.0	35	14	Mexico	206.4	2.2	16
15	Taipei, Chinese	182.4	2.0	21	15	Taipei, Chinese	168.4	1.8	32
16	Singapore	179.6	2.0	25	16	Singapore	163.9	1.7	28
	domestic exports	98.6	1.1	24		retained imports a	82.8	0.9	30
	re-exports	81.0	0.9	26					
17	Spain	178.6	2.0	14	17	Austria	117.8	1.2	18
18	Malaysia	126.5	1.4	21	18	Switzerland	111.6	1.2	16
19	Saudi Arabia b	126.2	1.4	35	19	Australia	109.4	1.2	23
20	Sweden	122.5	1.3	20	20	Malaysia	105.3	1.1	26
21	Switzerland	118.5	1.3	18	21	Sweden	99.3	1.0	19
22	Austria	117.4	1.3	21	22	Turkey	97.5	1.0	41
23	Ireland	104.3	1.1	12	23	India	97.3	1.0	37
24	Thailand	97.4	1.1	21	24	Russian Federation c	96.3	1.0	27
25	Brazil	96.5	1.1	32	25	Thailand	95.4	1.0	26
26	Australia	86.4	0.9	21	26	Poland	89.2	0.9	31
27	United Arab Emirates	82.8	0.9	23	27	Czech Republic c	69.5	0.7	34
28	Norway	81.8	0.9	21	28	Denmark	68.2	0.7	19
29	Denmark	76.8	0.8	15	29	Brazil	65.9	0.7	30
30	India	75.6	0.8	32	30	Ireland	60.7	0.6	13
31	Poland	74.9	0.8	39	31	Hungary	59.3	0.6	24
32	Indonesia	72.3	0.8	13	32	South Africa b	57.1	0.6	39
33	Czech Republic	68.7	0.8	41	33	Portugal	54.9	0.6	16
34	Turkey	63.1	0.7	34	34	Indonesia	54.9	0.6	30
35	Finland	61.3	0.7	15	35	Greece	52.6	0.6	17
36	Hungary	54.9	0.6	27	36	Finland	50.8	0.5	20
37	South Africa	46.0	0.5	26	37	Norway	48.1	0.5	22
38	Iran, Islamic Rep. of	44.4	0.5	31	38	United Arab Emirates	47.6	0.5	21
39	Philippines	39.7	0.4	7	39	Saudi Arabia	44.6	0.5	21
40	Israel	38.5	0.4	22	40	Israel	42.9	0.5	18
41	Portugal	35.8	0.4	13	41	Philippines	42.3	0.4	7
42	Argentina	34.5	0.4	17	42	Iran, Islamic Rep. of	34.7	0.4	33
43	Bolivarian Rep. of Venezuela b	34.2	0.4	43	43	Romania	32.7	0.3	36
44	Ukraine	32.7	0.4	42	44	Viet Nam	31.1	0.3	23
45	Algeria	32.3	0.4	31	45	Slovak Republic c	29.5	0.3	31
46	Chile	32.0	0.4	49	46	Ukraine	29.0	0.3	26
47	Nigeria	31.1	0.3	57	47	Chile	24.9	0.3	28
48	Kuwait	28.7	0.3	39	48	New Zealand	23.2	0.2	25
49	Slovak Republic	27.5	0.3	26	49	Argentina	22.3	0.2	61
50	Viet Nam	25.6	0.3	27	50	Iraq	21.3	0.2	114
	Total of above d	8639.8	94.4	-		Total of above d	8795.2	92.6	-
	World d	9153.0	100.0	21		World d	9495.0	100.0	21

a Retained imports are defined as imports less re-exports.
b Secretariat estimates.
c Imports are valued f.o.b.
d Includes significant re-exports or imports for re-export.

Source: World Trade Organization, 2006

Figure 1.3 Leading Exporters and Importers in World Trade in Commercial Services: 2004 (in billions of dollars and percents)

Rank	Exporters	Value	Share	Annual percentage change	Rank	Importers	Value	Share	Annual percentage change
1	United States	318.3	15.0	11	1	United States	260.0	12.4	14
2	United Kingdom	171.8	8.1	18	2	Germany	193.0	9.2	13
3	Germany	133.9	6.3	15	3	United Kingdom	136.1	6.5	14
4	France	109.5	5.1	12	4	Japan	134.0	6.4	22
5	Japan	94.9	4.5	25	5	France	96.4	4.6	18
6	Spain	84.5	4.0	11	6	Italy	80.6	3.8	10
7	Italy	82.0	3.9	17	7	Netherlands	72.4	3.5	11
8	Netherlands	73.0	3.4	16	8	China	71.6	3.4	31
9	China	62.1	2.9	34	9	Ireland	58.4	2.8	12
10	Hong Kong, China	53.6	2.5	18	10	Canada	55.9	2.7	12
11	Belgium	49.3	2.3	14	11	Spain	53.7	2.6	18
12	Austria	48.3	2.3	14	12	Korea, Republic of	49.6	2.4	25
13	Ireland	46.9	2.2	24	13	Belgium	48.3	2.3	14
14	Canada	46.8	2.2	11	14	Austria	47.1	2.2	14
15	Korea, Republic of	40.0	1.9	27	15	India	40.9	2.0	...
16	India	39.6	1.9	...	16	Singapore	36.2	1.7	23
17	Sweden	37.8	1.8	25	17	Denmark	33.4	1.6	18
18	Switzerland	36.8	1.7	11	18	Sweden	33.0	1.6	15
19	Singapore	36.5	1.7	19	19	Russian Federation	32.8	1.6	24
20	Denmark	36.3	1.7	15	20	Taipei, Chinese	29.9	1.4	20
21	Greece	33.2	1.6	37	21	Hong Kong, China	29.8	1.4	16
22	Luxembourg	33.1	1.6	34	22	Australia	25.6	1.2	22
23	Norway	25.9	1.2	21	23	Norway	24.0	1.1	21
24	Taipei, Chinese	25.5	1.2	11	24	Thailand	23.0	1.1	28
25	Australia	24.8	1.2	20	25	Luxembourg	22.3	1.1	35
26	Turkey	23.8	1.1	25	26	Indonesia a	21.3	1.0	...
27	Russian Federation	20.2	0.9	25	27	Switzerland	21.1	1.0	10
28	Thailand	18.9	0.9	21	28	Mexico	19.3	0.9	10
29	Malaysia	16.7	0.8	24	29	Malaysia	18.8	0.9	8
30	Israel	14.2	0.7	16	30	Brazil	16.1	0.8	12
31	Egypt	14.0	0.7	30	31	United Arab Emirates a	13.4	0.6	...
32	Mexico	13.9	0.7	12	32	Greece	13.4	0.6	25
33	Portugal	13.8	0.6	21	33	Israel	13.3	0.6	13
34	Poland	13.3	0.6	19	34	Poland	12.3	0.6	17
35	Brazil	11.5	0.5	20	35	Finland	11.8	0.6	18
36	Hungary	10.1	0.5	17	36	Saudi Arabia	11.0	0.5	39
37	Czech Republic	9.7	0.5	25	37	Turkey	10.3	0.5	33
38	Croatia	9.6	0.5	11	38	Hungary	10.0	0.5	11
39	Finland	8.9	0.4	14	39	Czech Republic	9.1	0.4	26
40	South Africa	8.1	0.4	10	40	South Africa	9.1	0.4	16
	Total of above	1950.0	91.7	-		Total of above	1900.0	90.6	-
	World	2125.0	100.0	18		World	2095.0	100.0	17

a Secretariat estimate.
Note: Figures for a number of countries and territories have been estimated by the Secretariat. Annual percentage changes and rankings are affected by continuity breaks in the series for a large number of economies, and by limitations in cross-country comparability.

Source: World Trade Organization, 2006

not export. According to the U.S. Department of Commerce, less than 10 percent of all American manufacturers currently sell their products overseas.

 Whether you run your business from your home or as an expansion of an existing domestic manufacturing firm, an import/export business often requires little capital investment for start-up. Of course it can grow into a giant business with billions of dollars in annual sales. An import/export business also offers great opportunities to travel and to enjoy the prestige of working with clients from all over the world.

Where Do Importers and Exporters Trade?

Everyone is trading internationally. And once trade begins with one country, new opportunities spring out of nowhere. A business person who successfully starts importing very soon learns of exporting opportunities and vice versa. In any case, a whole lot of money can be made. More than $11 trillion wouldn't be traded worldwide if it weren't profitable to do so.

The World Trade Organization (WTO)

Created on January 1, 1995, the World Trade Organization (WTO), with equal status alongside the World Bank and the International Monetary Fund, has strengthened global trade. It is the only international organization that deals with the rules of trade between nations. At its heart are the WTO agreements, negotiated and signed by the bulk of the world's trading nations and ratified by their parliaments. As of 2005, it has over 149 national members making it easier to do business across borders by reducing tariffs and harmonizing laws and practices that are barriers to trade. The WTO's goal is to help producers of goods and services, exporters and importers, conduct their business.

Cyber Trading

There is no president or congress of the Internet, and it has no boundaries; therefore, cyber communication is the international trader's connection without barriers (see Chapter 4).

World Trade Centers Association (WTCA)

Founded in 1970, the World Trade Centers Association (WTCA) is a not-for-profit, nonpolitical association dedicated to the establishment and effective operation of world trade centers as instruments for trade expansion. To date, the WTCA membership about 300 centers in 75 countries. These world trade centers service more than 750,000 international affiliated businesses.

World trade centers, dedicated to providing services to facilitate international trade, are located in over 170 cities with about 100 more in the planning stages. In other words, they are in virtually every major trading city in the world. To learn more about world trade centers, see Chapter 9.

Trade Integrations

Trade integrations are preferential arrangements between two or more nations to facilitate commerce across borders.

North America

The North American Free Trade Agreement (NAFTA)—the world's largest trading bloc—is expanding to include many of the nations of the Caribbean basin and South America.

Europe

The European Union (EU) formed a single internal market that has resulted in the removal of essentially all physical, technical, and fiscal barriers to the exchange of goods and services within the European common market. The EU is now becoming larger to include some of the newly independent states of Central and Eastern Europe. Some of the changes agreed to are:

- A common value-added tax
- Deregulation of transportation
- Establishment of minimum industrial and safety standards
- Broadening of the EU-wide bidding process for government procurement

Asia

The Asian/Pacific Basin nations of Australia, New Zealand, Japan, and the "Tigers" (South Korea, Taiwan, Hong Kong, Singapore, and Thailand) are the countries that today present the greatest trade opportunities. Trade in this region has expanded faster than any other part of the world.

China and India

China and India are the two most populated countries and are making special progress in international trade. They are worthy of focused research—they are doing business!

Africa

The latest world trade emphasis is focused on the countries of the African continent, particularly those south of the Sahara where there are vast untapped resources and a need for modernization and economic development.

Why Get into Trade?

There are three big reasons to get into the trade game:

1. Imports bring big profits.
2. Exports make big profits.

3. The world is interdependent. People have awakened to two realities—that people of each nation rely on people of other nations to exchange goods, services, and ideas—and that free trade creates jobs.

Those who are winning the trade game know that, regardless of national deficits or surpluses, the time is always right for an import/export business to make profits. The winners simply swing with political and economic changes over which they have little or no control.

Success Stories

This book does not guarantee financial success—there are too many variables such as management, financial capitalization, and determination; however, the following are a few stories you might find interesting and stimulating. The intention is to motivate and offer a few ideas that might work for you.

Hollywood USA

The president and CEO of a small New Jersey company with a Beverly Hills connection swears that it's true that customers in the Middle East are wild for products bearing American brand names and splashes of red, white, and blue on their packaging. His line of Hollywood USA high-quality body sprays, creams, baby products, deodorants, and shampoos has found buyers around the world—in Africa, Latin America, and, of course, the Middle East.

From Air to H$_2$O

Even in the driest part of the world, Hisham Fawzi's worldwide government customers don't wait for rain to quench their thirsts. As president and chairman of Excel Holdings, a small firm in Leesburg, Virginia, Fawzi develops and markets a patented line of machines that convert moisture from the air into drinkable water. Excel Holdings currently markets its products in 14 countries with more potential customers in the waiting. Most of his customers are foreign governments or international organizations that often finance water purification efforts.

Pumpkin Maternity

While touring the Netherlands, a rock musician thought about her sister and her best friend, both pregnant and complaining that they had nothing to wear. She knew exactly what was needed—hip, quality maternity clothes that reflect today's fashions.

Two months later the Pumpkin Maternity catalog was printed, and she was in business. Two years later, she has thriving mail-order and Web site sales. You can check out Pumpkin Maternity at www.pump kinmaternity.com and www.babystyle.com.

Down Under

Since 1991, Amy Frey has helped Australian manufacturers gain a niche in the lucrative North American market through her small business, ATC International. Frey nurtured her company from its humble origins in a spare bedroom to a 6,000-square-foot warehouse outside Washington, DC. From there, her four-person team provides market research, business management, distribution, and logistic services to clients in Australia and New Zealand.

Palomar Technologies

Palomar Technologies is a high-tech company headquartered in San Diego, California. It is the premier supplier of high-precision microelectronic assembly equipment in the world. Palomar provides best-in-class solutions for microelectronic component manufacturers worldwide. The unique concentration of telecom and bio-med companies in the San Diego region is renowned worldwide and provides instant credibility for a high-tech company such as Palomar to compete against foreign suppliers for design, process development, custom manufacturing, and service business.

International Consulting Group

The International Consulting Group serves the Mexico–United States border area. Since its start-up in the mid-1980s, it has offered services to expand into Mexico or Latin America. The group assists clients with informed ideas and services that best suit their specialized needs in researching and penetrating markets.

Dog Feeders and Alibaba.com

This company started production of high-end dog feeders and learned that it's almost impossible to compete with the big guys if you don't produce offshore. Start-ups don't usually have the capital for actually going to China and visiting potential business partners before closing the deal. So instead, this company went to Alibaba.com and found the system very easy to use and helpful. It posted its need to find suppliers in Asia on Alibaba's Web site and started making contacts immediately.

DriveCam International

Headquartered in San Diego, California, DriveCam reduces claims costs and saves lives by improving the way people drive. The company's product mitigates risk by improving driver behavior and assessing liability in collisions. Combining sights and sounds, expert analysis, and driver coaching, its approach has reduced vehicle damages, worker's compensation, and personal injury costs by 30 to 90 percent for more than 40,000 commercial, government, and consumer vehicles.

Launched in February 1998, DriveCam has received three patents for its innovative design with additional patents pending. By 2005, the company was ranked number 67 in the Inc. 500. Focusing on improving risky driving behavior by predicting and preventing crashes, DriveCam's exception-based video event recorder is mounted on the windshield behind the rearview mirror and captures sights and sounds inside and outside the vehicle. The company operates in 10 countries in North America, Europe, Africa, Australia, and Asia.

Candleworks

Located in Iowa City, Iowa, Candleworks is a company that makes and markets natural home fragrances and aromatherapy candles internationally. It was born out of struggle, has survived, and earned $800,000 in sales in their first year.

The next chapter explains how to launch a profitable transaction—the first steps of your import/export project—and speed you on your way toward international trade opportunities with profits and success.

CHAPTER 2

LAUNCHING A PROFITABLE TRANSACTION

Some perceive the import/export transaction process as an obstacle, but don't let that deter you. The truth is that anyone can grasp the nuts and bolts of international trade. The bridge from producers to buyers has existed for many years, and it has been tested and retested. By investing some time and money in yourself, you can easily learn this process.

This chapter addresses the first six commonalities of the importing and exporting transaction. If you understand the steps outlined below, your import/export business will get off to an excellent start on the road to early profitability.

1. Terminology
2. Homework
3. Choosing the product
4. Making contacts
5. Market research
6. What's the bottom line?

Don't mistakenly assume that the order presented in this book represents a hierarchy of importance, or that these steps are in the precise order of every import/export project. In reality, sometimes things happen simultaneously.

Terminology

Because of increasing international interdependency, trade literacy has become as important in modern business as Internet and computer literacy. As you progress in your reading, refer frequently to the extensive glossary of commonly used terms found at the end of this book. Many of these terms are also defined when they first appear in the text. Don't be frightened by the new terminology—you can learn it!

Homework

Research is one of the keys to winning the trade game! Even if you have some experience in international trade, it's unwise to jump into an unresearched project. In fact, it's not unusual to spend several weeks learning about the product and its profit potential before getting serious. Think of it as an investment to reduce the number of inevitable mistakes.

Choosing the Product or Service

The question asked most often is, "What product should I select to import or export? Should it be rugs or machinery?" Of course, if your firm already manufactures merchandise or provides a service, that product or service is what you sell. But for your own import/export business, your job will be to sell someone else's product or service. In other words you will be the middleman.

The Personal Decision

Most people begin with a single product or service that they know and understand or have experience. Others begin with a line of products or define their products in terms of an industry with which they are familiar. Above all, product selection is a personal decision, but the decision should make common sense. For example, if you aren't an engineer, don't begin by exporting gas turbine engines. Or, if you are an electronics engineer, don't start with fashionable textiles. A good example is the American house painter who began making excellent profits exporting a line of automated painting equipment to Europe. He knew the equipment before he began exporting.

Start your business with a product or service with which you have an advantage. You can gain that advantage because of prior knowledge, by doing library research about a product, by making or using contacts, or by understanding a language or culture.

HOT TIP

In the beginning, keep it simple.

The Technical Marketing Decisions

Keep in mind that the product you select may need to be adapted to the cultures of other countries.

- *Product standards.*   ISO is an organization that harmonizes world product standards such as flammability, labeling, pollution, food and drug laws, and safety standards. ISO 9000 (product registration) and ISO 14000 (environmental management registration) are the international quality assurance series. At the time of publication of this edition they have been in effect for more than 13 years and are unlikely to go away.

Therefore, it is important to check your products for compliance. Be sure to check www.iso.org
- *Technical specifications and codes.*   Most of the world uses 220 V, 50 Hz but products used in the United States are 120 V, 60 Hz. Similarly, most of the world uses the metric system of weights and measures. Determine how you can convert your product to meet the appropriate specifications and codes.
- *Quality and product life cycle.*   In the life cycle of product innovation, new products are typically introduced first to developed countries leaving an opportunity for sales of earlier models to least-developed countries. Assess the stage in the life cycle in which you find your export/import product.
- *Other uses.*   Different countries use some products for purposes different from those that we apply here. For example, motorcycles and bicycles are largely recreation vehicles in the United States, but in many countries they are the primary means of transportation.

What Is World Class?

What does it mean to have *world-class products*? Don't deceive yourself. Some things are better than others; you know it, we all know it. *World class* means there may be something as good, but there is nothing better in the world. But some markets can't absorb world class, so make sure that the products and services you select are right for your market.

Developed countries. Distinguishes the more industrialized nations, including all member countries of the Organization for Economic Cooperation and Development (OECD) from "developing"—or "less developed"—countries.

Least-developed countries. Forty-nine of the world's poorest countries are considered by the United Nations to be the least developed of the least-developed countries. Most of them are small in terms of both area and population, and some are land-locked or small island countries. They are generally characterized by:

➤ Low per capita incomes, literacy levels, and medical standards
➤ Subsistence agriculture
➤ Lack of exploitable minerals and competitive industries

Many least-developed countries are in Africa (see Chapter 12), but a few, such as Bangladesh, Afghanistan, Laos, and Nepal, are in Asia. Haiti is the only country in the Western Hemisphere classified by the United Nations as "least developed."

Making Contacts

Importers and exporters need contacts to get started. The exporter must convince a domestic manufacturer of his or her ability to sell the manufacturer's product or service internationally. The importer, on the other hand, must find an overseas manufacturer or middleman from whom to buy the product or service.

Contacts are classified in two categories. The two ways to make contacts overlap, and they can be used to expand your import/export network:

1. *Sourcing* (finding) a manufacturer or provider of the product or service you wish import or export
2. *Marketing* (selling) that product or service

Sourcing Contacts

If you are an exporter, any product or service you select falls into an industry classification, and that industry very likely has an association. Almost every industry has a publication—if not a magazine, at least a newsletter. Begin looking for manufacturers of your product or service in the appropriate industry publication. Under "Information Sources" in Chapter 7, you will find other information that may help you make contacts for products to export.

Contacts for importers are only slightly more difficult to obtain. Assuming you know in which country your product is manufactured, you need a contact in that industry in that country. Start with the nearest consulate office and then contact that country's international chamber of commerce. You can also make contacts through your embassy or through a corresponding industry association. Furthermore, you can make direct contact with the government of the country in which you have an interest.

Next, establish communications with the overseas contact to seek further information or to ask for product samples and prices. You can make contact by letter or by electronic means such as fax or e-mail. (See "Communications" in Chapter 3.)

Eventually, you will need to take a trip to the country with which you intend to trade. It will make a big difference. (Travel is also discussed in Chapter 3.)

Marketing Contacts

Marketing methods and channels of distribution are similar in most countries. Agents, distributors, wholesalers, and retailers exist everywhere, and you make marketing contacts through these channels.

For domestic marketing contacts, use trade shows, direct sales, direct mail, and manufacturer's representatives, as well as swap meets, flea markets, home parties, or wholesalers. Most governments will also help you find contacts.

Foreign sales representative. A representative or agent residing in a foreign country who acts as a salesperson for a U.S. manufacturer, usually for a commission. Sometimes referred to as a *sales agent* or *commission agent*.

Distributor. A firm that: (1) sells directly for a manufacturer, usually on an exclusive basis for a specified territory, and (2) maintains an inventory of the manufacturer's goods.

The international marketeer (trader) also can make contacts through world trade centers (WTCs) (see Chapter 9), trade shows, direct sales, a distributor, or an agent who is the equivalent of a manufacturer's representative. Trade fairs or shows are often the single most-effective means to make contacts and to learn about products, markets, competition, potential customers, and distributors. The term *trade show* or *fair* includes everything from catalog shows through local exhibits to major specialized international industry shows. At these shows, exhibitors offer literature and samples of their products.

Lists of worldwide trade shows and international conferences are available from most large airlines as well as from the U.S. Department of Commerce and Chamber of Commerce (COC). Your industry association will know when and where the appropriate trade shows take place. Table 2.1 offers a range of ideas that should assist you, the importer or exporter, in making either sourcing or market contacts.

Market Research

Market research is vital to the success of your import/export business. Is your product salable? Does anyone care? You must be able to sell enough of the product or service to justify undertaking the import/export project. If you are presenting a new product, you may have to create a market. But a good rule of thumb for the new import/export business is, "If the market isn't there, get out of the project and find another product."

Table 2.1 Making Contact

	Source	Market
Import	Consulate offices International COC Industrial organizations Foreign governments WTCA The Web (Internet)	Swap meets Direct mailers Mail orders Home parties Trade shows Wholesalers Associations Representatives Retailers U.S. government WTCA The Web (Internet)
Export	*Thomas Register* *Contacts Influential* *Yellow Pages* U.S. Department of Commerce Trade journals Trade associations WTCA The Web (Internet)	Distributors Trade shows Retailers Foreign governments U.S. Department of Commerce Direct mailers United Nations USAID Sell Overseas America *Business America* State trade promotion offices *Journal of Commerce* WTCA The Web (Internet)

Exporter Checklist

International market research will save money and time. Unfortunately, too many newcomers plunge into import/export without determining whether they can sell the product at a profit.

Following are checklists of research items for importers and exporters:

- Is there already a market for the product?
- What is the market price?
- What is the sales volume for that product?
- Who has market share, and what are the shares?

- What is the location of the market; what's its size and population? (Note that people in major urban areas generally have more money than people do elsewhere.)
- What are the climate, geography, and terrain of the market country?
- What are the economics of the country, its gross national product (GNP), major industries, and sources of income?
- What is its currency? How stable is it? Is barter commonplace?
- Who are the employees of the country? How much do they earn? Where do they live?
- Is the government stable? Is it friendly to Americans? Does the country have a good credit record?
- What are the tariffs, restrictions, and quotas?
- What are the other barriers to market entry, such as taxation and repatriation of income?
- What language is spoken there? Are there dialects? Does the business community speak English?
- How modern is the country?
- Do people there use the Internet?
- Do they have electric power?
- How do they move their goods?
- How good is the hard infrastructure (roads, trains, etc.)?
- What about the soft infrastructure (schools, etc.)?
- Does the country manufacture your product? How much does it produce? How much is sold there?
- What kind and how much advertising is generally used? Are there local advertising firms? Are there trade fairs and exhibitions?
- What distribution channels are being used? What levels of inventory are carried? Are adequate storage facilities available?
- Who are the customers? Where do they live? What influences the customers' buying decisions? Is it price, convenience, or habit?
- What kinds of services are expected? Is the custom to throw away or repair? Can repair services be set up?
- What about competition? Does the competition have sales organizations? How does it price?

Importer Checklist

- What are the property rights implications?
- Is there already a market for the product?
- What is the market price?
- What is the sales volume for that product?
- Who has market share, and what are the shares?
- What is the location of the market; what's its size and population? (Major urban areas are generally where the people have more money than elsewhere.)
- Who are the wholesalers?
- What sort and how much advertising is generally used? Are there local advertising firms? Are there trade fairs and exhibitions?
- What distribution channels are being used? What levels of inventory are carried? Are there adequate storage facilities available?
- Who are the customers? Where do they live? What influences the customers' buying decisions? Is it price, convenience, or habit?
- What kinds of services are expected? Is it the custom to throw away or repair? Can repair services be set up?
- What about competition? Does the competition have sales organizations? How does it price?

The answers to these questions are available through most good libraries, your equivalent of the U.S. Department of Commerce, your Chamber of Commerce, or private market research companies. (See Chapters 7 and 8 for a list of export and import information sources.)

What's the Bottom Line?

Profit is an internal, individualized decision that varies from product to product, industry to industry, and within the market channel. Desirable profit relates to the goals you plan for your import/export business. For instance, one person's goal might be to cover expenses, take a small salary, and be pleased if the business supports travel to exotic places. Another might have the goal to expand the business to eventually become a major trading company. Yet another might set a goal to work for only five or six years, sell the business at a profit, and retire on the capital gain.

This segment of the chapter discusses the profit aspects of international trade, beginning with initial quotations, terms of sale, the market channel, and pricing.

Initial Quotations

Initial quotes begin either with a request for quotation (RFQ) sent by the importer to the exporter or with an unsolicited offer from the exporter. A simple letter or e-mail can be a request for a quotation. Figure 2.1 shows a sample letter of inquiry.

Figure 2.1 Typical Letter of Inquiry

Our Company, Inc.
Hometown, U.S.A.

Ref:
Date:

XYZ Foreign Co.
2A1 Moon River
Yokohama, Japan

   Our company is a medium-sized manufacturing company. We are interested in your products.

   Please send us a pro forma invoice for five of your machines, CIF Los Angeles. Please indicate your payment terms and estimated time of delivery after receipt of our firm order.

Sincerely,

W.T. Door
President

The pro forma invoice, a normal invoice document visibly marked "pro forma," is the method most often used to initiate negotiations. This provisional invoice is forwarded by the seller of goods prior to a contemplated shipment; it advises the buyer of the kinds and quantities of goods to be sent, their value, and important specifications (weight, size, etc.). Its purpose is to describe in advance certain items and details, and it contains the major elements of a contract, which will be used later in shipping and collection documents such as letters of credit (discussed in Chapter 5).

Keep in mind that everything in a pro forma invoice is negotiable, so carefully think through any terms entered on this document. Once accepted by the purchaser, it becomes a binding sales agreement or legal contract, and the seller is bound to the terms stated. Figure 2.2 is an example of a pro forma invoice which shows the key elements of the contract which are:

- Product description and specifications
- Material costs
- Price
- Quantity
- Shipping costs
- Delivery terms
- Procedures

Terms of Sale

In international business, suppliers use pricing terms, called *terms of sale*. These pricing terms quite simply define the geographical point where the *risks* and *costs* of the exporter and importer *begin* and *end*.

The International Chamber of Commerce (ICC) has, over time, developed a set of international rules for the interpretation of the most commonly used trade terms called INCOTERMS. If, when drawing up the contract, both buyer and seller specifically refer to INCOTERMS, they can be sure of clearly defining their respective responsibilities. In

Figure 2.2 Typical Pro Forma Invoice

XYZ Foreign Co.
2A1 Moon River
Yokohama, Japan

Our Company, Inc.
Hometown, U.S.A.

Purchase Order Date:
Invoice Date:
Invoice Ref.No.:
  PRO FORMA 00012

Terms of Payment:
  Confirmed
  Irrevocable Letter of Credit
  Payable in U.S. dollars

Invoice To:
Ship To:
Forwarding Agent:

Via: Country of Origin:

QUANTITY	PART NO.	DESCRIPTION	PRICE EACH	TOTAL PRICE
10	A2Z	Machines	$100.00	$1,000.00

Inland freight, export packing & forwarding fees	$ 100.00
Free alongside (FAS) Yokohama	$1,100.00
Estimated ocean freight	$ 100.00
Estimated marine insurance	$ 50.00
CIF Long Beach	$1,250.00

Packed in 10 crates, 100 cubic feet
Gross weight 1000 lbs.
Net weight   900 lbs.
Payment terms: Irrevocable letter of credit by a U.S. bank.
Shipment to be made two (2) weeks after receipt of firm order.
Country of Origin: Japan
We certify this pro forma invoice is true and correct.

Issu A. Towa
President

so doing, buyer and seller eliminate any possibility of misunderstanding and subsequent dispute. A copy of INCOTERMS 2000 (effective January 1, 2000) can be ordered in 31 languages for about 40 Euros or US$50 via the Internet (Web site: www.iccbooks. com); it is available as a paper or as an e-book. You can also write to: The ICC Publishing Corporation, Inc., 156 Fifth Ave., Suite 417, New York, NY 10010; telephone 1-212-206-1150; fax (212) 633-6025; e-mail: pub@iccwbo.org

There are many variant terms of sale. INCOTERMS organizes them into four groups: "E group" for Ex words; "F group" for FCA, FAS, and FOB; "C group" for terms where the seller has to contract for carriage (CFR, CIF, CPT, CIP); and "D group" for terms in which the seller has to bear all costs and risks to bring the goods to the place of destination (DAF, DES, DEQ, DDU, and DDP).

Among all these terms there are four—EXW, FAS, CIF, and DAF—that are most commonly used. Figure 2.3 graphically shows how these terms function.

Figure 2.3 Where the Risks and Costs (Obligations) Begin and End

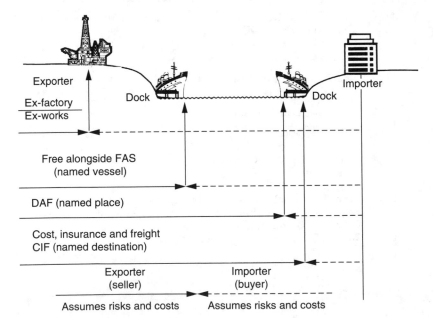

EXW is used with a named place or point of origin. Examples are Ex-Factory (named place) and Ex-Works (named place). These terms mean that the seller agrees to cover all charges to place the goods at a "specified delivery point." From that point on all other costs are the buyer's responsibility.

FAS (free alongside a ship) is usually followed by a named port of export. A seller quotes this term for the price of goods that includes charges for delivery alongside a vessel at the port. The buyer is responsible thereafter.

CIF (cost, marine insurance, freight) is used with a named overseas port of import. The seller is responsible for charges up to the port of final destination.

DAF (delivered at frontier) is used with a named place of import. The seller delivers when the goods are placed at the disposal of the buyer on the arriving means of transport. The goods are not unloaded; they are cleared for export but are not cleared for import at the frontier—that is, they must still pass the customs border of the named adjoining country.

Marine insurance. An insurance that will compensate the owner of goods transported on the seas in the event of loss if such loss would not be legally recovered from the carrier. Also covers overseas air shipments.

Specific delivery point. A point in sales quotations that designates specifically where and within what geographical locale the goods will be delivered at the expense and responsibility of the seller (e.g., FAS named vessel at named port of export).

The Market Channel

In general the international market channel includes:

- The manufacturer
- The foreign import/export agent

Figure 2.4 Market Channel

- Any distributors (wholesalers)
- Any retailers
- The buyers or customers

Figure 2.4 shows how this might look.

Pricing for Profit

The price of your product should be high enough to generate a suitable profit but low enough to be competitive. Ideally, the importer or exporter should strive to buy at or below factory prices. This can be done by eliminating the manufacturer's cost of domestic sales and advertising expenses from the overseas price.

Each step along the market channel has a cost. If a product is entirely new to the market or has unique features, you may be able to command higher prices. On the other hand, to gain a foothold in a very competitive market, you can use marginal cost pricing. *Marginal cost pricing* is the technique of setting the market entry price at or just above the threshold at which the firm would incur a loss. [Under GATT (General Agreement on Tariffs and Trade) rules, now an integral part of the WTO, it is illegal to dump—that is, gain market share—by incurring a loss.]

Most new importers/exporters simply use the domestic factory price plus freight, packing, insurance, and so on. Depending on the volume and value of the transaction, the buyer and seller may mutually agree on which currency they will use. However, there are a number of countries where the seller or buyer will prefer to use U.S. dollars or Euros for their transaction or, depending on the volume and value of the transaction, they may agree to a currency basket.

It is important that you understand not only the elements that make up your price, but also those of your overseas trading associate. Remember there are no free lunches; everything has a cost.

Figure 2.5 illustrates how a product might move from one country to another by an importer or exporter. In particular, it shows how the

Figure 2.5 Pricing Model

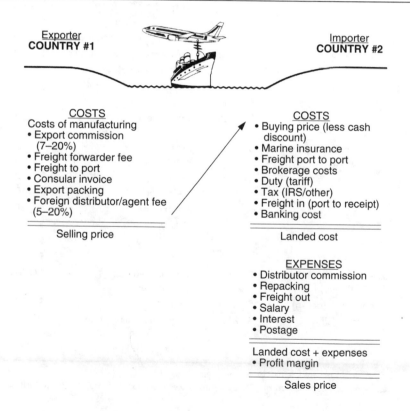

Exporter	Importer
COUNTRY #1	**COUNTRY #2**

COSTS
Costs of manufacturing
• Export commission (7–20%)
• Freight forwarder fee
• Freight to port
• Consular invoice
• Export packing
• Foreign distributor/agent fee (5–20%)

Selling price

COSTS
• Buying price (less cash discount)
• Marine insurance
• Freight port to port
• Brokerage costs
• Duty (tariff)
• Tax (IRS/other)
• Freight in (port to receipt)
• Banking cost

Landed cost

EXPENSES
• Distributor commission
• Repacking
• Freight out
• Salary
• Interest
• Postage

Landed cost + expenses
• Profit margin

Sales price

selling price in one country becomes the buying price in the other. Typical commission percentages are between 7 and 20 percent for an export middleman and between 5 and 20 percent for an import middleman (in other words, a foreign distributor or agent), although commissions may be as low as 1 percent and as high as 40 percent. The key issues are the price of the product and the number of units (sales

Table 2.2 Examples of Cost Elements

Terms of Sale: CIF

Export		Import	
Cost Elements	**Cost**	**Cost Elements**	**Cost**
Factory cost of 100 units @ $100/unit	$10,000	Landed cost (CIF)	$14,105
Expenses:			
		Duty @ 5.5%	$ 776
		Tax (IRS or other)	$ 150
Brokerage costs	$ 100	Brokerage clearance fees	$ 50
Export packing	$ 150	Reforwarding from broker	$ 100
Freight to port	$ 500	Banking charges	$ 50
Consular invoice	$ 50	Letter of credit @ 1/4%	$ 75
Freight forwarder fee	$ 150		
*Export agent commission @ 15% of cost	$ 1,500	Total landed cost	$15,306
†Foreign agent commission @ 5% of cost	$ 500	Expenses Warehouse	$ —
		Repacking	$ 100
		Freight out	$ 100
		Advertising	$ 500
		*Salary	$ 1,410
		Interest	$ —
		Postage	$ 100
Marine insurance ($12,950 @ $1.20 per $100 value	$ 155	Total landed plus expenses	$17,516
Transportation (ocean)	$ 1,000	Unit cost	$175.16
Landed cost (CIF)	$14,105	Suggested selling price @ 100% markup	$350.32
		Profit on 100 units	$17,516

*Only if an export middleman or import agent is used.
†Calculated at a commission of 10% of buying price: Markup (%) = Sell cost/cost × 100.

Figure 2.6 Export Costing Worksheet

Reference Information
Our reference_____   Customer reference_____

Customer Information
Name _____   E-mail_____
Address _____
_____   Fax_____

Product Information
Product _____   Dimensions ____ × ____ × ____
No. of units _____   Cubic measure _____ (sq. in.)
Net weight _____   Total measure _____
Gross weight _____

Product Charges
Price (or cost) per unit _____ × units _____ Total _____
Profit (or markup)   _____
Sales commissions   _____
FOB, factory   _____

Fees–packing, marking, inland freight   _____
Freight forwarder   _____
Financing costs   _____
Other charges   _____
Export packing   _____
Labeling/marking   _____
Inland freight to   _____
FOB, port city (export packed)   _____

Port Charges
Unloading (heavy lift)   _____
Loading (aboard ship)   _____
Terminal
  Consular document (check if required) _____
  Certificate of origin (check if required) _____
  Export license (check if required) _____
FAS vessel (or airplane)   _____

Freight
Based on_____ Weight_____ Measure_____
Ocean _____ Air _____
Rate _____ Minimum_____ Amount _____

Insurance
Coverage required _____
Basis _____ Rate _____ Amount _____
CIF, port of destination

Figure 2.7 Import Costing Worksheet

Reference Information
Our reference _____   Customer reference _____

Customer Information
Name_____   E-mail_____
Address _____
                _____   Fax_____

Product Information
Product _____   Dimension _____ × _____ × _____

No. of units _____   Cubic measure _____ (sq. in.)
Net weight _____   Total measure _____
Gross weight _____

Note: If quote is FOB factory, use export
Costing sheet to determine price at
CIF, Port of destination

Landed cost (CIF, port of destination)   _____
Customs duty   _____
Customs house broker fees   _____
Banking charges   _____
Taxes: federal   _____
       state   _____
       other   _____

Total landed   _____

Expenses   _____
Inland freight (from port city)   _____
Warehouse costs   _____
Repacking   _____
Inland freight (from warehouse)   _____
Advertising/promotion   _____
Overhead (% of annual)   _____
Salary (% of annual)   _____
Loans (principal/interest)   _____

Total landed plus expenses   _____

Unit cost   _____

Selling price   _____
Margin _____%

Profit   _____

volume) that you can sell. If, for instance, the product is a big-ticket item (i.e., having a high sales price), the commission percentage may be quite low, but a small percentage of a million-dollar sale can be very good business.

Table 2.2 shows a set of fictitious cost elements associated with a CIF quotation which corresponds to the steps shown in Figure 2.5. Figures 2.6 and 2.7 are offered as work lists to aid you in accurate costing of your product.

Is there sufficient profit at the *volumes* (number of units) you can sell to make it worth your while and meet your personal profit goals? Recall that the same amount of work goes into importing or exporting a product that makes no profit as one that makes a good profit.

HOT TIP

A word of caution for manufacturers: If at first exporting doesn't appear profitable, check your manufacturing costs. It may be necessary to import less costly components in order to compete internationally.

Be satisfied that you have a viable project. Then take the next step to lay out a long-range market plan. The next chapter explains how to develop that plan and then how to put it into action to make a transaction.

CHAPTER 3

PLANNING AND NEGOTIATING TO WIN

If you have a marketable and profitable product or service that will sell in sufficient volume, you now are ready to commit resources (time and money) to the project. But before you do, make sure you complete the following homework steps:

1. Develop a market plan
2. Prepare for negotiations
3. Understand the tips and traps of culture
4. Consider intellectual property rights
5. Learn about communications
6. Get ready to travel

Face up to the fact that international marketing is a step up from domestic marketing because it involves more complexity. The more countries, languages, and cultures with which you become involved, the more your planning will require special attention. Don't hesitate to call in consultants and other experts to read over your plan and offer criticism. This can pay off and save you money in the long run.

The Market Plan

You have determined that your project is viable; now write a long-range market plan, and then execute it.

A *market plan* is simply a process, recorded on paper, that allows you to think through the many logical ways to reach buyers and convince them to agree to a sale. It is important to integrate the international market plan with the firm's overall strategic business plan. See Chapter 6 ("How to Set Up Your Own Import/Export Business") for details about how to write a business plan.

Follow the following logical, step-by-step process to write your market plan:

1. *Objectives:*
   Examples:

   - Sales of $XXX,XXX by the end of the second year
   - Expansion into countries A and B by the end of the third year

2. *Specific tactics:*
   Examples:

   - Radio advertising in two cities
   - Three direct mailings to each company or person on a specific list
   - Develop an Internet Web site and advertise the address

3. *Schedule of activities or action plan:*
   Examples:

   - A list of trade shows indicating those that you will attend, including dates and duration of trips to visit overseas distributors, with their names, addresses, and phone numbers
   - Specific assignments of responsibility (an essential feature of an action plan)

4. *Budget for accomplishing the action plan:*

   - Include every conceivable cost associated with marketing the product. This is where most start-up firms underestimate. Initial marketing costs will be high.

Segmenting the Market

Marketing segmentation enables an import/export organization to choose its customers and fashion its marketing strategy based both on identified customer wants and requirements, and on response to the startup's specific desires and needs. You should visualize segmentation on both a macro and a micro level.

> *Macro.* From the Greek word *makros* meaning long. It is a combining form meaning large.
> *Micro.* From the Greek word *mikros* meaning small. A combining term meaning little, small, microscopic.

Macro Segmentation

Macro segmentation divides a market by such broad characteristics as industry shipments, location, firm size, and the like. An import macro segment might be dividing a city into marketing segments. On a larger scale, it might involve dividing the United States into regions, prioritizing those regions, and then developing a micro plan for each region.

Export macro segments might include prioritizing of continents or of countries within a continent; better yet, export macro segments might sort by language, purchasing power, or cultural preference.

Micro Segmentation

Micro segmentation finds the homogeneous customer groups within macro segments and, therefore, attempts to find out who makes the decisions for each homogeneous group. Micro segmentation pinpoints where (by address) and who (by name) can say yes to a buying decision. From this analysis, a promotional strategy can be designed to target the decision-making units (DMUs).

An import micro segmentation might take the data from your market research effort and identify where the wholesalers are located. If you list and prioritize these decision makers by name and address, you would have a logical and specific plan of attack for your marketing effort.

Your market plan and schedule should cover a three- to five-year period, depending on the kind of product(s) you market, your competitor(s), and your target market(s). Be sure to write this plan no matter how small the import/export project. Only when it is in writing will it receive proper attention and adequate allocation of funds.

Executing the Market Plan

Next comes the fun—putting the plan into action and actively marketing the product through trade shows, advertisements, television promotions, and direct mail, all in accordance with your budgeted plan. Remember that nothing happens in a business until something is sold.

Personal Sales

The two basic approaches to selling internationally for both imports and exports are direct and indirect sales. Using the *direct sales method*, a domestic manufacturing firm has its own marketing department that sells to a foreign distributor or retailing firm and is responsible for shipping the goods overseas. The *indirect sales method* uses a middleman, who usually assumes the responsibility for moving the goods. This is where your import/export business fits into the picture. You may sell directly to retailers or to distributors/wholesalers. Regardless of where your targeted DMU is in the market channel, keep in mind that international sales are just like domestic sales: someone makes personal contact and presents a portfolio, brochure, price list, and/or sample to decision makers (potential buyers) who can say yes.

HOT TIP

Making sales requires persistence and determination. Follow up, and then follow up again.

Trade Shows (Fairs)

If you're attending a trade fair or show for the first time, consider using it as the keystone of your sales trip. Allow time afterward to visit companies you meet at the fair.

The international trader attends trade shows for five basic reasons:

1. To make contacts
2. To identify products for import or export
3. To evaluate the competition (often done without exhibiting)
4. To find customers and distributors for import or export
5. To build sales for existing distributors

HOT TIPS: TRADE FAIRS

- If you are exhibiting to sell, don't over commit. You may get more business than you can handle reasonably.
- If you are searching for products to import, don't buy until you have done your homework!
- Take more business cards to the trade show than you think you will need. Have your fax number, Web site, and e-mail address on your card.
- Obtain language translation/interpreter help from a local university or college.
- If you are exhibiting to sell, consider prior advertising to let potential customers know that you will be there.

Trade Missions

Trade missions are trips made for the express purpose of promoting and participating in international trade. State, province, and local governments organize several kinds of trade missions for exporters.

Special Missions

These are organized and led by government officials with itineraries designed to bring you into contact with potential buyers and agents. You pay your own expenses and a share of the costs of the mission.

Seminar Missions

Similar to the specialized trade mission, seminar missions add several one- or two-day technical presentations to the trip by a team of industry representatives.

Industry-Organized, Government-Approved Trade Missions

Though these missions are organized by chambers of commerce, trade associations, or other industry groups, government officials often provide assistance prior to and during the trip.

Catalog Shows and Video/Catalog Exhibitions

These are the least expensive way to develop leads, to test markets, and to locate agents because you don't have to be there. You simply send along product catalogs, brochures, and other sales aids to be displayed at exhibitions organized by governments and consultants.

Video/catalog exhibitions are ideal for promoting large equipment and machinery which are costly to ship.

Trade Show Central

This is a free Internet service that provides information on more than 50,000 trade shows, conferences, and seminars. It has 5,000 service providers and 8,000 venues and facilities around the world (www. tscentral.com).

Advertising

All companies advertise to communicate with customers. Exporters and importers must ask themselves whether advertising is both important to sales and affordable. The assistance of an agency familiar with the market environment you wish to target could be critical to the success of your advertising campaign. Some countries do not carry television and radio advertising. Additionally, cultural differences often require more than a simple translation of promotional messages.

In countries where illiteracy is high, you may prefer to avoid written forms of advertising such as magazines and concentrate instead on outdoor advertising such as billboards, posters, electric signs, and street car or bus signs. These reach wide audiences in most countries.

Distributors

A *distributor* is a merchant who purchases merchandise from a manufacturer at the greatest possible discount and then resells it to retailers for profit. The distributor carries a supply of parts and maintains an adequate facility for servicing. The distributor buys the product in its own name, and payment terms are often arranged on a credit basis. A written contract usually defines the territory to be covered by the distributor, the terms of sale, and the method of compensation (see "Avoiding Risk" in Chapter 5). The work is usually performed on a commission basis, without assumption of risk, and the representative may operate on either an exclusive or a nonexclusive basis. The contract is established for a specific time frame such that it may be renewable based on satisfactory performance.

As with domestic sales, foreign retailers usually buy from the distributor's traveling sales force, but many buy through catalogs, brochures, or other literature.

Importers and exporters seldom sell directly to the end user. It is not recommended because: (1) it is time consuming, and (2) it leads to goods being impounded or sold at auction when the buyer doesn't know his or her own trade regulations.

Overseas Trader's Checklist

What you want from a foreign representative is:

- A solid reputation with suppliers and banks
- Financial strength
- Experience with the product or a similar product
- A sales organization
- Modern communications such as Internet, fax, and so on
- A sales record of growth
- Customers
- Warehouse capacity
- After-sales service capability
- Understanding of regional culture and business practices
- Knowledge of both English and the language of the country
- Knowledge of marketing techniques (promotion, advertisement, etc.)

Trading Partner's Checklist

What the foreign representative wants from you is:

- Excellent products
- Exclusive territories
- Training
- Parts availability
- Good warranties
- Advertising and merchandising support

- Credit terms, discounts, and deals
- Commissions on direct sales by the manufacturer in the distributor's territory
- Minimum control and/or visits
- Freedom to price
- Dealing with one person
- Security that the product will not be taken away once it is established in the territory
- The right to terminate the agreement when he or she pleases

Negotiations

Bargaining is a custom to people of many nations. But culturally nothing comes less naturally to Americans. The United States is a nation that operates on a fixed-price system, and most buyers have grown up with the notion of purchasing off the shelf at the price offered or not buying at all. Of course, comparative shopping is native to everyone's buying psyche, so when the international stakes and the competition increase, often companies from nations that are born cultural negotiators begin to force your hand. Your instincts should provide some basis for taking the right action and you can make the right moves if you prepare. An agent/distributor contract should be considered and should include issues of industrial property rights, territory covered (exclusive and nonexclusive contracts), the problems of terminating the contract, and the possibility of the host country switching from contract laws to labor laws according to the comparative size of the principal's company and distributor's company.

Preparations

Unfortunately, all too many people wander into international bargaining situations with no plan and no idea of how to proceed. For some, lack of preparation is the result of a sense of superiority, but for most it's pure ignorance about the number and competence of the ferocious competitors out there scouring the world for scraps of business.

The first step in preparing for international negotiations is to develop a complete assessment of your firm's capabilities. Analyze your strengths and weaknesses, particularly in terms of managerial skills, product delivery, technical abilities, and global resources.

Next, analyze your target—the company or country you intend to sell your product to. Keep in mind that the human and behavioral aspects of your negotiations will be vital. For example:

- Understand the place in the world where you will be traveling.
- Know its culture, history, and political processes.
- Play particular attention to the importance of face-saving to the people of the country where you will be negotiating.
- What is the host government's role in negotiations?
- How important are personal relations?
- How much time should you allow for negotiations?
- Be sure that the final agreement specifies terms for the cost, quality, and delivery of the product. Quality can be assured only by inspection of the actual product, but cost and delivery terms are the result of a quote agreed to by the seller.

In Japan, young executives role-play negotiations before they make an initial quote. They form teams, sit around a table with a chalkboard nearby, and pretend to negotiate the deal. Each team has a set of negotiating alternatives related to the country they are pretending to represent. Sometimes they cut their offer price by 10 percent; if that doesn't work, they cut it by another 5 or 10 percent. Other ploys are: (1) offering loans with lower interest rates than their competitors; (2) offering better after-sales service warrantees; or (3) providing warehouses for parts. Sometimes even the cost of advertising can make the difference in the sale.

Agreeing to a Contract

After obtaining the initial quotations as explained in Chapter 2, the next step in any international business arrangement is to reach an agreement or a sales contract with your overseas partner.

Negotiating is integral to international trade, and an importer/exporter should be ready to offer or ask for alternatives using simple letters, faxes, or e-mails. In the highly competitive international business world, a trader's ability to offer reasonable terms to customers may mean the difference between winning and losing a sale.

Exporters are finding it increasingly necessary to offer terms ranging from cash against shipping documents to time drafts, open accounts, and even installment payments spread over several years. More sophisticated business arrangements such as countertrade, which includes barter, product buyback, counterpurchase, and after-sales service, are also negotiables. Figure 3.1 illustrates the concept.

Figure 3.1 Countertrade

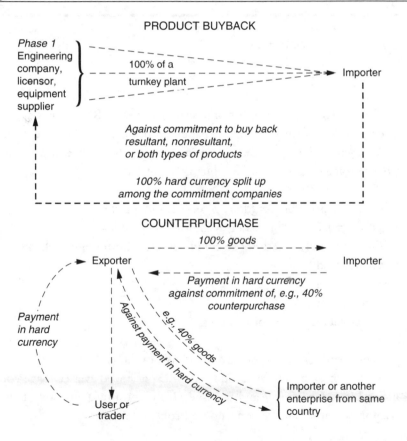

Countertrade. A general international trade term for a variety of methods to conduct reciprocal trade in which the seller is required to accept goods or other instruments of trade, in partial or whole payment for its products.

Barter. Trade in which merchandise is exchanged directly for other merchandise without the use of money.

Product buyback. Principally applicable for the construction and supply of plant and equipment. Major characteristic is its long-term aspect.

Counterpurchase. One of the most common forms of countertrade in which the seller receives cash but contractually agrees to buy local products or services as a percentage of cash received and over an agreed period of time.

The trader must have a list of alternatives ready. Keep negotiations open and don't firm them up on paper until a general agreement has been reached. The following is a partial list of alternatives and conditions you may wish to consider during negotiations:

- Quantity price breaks (don't offer just one price)
- Discounts for cash deals or even down payments
- Offer countertrade to those countries short on foreign exchange
- Guaranteed loans
- Low-interest loans
- Time payments
- Home factory trips for training

Let your banker, freight forwarder, or customs house broker review the final offer or quotation. A second pair of experienced eyes can save you money. (See Chapters 7 and 8, respectively, for an explanation of the freight forwarder and customs house broker.)

Foreign Corrupt Practices Act (FCPA)

During your negotiations, make sure you stay on the right side of the Foreign Corrupt Practices Act (FCPA) of 1977, amended by the International Anti-Bribery and Fair Competition Act of 1998. In essence, this act makes it illegal for companies to bribe foreign officials, candidates, or political parties. Make certain that everything in the contract has a price. Don't get caught making illegal payments or gifts to win a contract or sale. Two kinds of penalties can be imposed for violation of the FCPA, criminal and civil.

Criminal Penalties

The following criminal penalties may be imposed for violations of the FCPA's antibribery provisions. Corporations and other business entities are subject to a fine of up to $2 million. Officers, directors, stockholders, employees, and agents are subject to fines of up to $100,000 and imprisonment for up to five years. Moreover, fines under the Alternative Fines Act may be quite a bit higher; the actual fine may be up to twice the benefit that the defendant sought to obtain by making the corrupt payment. You should also be aware that fines imposed on individuals may *not* be paid by their employer or principal.

Civil Penalties

The U.S. Attorney General or the SEC, as appropriate, may bring a civil action for a fine of up to $10,000 against any firm *as well as* any officer, director, employee, or agent of a firm, or stockholder acting on behalf of the firm, who violates the antibribery provisions. The specified dollar limitations are based on the egregiousness of the violation, ranging from $5,000 to $100,000 for a natural person, and $50,000 to $500,000 for any other person.

The law does not address itself to "facilitating payments," those small amounts used to expedite business activities euphemistically called in various countries: "mordida," "grease," "bakshish" (small amount of money), "rashoa" (big amount of money), "cumsha," or "squeeze." Nevertheless, great care should be exercised in this regard as well.

Tips and Traps of Culture

The very thought of doing business in a foreign culture can be a major barrier to negotiations, but it shouldn't be. After all, traders are known for their spirit of curiosity, inquisitiveness, and risk taking.

Developing overseas alliances does present new elements of risk and due diligence, along with the inherent challenges brought by distance, differing cultural motivations and priorities, and the effective integration of differing approaches and objectives. But that's also what brings the rewards.

Can one culture be superior to another? Political systems, armies, navies, and even economic systems may be superior, but cultures cannot.

The best way to appreciate another culture is to "walk in the other person's shoes"; that is, visit or live in the country and get a feel for the similarities and differences. Short of that, this section of this chapter is the next best thing, because its purpose is to help you break through culture barriers. You are cautioned that, to be effective in your business dealings, it is essential to be prepared. Do your homework before you interact in a new country, and then get on with doing business.

Does understanding foreign cultural values really make a difference? You bet it does! One person who had traveled overseas regularly and had made friends in many countries said, "They're more like us than they're different." What he meant was that they like kids, they want them to be educated, they understand business, and they work hard. What he didn't say was that it's the differences that affect attitudes, so much so at times that some managers won't even consider entering the market to do business with "them."

What Is Culture?

Culture is a set of meanings or orientations for a given society or social setting. It's a complex concept because there are often many cultures within a given nation. For an international business person, the definition is more difficult because a country's business culture is often different from its general culture. Thus the environment of international business is composed of language, religion, values and attitudes, laws, education, politics, technology, and social organizations that are different.

Whatever a nation's culture, it works for the people who live there. In order to function within it, you must get on the bandwagon.

The Japanese do it very well. They learn how to penetrate foreign markets by sending their managers to live and study in "the other person's shoes." Their mission is to develop relationships with contemporaries that will last for years. The Japanese don't try to change the way of life in the other country; they learn about it. When they go home, they are specialists in marketing and production in the country they researched.

It's a country's culture that regulates such things as sexuality, child rearing, acquisition of food and clothing, and the incentives that motivate people to work and buy products. All these things are of course major factors in marketing products.

The Nine Elements of Business Culture

Business culture is secondary to a country's general culture, but it provides the rules of the business game and explains the differences and the priorities.

Relationships

Relationships developed over a long period of time are the thing that reduces mistrust. To meet this challenge, you need to understand the countries, their people, and the cultures where you intend to do business.

Language

Ask international business people what language they speak, and they will say that they speak the language of the customer.

Language is one of the things that sets humans off from other forms of life. It is the way you tell others about your history and your intentions for the future. Language is the means of communicating within a culture. For people in a given culture, their language defines their socialization.

Body Language

Body language is the subtle power of nonverbal communication. It's the first form of communication you learn, and you use it every day to tell other people how you feel about yourself and them. This language includes your posture, gestures, facial expressions, costumes, the way you walk, and even how you view time, material things, and space.

Religion

Religion plays a major part in the cultural similarities and differences of nations. In itself religion can be a basis of mistrust and a barrier to trade. Religion is often the dominant influence for the consumer of products. Such things as religious holidays determine buying and consumption patterns. Knowing what is forbidden and what a society expects as a result of its various religions influences market strategy.

Values and Attitudes

The role of values and attitudes in international business is difficult to measure, but vital to success. Work ethic and motivation are the intangibles that affect economic performance.

Values of a society determine its attitudes toward wealth, consumption, achievement, technology, and change, and you must evaluate in terms of the host culture. Researching attitudes about openness and the receptivity to new technology is essential to marketing.

Laws and Legal Environment

The laws of a society are another dimension of its culture. They are the rules established by authority and society. On the one hand, laws provide an opportunity to handle the mistrust of doing business across international boundaries; on the other hand, they can become barriers and constraints to operations. The laws of nations are often greatly different. About half the nations of the world are under a form of code or common law, but the other half are under Muslim, communist, or indigenous laws. In actuality, none of the world's legal systems are pure—each nation has its own unique laws, but one can find many similarities and mixtures among each classification.

For most dealings you will be primarily interested in the law as it relates to contracts, but always view litigation as a last resort. Settle disputes in other ways if possible. Litigation is only for the stupid and the rich, because it usually involves long delays during which inventories are tied up and trade is halted. Lawsuits are costly, not just because of the money but also because of the broken relationship that results. Most international commercial disputes can be solved by conciliation, mediation, and arbitration. The International Chamber of Commerce provides an arbitration service that can often be written into a sales contract for use should the unspeakable happen.

Education

Culture shapes our thoughts and emotions. Motivation is influenced by our education as well as other things such as values and religion which we have already discussed. The biggest international difference is the educational attainment of the populous. The next biggest difference is the educational mix. In some countries such as the United States there is little difference in the mix. Practically all Americans are educated from kindergarten through twelfth grade. In the United States education is no longer a function of wealth, but this is not so in many other countries. It is not unusual to find only the elite of some nations educated to the levels Americans assume for all people. The impact of education is therefore profound for marketing products as well as for establishing relationships, because good communications are often based on relative education capacities and standards.

Technology

The most recent change in technology is our growing control over transportation, energy, and information communications including the

Internet. The word *technology* begets concepts such as science, development, invention, and innovation. Some older languages don't even have words to express these concepts. Understanding the technological gaps among nations is an essential element to exporting products across borders. Wide gaps still exist between the most advanced nations and those that are still what we call "traditional societies." The implications are that you might need to consider such things as training needs for technology transfer and the impact of that transfer on social environments. You should always look at technology from the importing country's point of view.

Social Organization

Social stratification is the hierarchy of classes within a society—the relative power, social priorities, privilege, and income of those classes. Each class within a system has somewhat different and distinct tastes, political views, and consumption patterns. Many countries have a socio-religious ideology that allows rank to be intrinsic and inherited biologically. This implies that different categories of humans are culturally defined as if consisting of different worth and potential for performance. Regardless of how you react to such noncompetitive socialization, such ideas are predictable in some countries. Faced with such a system of socio-religious rank, it is essential that you learn how to deal with it—not attempt to change it.

Practical Applications

Now that you have an appreciation of culture, let's take a look at the practical side.

Most business trips are usually short term. Nevertheless, it's important to understand as much about the culture of a country as possible, even when you're just visiting. To begin, let's look at some generalities—some ideas that will help you make a good impression no matter where you're doing business.

Saving face is not just an Asian concept, although it is particularly sensitive in Asian countries. Avoiding embarrassment to others, particularly ranking persons, is essential wherever you are in the world.

People of any country like to talk about their own land and people. If you ask questions that demonstrate genuine interest, it will cultivate their respect toward you. But no one likes critical questions such as, "Why don't you do it this way?" Or, "How come you do it that way?" Above all they don't want to hear how much better it is where you come from.

First impressions do count, and the wrong first impression can stop your business deal in its tracks. Bad first impressions are all but impossible to overcome. Following are some tips that will help you make that good first impression:

1. Smile! It's the universal business language and helps to avoid many problems.
2. But smile right. The smile in which the lips are parted in a sort of an ellipse around the teeth comes across as phony and dishonest. Smile easily—where your full teeth are exposed and the corners of your mouth are pulled up. This kind of smile says, "Hi, I'm pleased to meet you!"
3. Grooming is important all over the world. Studies indicate that most people are more attracted to others who are neat, well groomed, and crisply dressed.
4. Flash your eyebrows. That is, in most cultures raising the eyebrows almost instinctively in a rapid movement and keeping them raised for about a half-second is an unspoken signal of friendliness and approval.
5. Lean forward. Liking is produced by leaning forward.
6. Look for similarities. People tend to like others who are like them, so common experiences and interests are often a starting point for producing liking.
7. Nod your head. People like other people who agree with them and are attentive to what they are saying.

8. Open up. A position in which your arms are crossed in front of your chest may project the impression that you're resisting the other person's ideas. Open, frequently outstretched arms and open palms project the opposite.

Tips for Women

Following are some tips that might be especially useful for women travelers:

1. Never give a man a gift, no matter how close the business relationship. A small gift for his family might do.
2. Give gifts from the company, never from you.
3. If you are married, use Mrs. when overseas, even if you don't at home.
4. Avoid eating or drinking alone in public. Use room service, or invite a woman from the office where you are doing business to join you at a restaurant.
5. If the question of dinner arises and is useful to cement the deal, avoid any doubts by inviting your counterpart's family.
6. Make a point to mention your husband and ask about your male counterpart's family. Some business women who are not married invent a fiancé or "steady" back home.
7. Turn off flirtations immediately with a straightforward no.
8. Be aware of the culture, and dress to fit it as closely as your wardrobe will permit. Conservatism works.

About Jokes

People of every country enjoy humor, and they all have their funny stories, but explaining complicated jokes to business people who don't share your culture can be very tricky. Here are a few tips and traps:

1. Do remember that each culture reacts differently to jokes.
2. Don't tell foreigners a joke that depends on word play or punning.

3. Do be careful about the subject of your joke. It could be taken seriously in a culture different from your own.
4. Do be informed about the sensitive issues in the country where you are visiting.
5. Do ask to hear a few local jokes. They will give you a sense of what's considered funny.
6. Do tell jokes; everyone enjoys a good laugh.

Intellectual Property Rights

"The Chinese stole my stuff! They just drove down the road, passed our factory, and copied our trademark. It took us two and a half years and $5,000 to get it back," said one executive. On the other hand, because this company had the trademark registered, no one else in the United States could use it, and the litigation against the guilty Chinese firm was considerably easier than it would have been without proper registration.

Intellectual property is a general term that describes inventions or other discoveries that have been registered with government authorities for the sale or use by their owners. Such terms as *patent, trademark, copyright* fall into the category of intellectual property.

You can obtain information about patents and trademarks from the World Intellectual Property Organization (WIPO) at www.wipo.int or the U.S. Patent Office by going to its Web site at www.ustpo.gov, calling (800) 786-9199, faxing 571-273-3245, e-mailing USPTOinfo@USPTO.gov, or writing:

Patent and Trademark Office
Crystal Plaza 3, Room 2C02
Division of Patents and Trademarks
Washington, DC 20231

The booklet titled *General Information on Patents* can be ordered from the Government Printing Office online at www.uspto.gov/web/offices, or you can call 1-800-786-9199, fax 571-273-3245, or e-mail usptoinfo@ustpo.gov. Table 3.1 is a summary of the basic elements of intellectual rights in the United States.

Table 3.1 Intellectual Property Rights

	Patents	Copyrights	Trade and Service Marks	Trade Name	Trade Dress	Trade Secrets
Duration (years)	14–17 years	Life + 50 years	As long as in use	As long as in use	As long as in use	Until public disclosure
How	Apply to patent office	By original creation in permanent form	By use	By use	By use	By security measures
Requirements	Useful/novel	Non-functional original creation	Fanciful and distinguishing	Non-confusion with others	Fanciful, non-functional	Not known
Prevents	Manufacturer use or sale	Copying or adapting	Confusing or misleading use	Confusing or misleading use	Confusing or misleading use	Disclosure
Protects	Utility and design attributes	Authorship	Reputation and goodwill	Goodwill	Reputation	Info for competitive advantage
Examples	Product/mechanism/ process/style	Label design/ operating manual	Coca-Cola	Computer Land, Inc.	Container shape	Formula
Legal costs	$1,500–$3,000	$10–$100	$100–$400			

Patent Registration

You should recognize that patent registration in the United States does not protect your product in a foreign country. In general, protection in one country does not constitute protection in another. The rule of thumb is to apply for and register all intellectual property rights in each country where you intend to do business. Registration can be expensive; therefore, several multilateral organizations have been formed that make registration possible for all member countries.

The Community Patent

The *community patent*, also known as the European community patent or EC patent, is a patent measure being debated within the European Union. It would allow individuals and companies to obtain a unitary patent throughout the European Union. The community patent should not be confused with European patents, which are granted under the European Patent Convention. European patents, once granted, become a bundle of nationally enforceable patents in the designated states.

The community patent is intended to solve granting and enforcement by providing a patent right that is consistent across Europe. This fulfills one of the key principles of the internal market in that the same market conditions exist wherever in Europe trade is carried out— different patent rights in different countries distort this principle.

In view of the difficulties in reaching an agreement on the community patent, other legal agreements have been proposed outside the European Union legal framework to reduce the cost of translation (of patents when granted) and litigation, namely the London Agreement and the European Patent Litigation Agreement (EPLA).

European Patent Convention

The Convention on the Grant of European Patents of October 5, 1973, commonly known as the *European Patent Convention* (EPC), is a multilateral treaty instituting the European Patent Organization and providing an autonomous legal system according to which European patents are granted. Once granted, a European patent becomes equivalent to a bundle of nationally enforceable, nationally revocable patents, except for the provision of a time-limited, unified, postgrant opposition procedure. See www.epo.org/patents/law/legal-texts/html/epc/1973/e/ma1.html

There is currently no single European Union–wide patent. Since the 1970s, there has been concurrent discussion toward the creation of a community patent in the European Union. In May 2004, however, a stalemate was reached, and the prospect of a single European Union–wide patent is receding.

The EPC is separate from the European Union, and its membership is different: Switzerland, Liechtenstein, Turkey, Monaco, and Iceland are members of the EPO but are not members of the EU, while the opposite is true for Malta. The EPC provides a legal framework for the granting of European patents via a single, harmonized procedure before the European patent office. A single patent application may be filed at the European patent office in Munich, at its branches at The Hague or Berlin, or at a national patent office of a contracting state, if the national law of the state so permits. This last provision is important in countries such as the United Kingdom, in which it is an offense for a U.K. resident to file a patent application for inventions in certain sensitive areas abroad without obtaining clearance through the U.K. patent office first.

The Patent Cooperation Treaty

The *Patent Cooperation Treaty* (PCT) provides a unified procedure for filing patent applications to protect inventions internationally. A single filing results in a single search accompanied by a written opinion (and optionally a preliminary examination), after which the examination (if provided by national law) and grant procedures are handled by the relevant national or regional authorities. The PCT does not lead to the granting of an "international patent," which does not exist.

The states party to the PCT constitute the International Patent Cooperation Union. As of May 24, 2006, there were 132 contracting states.

Trademark Registration

Trademark registration is less costly and time consuming than patent registration.

1. The International Convention for the Protection of Industrial Property, better known as the Paris Union, is 90 years old and covers patents as well as trademarks. Under this convention six-month protection is provided a firm, during which time the trademark can be registered in the other member countries.
2. The Madrid Arrangement for International Registration of Trademarks has 22 members, but it offers the advantage that registration in one country qualifies as registration in all other member countries.

Communications

Although nothing substitutes for personal contact when developing an international marketing structure, this may not always be possible. Therefore, the tone of initial written communications is critical. It often makes the difference between a profitable long-term arrangement and a lost opportunity.

The Introductory Letter, Facsimile (Fax), or E-mail

Your introductory letter, fax, or e-mail most often can be written in your language, your potential buyers (or sellers) language, or in English. With the exception of Latin America, English has become the language of international business, but use simple words. If your communication must be translated and transmitted into a foreign language, make sure that you have it translated back to English by a third party before sending it. However proficient a person is in the other language, funny things can happen in translation.

From the beginning establish your company's favorable reputation and explain the relationship that you seek. Describe the product you want to market (export) or to purchase (import). Propose a personal meeting and offer the buyer a visit to your firm during the person's next visit to your country. Ask for a response to your letter. Figure 3.2 shows a sample letter of introduction.

Follow-Up Communications

As technology improves, more alternative forms of communications, including express delivery services, have become available, and choosing the best alternative may result in the competitive difference. Successful importing/exporting depends on reliable two-way communication. It is critical in establishing and running an import/export marketing network.

Telephone

Speech is the fastest way to convey ideas and receive answers. Voice communications allow for immediate feedback—quick response to fast-breaking problems or opportunities. Most countries can be dialed directly, and the rates for international telephone service depend on the time of day. While international telephone can be expeditious, it can be expensive if you have a lot to say.

Facsimile

Facsimile (fax), or telecopier service, remains one of the fastest growing means of business communication. The advantage of fax is that any image of up to $8\frac{1}{2}$ by 14 inches can be transmitted directly to the receiving unit. Letters, pictures, contracts, forms, catalog sheets, drawings, and illustrations—anything that would reproduce in a copy machine—can be sent.

On a historical note, facsimile is not new. It was invented over a century ago, in 1842, by Alexander Bain, a Scottish clockmaker. His device used a pendulum that swept a metal point over a set of raised metal letters. When the point touched a letter, it created an electrical charge that traveled down a telegraph wire to reproduce on paper the series of letters the pendulum had touched. Wire service photos were

Figure 3.2 Sample Letter of Introduction

> Our Company, Inc.
> Hometown, U.S.A.
>
>
> Ref:
> Date:
>
>
> XYZ Foreign Co.
> 2A1 Moon River
> Yokohama, Japan
>
>
> Gentlemen:
>
>
> Our Company, Inc., markets a line of highway spots. When se-
> cured to the centerline of highway, these spots provide for in-
> creased safety for motorists. We believe that these spots might
> interest foreign markets, especially the Japanese market. Our
> major customers include highway contractors and highway
> departments of the states of ABC and DEF.
>
>
> Our Company, founded in 1983, has sales of $1.5 million.
> Further details are given in the attached brochure. The at-
> tached catalogs and specification sheets give detailed informa-
> tion about our products.
>
>
> We are writing to learn whether: (1) XYZ Foreign Co. has a
> requirement to purchase similar products for use in Japan; and
> (2) XYZ Foreign Co. would be interested in representing Our
> Company in Japan.
>
>
> Don't hesitate to telephone if you need further details. We look
> forward to meeting with representatives of XYZ Foreign Co.
> about our highway spots.
>
>
> Sincerely,
>
>
> W. T. Door
> President

transmitted by fax as early as 1930. The U.S. Navy used them aboard ship during World War II for the transmission of weather data.

The earliest fax machines were clunkers and very expensive, taking more than 10 minutes to send a single page and costing more than $18,000. Today, dedicated facsimile terminals cost as little as $60. Their speed equates favorably to telex. Fax transmits over ordinary voice phone networks. Several private bureaus manage faxes as a worldwide service. There is no effective proof of delivery of a fax document. Although most businesses still maintain some kind of fax capability, the technology appears increasingly dated in the world of the Internet.

Internet

It wasn't that long ago that the Internet was just a public, amorphous collection of computer networks—a technofad made up of blending a few personal computers and citizen's band radio enthusiasts.

Today the Internet is the fastest growing and most exciting place to do business (see Chapter 4). New cross-indexing software and imaginative services are connecting the home computer masses to electronic commerce through Web servers and high-speed circuits into the World Wide Web.

This concept of linking buyers and sellers and elimination of paperwork will drive down the cost of transactions. The Internet has become the low-cost alternative to faxes, express mail, and other communications channels such as 1-800 telephone sales. Most international businesses have their own Web pages in more than one language. There are programs that will translate from one country's language to another.

The Internet knows no international boundaries—internauts are logging on from Bangkok to New York's Broadway. The network extends to all countries, and the most interesting part of it is nobody owns the Internet. The Internet is not guided by a single company or institution. The internet protocol (IP) allows any number of computer networks to link up and act as one.

On another historical note, the Internet is also not new. Its beginning was in the late 1960s when the Pentagon (American Defense

Department) asked computer scientists to find the best way for an unlimited number of computers to communicate—without relying on any single computer to be traffic cop. That way the system would not be vulnerable to nuclear attack. The outcome was the decision to fund experimental packet-switching communications using a transmission and control/internet protocol (TCP/IP) technology called ARPAnet that quickly expanded to dozens of universities and corporations. Programs were written to help people exchange e-mail and tap into remote databases. In 1983 ARPAnet was split into two networks, ARPAnet and Milnet, and the Pentagon mandated TCP/IP as the standard protocol. These two networks evolved into the Internet.

HOT TIP

Though print lacks speed (compared to voice), it provides written documentation that can be read and reread at the reader's pace and schedule.

Cables and Telexes

International mailgrams, telegrams, or cables can still be sent anywhere mail goes. These forms of communication require a complete mailing address, including any postal codes.

Cables are sent electronically to the major city nearest the recipient. There, the message may be telephoned and mailed, mailed only, or (in a few locations) delivered by messenger. Cables don't offer proof of delivery that a telex message does, and because of the extra handling, cables are significantly more expensive than telex messages. But a cable can be sent to anyone, anywhere.

There are still some telex terminals in government and business offices around the world. Their advantage is they can receive information automatically, even when unattended.

Communications Equipment

Electronic data transmission grew rapidly throughout the 1990s. In the new century data must flow easily and quickly back and forth among the importer/exporter and agencies, distributors, and customers. Electronic mail is now commonly delivered over international phone lines. Practically any computer can be interfaced with a modem via a cable, ordinary telephone, satellite, or microwave to any another computer or word processor anywhere in the world so long as the receiving country does not restrict or prohibit transborder data flows.

HOT COMMUNICATIONS TIPS

1. Write out your message and check it by reading it aloud.
2. Some situations in international business can be frustrating, so take care not to lose your temper and send a "zinger" that you'll regret later. Develop a cordial and professional style, and stick to it at all times. Try to draft replies in the morning when you are fresh. Whenever possible, let a second party read each message.
3. Send messages earlier in the day and earlier in the week to avoid the heavy calling periods and possible delay of your message.
4. Keep your messages brief, but avoid abbreviations that might not be understood.
5. Try to reply to every fax/telex/Internet message the same day it is received, even if only to give a date when a more complete reply will be sent. Keep in mind the differences in time zones between countries.
6. Use "ATTN: Name" rather than "Dear Name." Also, almost all fax/Internet messages, by custom, end with "Regards," "Best regards," or occasionally "Cordially."

Travel

Mistrust across international borders can be a barrier to a successful import/export business. Therefore, visiting the country and the people who offer goods for your importation or the agents or distributors who market your export products is essential. These personal contacts remind us that we have more in common with people from other nations than differences. Travel to exotic places is not only fun, but it is a tax deductible expense of international trade as well.

HOT TIP

The Internal Revenue Service will look closely at travel expenses to make sure that you are actually doing business and not indulging your love of travel. For this purpose keep good records during your travels and make sure you profit from your trips.

Planning a Trip

You alone know your itinerary, how long you can stay in each place, and what you expect to accomplish, so lay out your own trip before turning it over to a travel agent. Make certain your local arrival time allows for time changes and scheduled business meetings. Also, allow time for rest prior to negotiating.

After you have planned out your trip, take it to the travel agent for booking. Allow three to five days and expect some changes. You may need to go through country B in order to get to country C.

Foreign Travel Information

Terrorism is a major concern to traveling traders, but it should not keep you from your work. To stay alert to any possible danger areas in the world, contact the Citizens Emergency Center, Office of American Citizen Service & Crisis Management at the U.S. Department of State, Washington, DC, at 202-647-5225. See www.travel.state.gov for important information on traveling abroad.

Five Traveling Tips

1. Travel light. The usual arrival sequence is immigration followed by customs. Be ready to open your luggage and sometimes declare each item. Smile!

2. Request business class to most countries; it's more comfortable than coach and less expensive than first class.

3. Unless you are familiar with the better hotels in a country, you are usually better off staying at one that is internationally recognized. Most major travel companies, agents, or your local library can give you the names of the best hotels.

4. Are you a bit overweight? Now is the time to drop a few pounds. The food may be the best in the world, but eat light and drink only sterilized water.

5. Plan for the changing time zones. Think ahead and determine the local time of arrival for the plane you have booked. Remember that time is reckoned from Greenwich, England, and watches are normally set to a particular zone time. Time is changed near the crossing of the boundary between zones, usually at a whole hour. If you know the time zone, you can calculate the local time. Figure 3.3 depicts international time zones as they appear at noon Eastern standard time.

Passports and Visas

A *passport* is a travel document that identifies the holder as a citizen of the country from which it is issued. In the United States, the Department of State issues passports. You can apply at your local U.S. post office. Although these may change, the cost for Americans 16 years of age and older is $92 which includes a passport fee of $50, a security surcharge of $12, and an execution fee of $30. For those younger than 16, the passport fee is $40 plus the other fees, totaling $82. You should allow about two to three weeks for processing.

The *visa* is an official endorsement from a country a person wishes to visit. You must receive it before entry into that country is permitted. Some nations don't require a visa. Check with your travel agent or the

Figure 3.3 International Time Zones

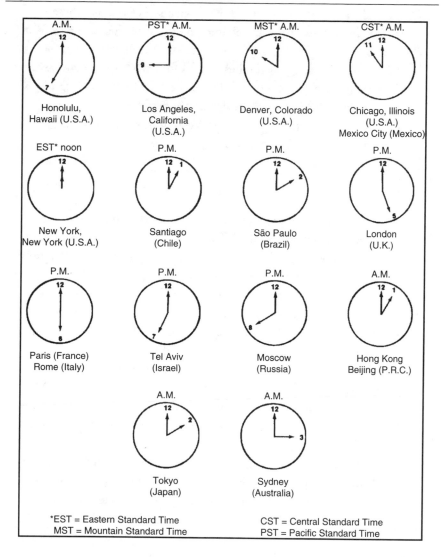

A.M.	PST* A.M.	MST* A.M.	CST* A.M.
Honolulu, Hawaii (U.S.A.)	Los Angeles, California (U.S.A.)	Denver, Colorado (U.S.A.)	Chicago, Illinois (U.S.A.) Mexico City (Mexico)
EST* noon	P.M.	P.M.	P.M.
New York, New York (U.S.A.)	Santiago (Chile)	São Paulo (Brazil)	London (U.K.)
P.M.	P.M.	P.M.	A.M.
Paris (France) Rome (Italy)	Tel Aviv (Israel)	Moscow (Russia)	Hong Kong Beijing (P.R.C.)
	A.M.	A.M.	
	Tokyo (Japan)	Sydney (Australia)	

*EST = Eastern Standard Time   CST = Central Standard Time
MST = Mountain Standard Time   PST = Pacific Standard Time

consul or embassy for the country you're planning to visit. You may prefer to give your passport and three photos to a visa service and let the service make the rounds of embassies. Count on waiting a week or more for the completion of this service.

Fares and Gratuities

On arrival in a country you have never visited before, ask the airline crew or counter personnel for such information as normal taxi fare from the airport to the hotel, sights to see, and local travel problems. Exchange your currency at the best rate. On departure use any excess local currency to pay your hotel bill. But be sure to save enough local currency for taxi fare and airport departure tax.

Smile and be cheerful as you pass through immigration and customs. A smile can head off a lot of problems.

Carnets

In over 69 countries your goods can go duty-free and extensive customs procedures may be avoided if you have an ATA (admission temporoire) carnet. See the list of 75 carnet countries in Appendix B and/or go to www.uscib.org for more information.

The ATA carnet is a standard international customs document used to obtain duty-free temporary admission of certain goods on an annualized basis into the countries that are signatories to the ATA Convention. Under the ATA Convention, commercial and professional travelers may take commercial samples; tools of the trade; advertising material; and cinematographic, audiovisual, medical, scientific, or other professional equipment into member countries temporarily without paying customs duties and taxes or posting a bond at the border of each country to be visited.

Applications for the ATA carnet are made to the Council for International Business in your country. In the United States, contact www.uscib.org or call 212-354-4480. Because countries are continuously added to the ATA carnet system, the traveler should contact the Council for International Business to learn if the country to be visited is included on the list. The list of over 97 nations and territories where the ATA carnet can be used (current as of 2008, www.ATAcarnet.com) may be found in Appendix B. The fee charged for the carnet depends on the value of the goods to be covered. A bond, letter of credit, or bank guarantee of 40 percent of the value of the goods is also required to cover duties and taxes that would be due if goods imported into a foreign country were not paid by the carnet holder. Typical processing fees are:

Shipment Value	Basic Processing Fee
Under $5,000	US$120
$5,000–14,999	US$150
$15,000–49,999	US$175
$50,000–199,999	US$200
$200,000–499,999	US$225
$500,000 and over	US$250

Further information can be found in the informative book published by the council titled *Carnet: Move Goods Duty-Free through Customs*.

If you don't get a carnet, check your samples at the airport with customs, but allow plenty of time to get them before the next flight.

The next chapter is intended to vault you into the cyber world. Read it and incorporate Internet sales into your project.

CHAPTER 4

SELLING WITH E-COMMERCE

This is one of the most important chapters of this book. Why? Because the Internet has redefined modern business!

Every day virtually every newspaper and television station in every country tells the story of how millions of computer users tap the global network for unparalleled access to communications, research information, and trade.

In its many forms, *e-commerce* may be defined as any commercial transaction carried out, facilitated, or enabled by the exchange of information electronically. The true value of the Internet and the World Wide Web that resides therein is that it is borderless.

Think of countries as if they were lakes without connecting canals; now with the Internet, people from one lake can swim easily to another lake where they can experience food, wares, and culture they could never before access.

The Internet and Your Business

The potential of the Internet for international e-commerce has been more than realized—big cross-border business is being conducted over the Web. The benefit to business is the capability to bring customers, vendors, and suppliers closer together and thus maximizing results. It promotes economies of scale, reduces operational costs, and improves customer service by enabling businesses to communicate directly with the client.

Background

Once the exclusive province of government and university researchers, the Internet has become an information nirvana for the common business person and is growing at a rate of about 10 to 20 percent each month.

Created in 1989 at CERN, a huge Swiss research laboratory, the Web began simply as a project to link scientists worldwide. But its intuitive, easy-to-use hypertextual design caused the Web to spread beyond its original user community. By accessing the Web with a browsing program, you can now tap a graphic environment in which you move between millions of Web sites that offer everything from sunglasses to Silly Putty. Most Web pages integrate images, sounds, and text to advertise their products and services.

In the 1950s the world sold things on Main Street; in the 1980s it was the mall; in the 1990s it was the superstore; but in the 2000s it is and will be at www.com. Why? Because, as Bill Gates, the founder of Microsoft, says, "The Net represents frictionless capitalism." (For a listing of Internet terms, see the glossary at the back of the book.)

The Global Marketing Opportunity

No supranational organization or head of state has been able to bring the world together, but the Web is uniting the world. Because there is no president or king of the Internet, small businesses can sell anywhere in the world.

The obvious advantage of the Internet is the ability to bypass the middle of the supply chain—that is, the many distributors, wholesalers, and storefronts of traditional business—to reach directly to the consumer. Now, customers (users and buyers) can be served directly, just like the old direct-mail marketing process but without the high cost of printing and postage. More importantly, the Internet knows no boundaries—it can reach the potential customer in every nook and cranny of the world, wherever a person can surf the Web.

The Cyber Trader

In 1998 there were $6.1 billion in consumer purchases were conducted over the Internet and about $15.6 billion in business-to-business sales. In 2001 the increase was 800 percent stronger, moving to more than $25 billion in consumer purchases and more than $200 billion in business-to-business sales. Yet today e-commerce is only 1 percent of total U.S. gross domestic product (GDP) and only 0.02 percent of total retail sales. Internet sales are expected to grow exponentially—in 2007, 1.319 billion people were using this method of communication.

The Changing Competition

The Web is also changing competition. Online businesses have an easier time locking in their customers with plenty of room for further growth. Consider geography, for example. As retailers expand, they must build storefronts and organize distribution networks, settling for smaller and smaller markets and having already hit the larger ones. The online competitor has the advantage because the business has instant reach. Costs of acquiring a customer in another city or country are the same as finding one locally.

Price is another way that the online business wins in the ever-changing competitive world. An online seller can undercut the non-Web player. In fact, some are even offering products and services for free while gaining their income through outside advertising.

Getting Started

Getting your business on the Web requires the least amount of financial capital; it simply requires what is known as a *virtual office*—that is, a computer or television, proper software, and a modem. This virtual office, which could be in the back room of your business, in your home, or on your lap when you're traveling, provides you with the adaptability and flexibility to enter your business environment on an equal footing with the largest companies. In other words, your business is no longer tied to a physical storefront or a desk—your Web page is your storefront. As long as you can plug into a telephone or cable line (or connect to a satellite), you can do business. You can even get faxes through your e-mail system by using services such as efax.com

The first step in obtaining a presence on the World Wide Web is the designing of a Web site, which is made up of a home page and several supplemental pages of information (see Figure 4.1). The home page is to the rest of your Web site as a book cover is to its contents. Because your business is international, you should consider allowing the user

Figure 4.1 Typical Home Page

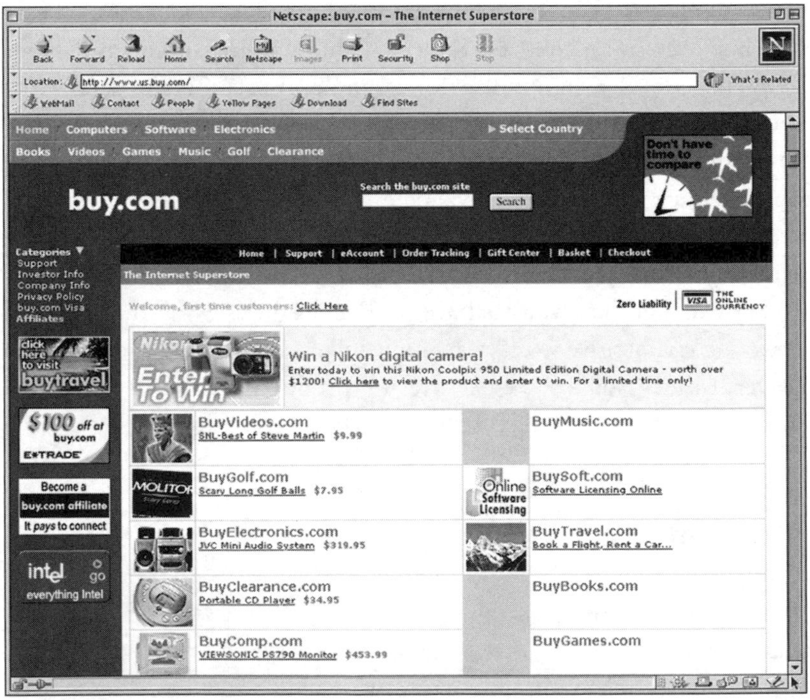

to click on a choice of languages—maybe English, French, Italian, Mandarin, and Hindi. Similarly, an early decision will be how many and which countries should you have a home page presence. For instance, Dell Computers has crossed national boundaries by having Web sites all over the world.

Home Page Presence

The home page design should be bold and visual but lean and mean, so that it can quickly capture attention yet be understood at a glance and lead the reader to the other pages of the site. Keep the home page simple. Don't clutter, and make it easy to navigate. The prospective customer who gets lost or confused while reading is quickly gone. Use your home page to make a few essential points like who you are, what you offer, and what's on the rest of the pages. Don't be too commercial. Internet protocol dictates that you offer some free information and entertainment first. Then you can ask for the sale.

No matter what you are selling, there are already many sites devoted to the same products or services. Know your competitors by searching them out. Learn what they have emphasized and what is working for them.

All too many businesses rush into this project without thinking it through. It is essential to plan ahead by identifying and honing your key messages and organizing them in a logical structure, developing a prototype page design, testing it on representative users, and refining it through successive iterations. Even after your Web site is up and running, revisit it often—keep it fresh by giving users something new and a reason to return.

KEYS TO SITE DESIGN

- Start slowly
- Place emphasis on content
- Make it easy for consumers to get around (navigate)
- Avoid using too many graphic elements

- Be entertaining
- Make your site graphically pleasing
- Reach sight-impaired readers
- Design for the overseas market by incorporating multiple languages
- Add pages to your site
- Accept credit cards
- Give payment options
- Make it easy to order
- Provide a shopping cart
- Provide links

Blogging

Blog is the contraction universally used for Weblog, a type of Web site in which entries are made (such as in a journal or diary) and displayed in reverse chronological order.

They often provide commentary or news on a particular subject, such as food, politics, or business. A typical blog combines text, images, and links to other blogs, Web pages, and other media related to the topic. Most blogs are primarily textual although some focus on photographs (photoblog), videos (vlog), or audio (podcast) and are part of a wider network of social media.

Early blogs were simply manually updated components of common Web sites. However, the evolution of tools to facilitate the production and maintenance of Web articles posted in chronological fashion made the publishing process feasible to a much larger, less technical population. Ultimately, this resulted in the distinct class of online publishing that produces blogs we recognize today. For instance, the use of some sort of browser-based software is now a typical aspect of blogging. Blogs can be hosted by dedicated blog hosting services, or they can be run using blog software, such as WordPress, blogger or LiveJournal, or they can run on regular Web hosting services, such as DreamHost.

While the great majority of blogs are noncommercial, full-time bloggers have struggled to find a way to make a profit from their work. The most common and simplest method is to accept targeted banner advertising. One form of advertising for bloggers is to promote merchandise from other sites. They receive a commission when a customer buys the item after following a blog link.

HISTORICAL NOTE

According to Wikipedia, the term *Weblog* was coined by Jorn Barger on December 17, 1997. The short form, *blog*, was coined by Peter Merholz, who jokingly broke the word *Weblog* into the phrase *we blog* in the sidebar of his blog Peterme.com in April or May of 1999. This was quickly adopted as both a noun and verb ("to blog," meaning "to edit one's Weblog or to post to one's Weblog").

You Can Create Your Own Web Site

Can you design your own Web site? Of course you can! Many people do. Learning HTML code is not difficult (see Figure 4.2); neither are FrontPage or DreamWeaver softwares. What is difficult is designing a Web page that captures the attention of customers. The technology of design is easy enough to learn, but the art of getting attention is not, so you might want to consider getting professional help.

SOFTWARE GUIDE

There are many software tools available to allow you to get your e-commerce project off the ground. Here is a list of some Internet software products; however, neither quality nor rank is implied—be aware the market is changing rapidly so these may not be around next year.

> Oracle Applications, (650) 506-7000, www.oracle.com
> Peoplesoft, (800) 380-7638, www.peoplesoft.com
> MySap.com, (610) 355-2500, www.sap.com
> Broadbase EPM, (650) 614-8301, www.broadbase.com
> BroadVision One-to-One, (650) 261-5900, www.broadvison.com
> Commerce Exchange, (212) 301-2500, www.interworld.com
> E-Speak and Chai Appliance Platform, (650) 857-1501
> The Kana Platform, (650) 298-9282, www.kana.com
> NetCommerce Family, (800) 772-2227, www.ibm.com
> Spectra and ColdFusion, (888) 939-2545, www.altaire.com
> Sun-Netscape Alliance, (650) 254-1900, www.netscape.com
> GoLive from Adobe, (800) 833-6687, www.adobe.com
> Homesite, (888) 939-2545, www.allaire.com
> FrontPage 2000, (800) 426-9400, www.microsoft.com
> WebLogic, (800) 817-4BEA, www.beasys.com
> Oberon E-Enterprise, (800) 654-1215, www.oberon.com
> Enfinity, (800) 736-5197, www.intershop.com
> Infranet, (408)343-4400, www.portal.com
> Quickbooks Internet Gateway, (650) 944-6000, www.quicken.com
> e-BIZ, (888) 4LUXENT, www.e-bixinabox.com

Or You Can Get Someone Else to Do It

Too many firms turn the task of creating a Web site over to a marketing director of the old school who never got past e-mail. What you need is a modern Internet geek who can design an entire online transaction from first look to showroom tour to a final handshake deal.

Like any other new endeavor, in every city there are people who specialize in Web page strategy and design. Many of these are recent college students who focused their training in this specialty. Others are affiliated with major advertising companies who have the advantage of the ad firm's years of experience and adapt it to the Web technology of modern communications.

HOT TIP

A *domain name* is what people type into search engines to find Web sites. Most companies use several domain names and aliases such as "Your-company.com" and others like "international business"—those appropriate to what people might type into a search engine to find your specialty or industry. The trick is to get your domain name to the top of the search engine list.

Figure 4.2 Example of HTML

Partial List of HTML Markup Tags

Markup Tags	Use of Tag
<A HREF="pagename.htm"> ... </A>	Create a link to another document
<A HREF="http://www.abc.com"> ... </A>	Create a link to another Web site
<A HREF="MAIL TO:you@xyz.com"> ... </A>	Create a link in order to send an e-mail message
<B> ... </B>	Boldface text
<BLOCKQUOTE> ... </BLOCKQUOTE>	Indents text from the left and right margins
<BODY> ... </BODY>	Encloses the body of the HTML document which is displayed by the browser
 	Creates a line break without extra space
<CENTER> ... </CENTER>	Centers text
<FONT COLOR = "X"> ... </FONT>	Allows use of different font colors e.g., <FONT COLOR = "red">
<FONT FACE = "X"> ... </FONT>	Allows use of different font styles e.g., <FONT FACE = "arial">
<FONT SIZE = "X"> ... </FONT>	Allows change of font size in running text e.g., <FONT SIZE="+2">
<H1> thru <H6> ... </H1> thru </H6>	First- through sixth-level headings
<HEAD> ... </HEAD>	Encloses the heading of the HTML document
<HR>	Creates a horizontal rule line
<HTML> ... </HTML>	Encloses the entire HTML document
<I> ... </I>	Italic text
<IMG SRC="xxx">	Used to insert an in-line image, e.g., <IMG SRC="pic.gif">
<LI>	Used to create list items
	Used in place of a space to create a nonbreaking space so line doesn't overflow line
<OL> ... </OL>	Used to create a numbered or ordered list
<P>	Creates a line break with extra space before start of next text block
<PRE> ... </PRE>	Retains the spacing that is keyed in the text within the tags
<TITLE> ... </TITLE>	Indicates the title of the HTML document
<U> ... </U>	Underlined text
<UL> ... </UL>	Used to create a bulleted or unordered list
<!-- ... -->	Used to insert nondisplayed comments in the HTML document

Note: For a complete listing of HTML codes, check the following Web site: http://www.willcam.com/cmat/html/crossname.html

(Continued)

Figure 4.2 (Continued)

Sample of Markup Tags

```
<HTML>
<HEAD>
<TITLE>My Home Page</TITLE></HEAD><BR>
<BODY>
<FONT SIZE="+2"><B><I>Welcome to...</B></I></FONT><BR>
<FONT SIZE="+3"><B><I>My Home Page</B></I></FONT><P>
<IMG SRC="4bird.gif"><P><P><P>
<FONT SIZE="+1">I'm<B>glad</B>you are visiting my home page.
<BR><BR>
<H1>Example of first-level heading</H1>
<H3>Example of third-level heading</H3><P>
<!--This comment will not print on the Web page-->
Following are list items:<BR>
<UL>
<LI>List item #1<BR>
<LI>List item #2<P>
</UL>
<PRE>      A PRE tag allows you to control placement
</FONT></PRE><P>
Send an e-mail message to:
<A HREF="mailto:me@my-isp>me@my-isp</A>
<BR><BR></FONT>
<HR>
<CENTER>
<FONT SIZE="2">Copyright &#169 1996-97.companyname
</CENTER>
</BODY>
</HTML>
```

Essential Web Page Tags

```
<HTML>
<HEAD>
    Between the HEAD tags you put the title, meta
    tags, and other nonprinting information
<TITLE>Title of your page goes here</TITLE>
</HEAD>
<BODY>
    Between the BODY tags is where you put all
    information that will be visible on your Web page.
</BODY>
</HTML>
```

Getting Out There

It is one thing to have a Web site; it's another that customers know it exists and how to find it. First of all, put your Web site and e-mail addresses on your brochures, flyers, trucks, ships, billboards, ads, stationery, and business cards. Next get your Web site address listed in an Internet business directory such as www.directory.net. There are many such directories, and many do not charge for inclusion. Another is to join a virtual mall—a group of Internet businesses using the metaphor of a shopping mall. Last but not least, be certain to get your address on as many search engines as possible.

Search Engines

Search engines compile lists for consumers who surf for a product. The trick is to get your address as high on the search engine list as possible. Because engines use different criteria, there are several strategies. First in importance is your domain name. For instance the term "international business" will bring domain names such as internationalbusiness.com or international-business.com or internationalbusiness.org to the top of the list. If your business domain name just used the initials of your company, you will find yourself near the bottom of the list. The right strategy is to use several domain names. The second trick is giving the right title of your Web pages. A title such as "ABCD company discount sunglasses" will come up closer to the top than just the company name. The next criterion is the HTML document. Sunglass.html will get you closer to the top than 1234.doc or abbreviated names.

TOP SEARCH ENGINES

37.com (searches 37 search engines at once)
google.com
Altavista.com
Infoseek.com
Excite.com
aol.com/netfind
hotbot.com

lycos.com
webscrawler.com
yahoo.com

Finding Foreign Markets

There are more than 200 million online users worldwide; over 100 million are in the United States and Canada. Even so, the potential market is phenomenal because everyone who has a computer or television set is getting on the Net.

Finding foreign buyers continues to be a market research problem. As always, start with the country or region. But where to look? Try the following databases:

STAT-USA/Internet. A service of the U.S. Department of Commerce, this is the site for the U.S. business, economic, and trade community. It provides authoritative information from the federal government. It includes access to the National Trade Data Bank (NTDB) for country and market research. (http://www.stat-usa.gov/)

Strategis. This is a Canadian government trade assistance site which has international trade information and statistics that can be turned into a graphic presentation of the top 10 markets for most products. Follow the international and trade links. (http://www.strategis.ic. gc.ca/engdoc/main.html)

The Central Intelligence Agency. The CIA Fact Book is one of the best sources of basic information on any country. (http://www.odci. gov/cia/ciahome.html)

The SBA Office for International Trade. Extensive links and training resources can be found at http://www.sbaoniine. sba.gov/OIT/ info/Iinks.html.

Michigan State University, Center for International Business and Education Research (CIBER). International Business Resources on the WWW. It has one of the best and most extensive sites for international markets, trade leads, and hotlinks on all aspects of global markets. (http://ciber.bus.msu.edu/busres.htm)

Tradeport. This is one of the most extensive international trade resources on the Internet. A free site with market information, guidance, and resource listing as well as trade leads and international events in the southern California area. (http://www.tradeport.org)

Finding Foreign Buyers

Of course there are over 400 trade lead sites: the United Nations (www.un.org) and the World Trade Centers Association (www.wtca.org) have lead services. To reach over 2 million traders, try these resources:

NEOS—National Export Offer Service. A comprehensive site for links and access to foreign buyers, directories, and guidance resources. (http://www.exportservices.com)

Europages. Contains information on 500,000 companies in 30 countries. Excellent place to search for companies to contact, by product or service search as buyers or for market research. (http://www.europages.com)

Clear Freight. Follow the trade lead links section for an extensive set of contacts and go back to the main page for freight forwarder information. (http://www.clearfreight.com)

Global Electronic Commerce Korea. Great site with links to many other countries with company directories. Try EC Links for an extensive list of other areas and trade lead sites. (http://www.commerce. ktnet.co.kr)

Beaucoup. A search engine directory that also lists country-specific searches and several directories in each country. (http://www.beaucoup.com)

Europeonline. A central access site to all countries in Europe in local languages and English, for business, financial, and general information. Access to European Union info and europages. (http://www.europeonline.com)

Trade Show Central. A free Internet service providing information on more than 50,000 trade shows, conferences, and seminars; 5,000 service providers; and 8,000 venues and facilities around the world. (http://www.tscentral.com/)

Government Procurement

Ever since the World Trade Organization formalized opportunities for bidding, government procurement competition has become worldwide. Here are a few valuable addresses:

www.wto.org/

www.arnet.gov

www.texas-one.org/market/newposts.html

www.financenet.gov/financenet/sales/saleint.html

www.Jetro.go.jp

www.govcon.com
www.sbaonline.sba.gov

Pricing and Marketing Your Product

Gone are the days of arbitrary pricing. Because the Internet offers worldwide openness, pricing without substance is gone forever. You must continually check the market and competition and provide additional services and features as necessary to maintain your price. Places to search are www.price.com or mysimon.com.

Marketing Techniques

The Internet is a place where creativity reigns. Here are some techniques that have been evolving as the Web has grown from childhood to adolescence:

- Set up a chat area or a blog
- Sell advertising on your page
- Create contests for your customers

- Build customer lists
- Offer a free catalog
- Offer coupons
- Provide information
- Publish a newsletter
- Sell access to your products and services
- Upload your annual report

Communications

If you don't have an e-mail address, you may as well pack up and move to the South Pole. In today's business world, an e-mail address is a must.

E-mail is currently being used 10 to 1 over postal services, and the rate of change is growing. Business contracts are being negotiated between nations via e-mail routinely. This author recently negotiated book contracts with a London publisher by e-mail.

Getting Paid

Yes, you can ask for cash, you can take checks, PayPal, or accept credit cards, but the world's standard method of payment for big sales is still the documentary letter of credit (see Chapter 6 for a more complete discussion). The Internet is able to combine technology with standard business systems to continue to use the letter of credit as an easy, trust-worthy payment method.

Internet technologies available include: document management software, document imaging, electronic mail, interactive forms within Web browsers, and password security protocols. One source of good information about this subject is www.AVGTSG.com, a company that specializes in payment solutions relating to the Internet.

Keeping in Touch

Things are changing so fast in international trade that most business people find it difficult to keep up. However, here are several publications that seem to keep up with the trends:

www.baidu.com

www.alibaba.com

www.taobao.com

www.AliPay.com

www.tradeport.com

www.aaatrading.com

www.exporter.com

www.worldtrademag.com

www.exporttoday.com

www.AVGTSG.com

www.pangaea.net

www.tradecompass.com

www.euromktg.com

www.fedex.com

www.dhl.com

www.bankamerica.com

www.worldbank.com
www.merklerweb.com/imall/imall/htm

What About the Future?

Eliminating cultural differences is one of the goals of Internet trade. Some people can't get past their feelings about differences (ethnocentrism) and therefore they don't trade with foreigners.

A text-based system suitable for smaller businesses with the same rules for everyone is needed. However, it should be one that would allow us to close a deal quickly, but not before we can check on performance and financial background. A corollary, and most important, the system must be secure.

Are you familiar with the Chinese Web site Alibaba.com (essentially a Chinese manufacturer's business directory)? This company has been growing at a phenomenal rate since about 2001 (along with others such a FITA, Europages, and tradeleads.com).

Alibaba is somewhat different from sites in other countries because it is continually finding new ways of leveraging technology to enhance its overall value proposition. Alibaba recently struck a deal with Microsoft to begin implementing real-time communications (essentially like MSN instant messenger) in its platform so that as buyers find potential suppliers, they can instantly form a dialogue. This essentially breaks new ground for the future of trade on the Internet—not because of where Alibaba is now but because of where it will be going. It signals a new paradigm in international trade.

E-commerce Law

The laws governing e-commerce are constantly changing. This author does not claim to be an expert in this area but encourages those participating in this important area of world business to become familiar with the latest methods. Here are a few sources you may find useful:

euro.ecom.cmu.edu/resources/elibrary/ecllinks.shtml

www.bakernet.com/ecommerce

www.knowthis.com/legal/internetlaw.htm

www.mbc.com/ecommerce/ecom_overview.asp

www.denniskennedy.com/resources/technology-law-central/ecomlaw.aspx

www.weblaw.co.uk

The next chapter further expands the concepts related to both import and export, developing the fundamentals needed to "complete the transaction," namely, financing, avoiding risk, shipping, and documentation.

Further Readings

Alfonsi, Benjamin, "Web globalization," IEEE Distributed Systems Online, Vol. No. 1, 2005.

Bishop, Mark, *How to Build a Successful International Web Site*, Coriolis Group Books, 1997. An excellent detailed instruction manual for creating an international Web site, including software for language editing and information on international search engines.

Block, David, "*Globalization, Transnational Communication and the Internet*," Institute of Education, London University, 2003.

Clarke, George R. G., and Scott J. Wallsten, "Evidence from Industrial and Developing Countries," World Bank Policy Research Working paper 3215, February 2004.

Cronin, Mary, *Doing More Business on the Internet*, Wiley, 1995.

Easton, Jaclyn, *Striking It Rich.com—Profiles of 23 Incredibly Successful Websites You've Probably Never Heard Of*, McGraw-Hill, 1998. A very exciting collection of accounts of a wide variety of Web sites and how they achieved success. This book contains the mistakes, ideas, and insights of different online businesses and provides a great understanding of what it takes to achieve success. Her active Web site contains updates on the subjects and keeps the book from being outdated.

Ellsworth, Jill, and Matthew Ellsworth, *The Internet Business Book*, John Wiley, 1994.

Emery, Vince, *How to Grow Your Business on the Internet* (3rd Ed.), Coriolis Group Books, 1996. A most comprehensive discussion of the best Internet business strategies, marketing strategies, and many aspects of online business, based on actual experience and several years of active participation in the field. Also has an active Web site.

Gilster, Paul, *The Internet Navigator*, John Wiley, 1993.

Lundquist, Leslie Heeter, *Selling Online for Dummies*, IDG Books Worldwide, 2000. A basic instruction manual for setting up business online and developing a Web site and the tools to enhance business results. Also comes with a package of software tools and tips.

Resnick, Rosalind, and Dave Taylor, *The Internet Business Guide* (2nd Ed.), Sams Publishing, 1995.

Schwartz, Evan, *Webonomics: Nine Essential Principles for Growing your Business on the World Wide Web*, Broadway Books, 1998. An excellent analysis about what works online and what does not work. Contains fundamental insights into Internet business, global or otherwise. Schwartz also publishes an e-mail newsletter for readers and subscribers.

Smith, Bud, and Frank Catalano, *Marketing Online for Dummies*, IDG Books Worldwide, 1998. A comprehensive guide to marketing strategies online and includes a software package with many tools.

CHAPTER 5

COMPLETING A SUCCESSFUL TRANSACTION

In Chapter 2 you learned the basics of start-up. Chapter 3 led you through the concepts of planning and negotiating a transaction. Then Chapter 4 explained how to compete using e-commerce. This chapter covers the remaining commonalties, that is, paying for the goods and physically moving them from one country to another.

Now, are you ready for the steps needed to complete an import or export transaction? They are:

1. Financing
2. E-banking
3. Avoiding risk
4. Letters of credit
5. Physical distribution (packing and shipping)
6. Documentation

Financing

To start, expand, or take advantage of opportunities, all businesses need new money sooner or later. By *new money* we mean money that we have not yet earned but that can become the engine for growth.

For the importer, financing offers the ability to pay for the overseas manufacture and shipment of foreign goods destined for the domestic market. For the exporter, financing could mean working capital to pay for international travel and the marketing effort. New money can also be loans to foreign buyers so that buyers can purchase an exporter's goods.

If the homework phase is done well and purchase orders for the product(s) are in hand, there is plenty of currency available—banks or factors are waiting to assist.

The Bank

Commercial banking is the primary industry that supports the financing of importing and exporting. Selection of a banking partner is an essential part of the teamwork required for international trade success. When shopping for a bank, look for the following:

1. A strong international department
2. E-banking
3. Speed in handling transactions (does it want to make money on your money—called the *float?*)
4. The bank's relationship with overseas banks (that is, does it have corresponding relationships with banks in the countries in which you wish to do business?)
5. Credit policy

HOT TIP

In the import/export industry there is a saying: "Walk on two legs." This means that you should choose carefully and then work closely with a good international bank and a customs broker/freight forwarder.

E-banking

Electronic banking (e-banking) is an umbrella term for the process by which customers perform banking transactions electronically without physically visiting an institution. The following terms all refer to one form or another of electronic banking:

- Personal computer (PC) banking
- Internet banking
- Virtual banking
- Online banking
- Home banking
- Remote electronic banking
- Phone banking

Personal computer banking, Internet, or online banking are the most frequently used designations. It should be noted, however, that the terms used to describe the various types of electronic banking are often used interchangeably.

This form of banking enables customers to execute transactions from a computer via a modem. The bank typically offers the customer a proprietary financial software program that allows the customer to perform financial transactions from his or her home computer. The customer then dials into the bank with his or her modem, downloads data, and runs the programs that are resident on the customer's computer.

Currently, many banks offer banking systems that allow customers to obtain account balances and credit card statements, pay bills, and transfer funds between accounts.

The alternative method is often called Internet banking. You enter your personal account on the bank's Web site with a coded personal identification number (PIN). Internet banking uses the Internet as the delivery channel by which, for example, we transfer funds, pay bills, view checking and savings account balances, pay mortgages, and purchase financial instruments and certificates of deposit. An Internet banking customer accesses his or her accounts from a browser—software that runs Internet banking programs resident on the bank's World Wide

Web server, not on the user's PC. A true Internet bank is one that provides account balances and some transactional capabilities to retail customers over the World Wide Web. Internet banks are also known as virtual, cyber, Net, interactive, or Web banks.

Online currencies such as PayPal and Internetcash have increased e-commerce sales to just under $16 billion per quarter in 2006, from about $6 billion in 1999.

PayPal and Internetcash work like this: A consumer funds an account by providing his or her bank or credit card information. The consumer can then send funds to anyone with an e-mail address. Funds from PayPal or Internetcash can be withdrawn by check or transferred to a bank account.

Some Internet banks exist without physical branches. In some cases, Web banks are not restricted to conducting transactions within national borders and have the ability to conduct transactions involving large amounts of assets instantaneously. According to industry analysts, electronic banking provides a variety of attractive possibilities for remote account access, including:

- Availability of inquiry and transaction services around the clock
- Worldwide connectivity
- Easy access to transaction data, both recent and historical
- Direct customer control of international movement of funds without intermediation of financial institutions in customer's jurisdiction

Forms of Bank Financing

Loans for international trade fall into two categories: secured and unsecured.

Secured Financing

Banks are not high risk takers. To reduce their exposure to loss, they often ask for collateral. Financing against collateral is called *secured financing* and is the most common method of raising new money. Banks will advance funds against payment obligations, shipment documents, or storage documents. Most common of these is advancement of funds against payment obligations or documentary title. In this case, the trader pledges the goods for export or import as collateral for a loan to finance those goods. The bank maintains a secure position by accepting as collateral documents that convey title such as negotiable bills of lading, warehouse receipts, or trust receipts.

Another popular method of obtaining secured financing is the *banker's acceptance* (BA). This is a time draft presented to a bank by an exporter. This differs from what is known as a *trade acceptance* between buyer and seller in which a bank is not involved. The bank stamps and signs the draft "accepted" on behalf of its client, the importer. By accepting the draft, the bank undertakes and recognizes the obligation to pay the draft at maturity and has placed its creditworthiness between the exporter (*drawer*) and the importer (*drawee*). Banker's acceptances are negotiable instruments that can be sold in the money market. The BA rate is a discount rate generally two to three points below the prime rate. With the full creditworthiness of the bank behind the draft, eligible BAs attract the very best of market interest rates. The criteria for eligibility are:

1. The BA must be created within 30 days of the shipment of the goods.
2. The maximum tenor is 180 days after shipment.
3. It must be self-liquidating.
4. It cannot be used for working capital purposes.
5. The credit recipient must attest to no duplication.

Shipping documents. Commercial invoices, bills of lading, insurance certificates, consular invoices, and related documents.

Draft. The same as a "bill of exchange." A written order for a certain sum of money to be transferred on a certain date from the person who owes the money or agrees to make the payment (the drawee) to the creditor to whom the money is owed (the drawer of the draft). See glossary for "date draft," "documentary draft," "sight draft," and "time draft."

Unsecured Financing

In truth, *unsecured financing* is only for those who have a sound credit standing with their bank or have had long-term trading experience. It usually amounts to expanding already existing lines of working credit. For the small importer/exporter unsecured financing will probably be limited to a personal line of credit.

Factors

A *factor* is an agent who will, at a discount (usually 5 to 8 percent of the gross), buy receivables. Banks do 95 percent of factoring; the remainder is done by private specialists. The factor makes a profit on the collection and provides a source of cash flow for the seller, albeit less than if the business had held out to make the collection itself.

For example, suppose you had a receivable of $1,000. A factor might offer you a $750 advance on the invoice and charge you 5 percent on the gross of $1,000 per month until collection. If the collection is made within the first month, the factor would keep only $50 and return $200. If it takes two months, the factor would keep $100 and return only $150, and so on.

The importer benefits from having the cash to reorder products from overseas. For a manufacturer, the benefit can be cash flow available for increased or new production.

Other Private Sources of Financing

The United States has several major private trade financing institutions, all in competition to support your export programs.

Private Export Funding Corporation (PEFCO)

The Private Export Funding Corporation (PEFCO) was established in 1970 and is owned by about 60 banks, 7 industrial corporations, and an investment banking firm. PEFCO operates with its own capital stock, an extensive line of credit from the U.S. government's EXIM Bank, and the proceeds of its secured and unsecured debt obligations. It provides medium- and long-term loans, subject to EXIM Bank approval, to foreign buyers of U.S. goods and services. PEFCO generally deals in sales of capital goods with a minimum commitment of about $1 million—there is no maximum. Contact: PEFCO, 280 Park Ave. (4-West), New York, NY 10017; phone: (212) 916-0300; fax: (212) 286-0304; e-mail: info@pefco.com; www.pefco.com

Overseas Private Investment Corporation (OPIC)

The Overseas Private Investment Corporation (OPIC) is a private, self-sustaining institution whose purpose is to promote economic growth in developing countries. OPIC's programs include insurance, finance, missions, contractors' and exporters' insurance programs, small contractors' guarantee programs, and investor information services. For more information: OPIC, 1615 M Street NW, Washington, DC 20527; phone: (202) 336-8400; fax: (202) 408-9859; www.opic.gov

Government Sources

Many nations are short on foreign exchange, and what they have is earmarked for priority national imports and to service large international credit commitments. Nevertheless, there are probably more sources of competitive financing available today to support exporting than at any other time in history. The major complaint is that not enough firms are taking advantage of the programs.

Small Business Administration (SBA)

All nations support the growth of small business. For example the U.S. government has a Small Business Administration (SBA), which guarantees that small companies that can show reasonable ability to pay can get 10-year working capital loans for not more than prime plus 4.25 percent. The maximum maturity may be up to 25 years, depending on the use of the loan proceeds. Interest rates can be negotiated between borrowers and lenders, subject to SBA maximums pegged at prime rate. The SBA's export revolving-line-of-credit guarantee program provides pre-export financing for the manufacture or purchase of goods for sale to foreign markets and to help a small business penetrate or develop a foreign market. The maximum maturity for this financing is 18 months. The SBA, in cooperation with the Export–Import Bank, participates in loans of between $200,000 and $1 million.

Export–Import (EXIM) Bank

For those exporters who have found a sale, but the buyer can't find the financing in her or his own country, the Export–Import (EXIM) Bank has funds available to provide credit support in the form of loans, guarantees, and insurance for small businesses. The Export–Import Bank of the United States is a federal agency to help finance the export of U.S. goods and services. Rates vary but are available for a 5- to 10-year maturity period.

Programs include medium- and long-term loans and guarantees that cover up to 85 percent of a transaction's export value with repayment terms of one year or longer. Long-term loans and guarantees are provided for over seven years but not usually more than 10 years. The Medium-Term Credit Program has more than $300 million available for small businesses facing subsidized foreign competition. The Small Business Credit Program also has funds available, with direct credit for exporting medium term goods; competition is not necessary. The EXIM Working Capital Program (EWCP) guarantees the lender's repayment on short-term capital loans for exports with 0- to 10-year repayment periods. Web site contact can be made at www.exim.gov.

The Agency for International Development (AID)

This organization, a subordinate division of the U.S. State Department, provides loans and grants to less-developed countries for both developmental and foreign policy reasons. Under the AID Development Assistance Program funds are available at rates of 2 and 3 percent over 40 years. The AID Economic Development Fund also has funds at similar interest rates. Generally, these funds are available through invitations to bid through the *Commerce Daily Bulletin*, a publication available from the Government Printing Office, Washington, DC 20402; phone: (202) 712-0600; fax (202) 216-3524; e-mail: inquiries@ usaid.gov; Web site: www.usaid.gov.

The International Development Cooperation Agency (IDCA)

This organization sponsors a Trade and Development Program (TDP), and loans funds on an annual basis so that friendly countries can procure foreign goods and services for major development projects. Often, these funds support smaller firms in subcontract positions.

Avoiding Risk

Doing business always involves some risk, so you should expect across-border business to be no different. A certain amount of uncertainty is always present in doing business across international borders, but much of it can be hedged, managed, and controlled. All major exporting countries have arrangements to protect exporters and the bankers who provide their funding support. Avoiding and/or controlling risks in global trade is an everyday occurrence for importers and exporters. Understanding the instruments available for avoiding risk is not difficult but is vital. There are essentially four kinds of risks:

- *Commercial risks.*   Not being paid; non-delivery of goods; insolvency or protracted default by the buyer; competition; and disputes over product, warranty, and so forth.
- *Foreign exchange risks.*   Foreign exchange fluctuations.
- *Political risks.*   War, coup d'état, revolution, expropriation, expulsion, foreign exchange controls, or cancellation of import or export licenses.

- *Shipping risks.* Risk of damage and/or loss at sea or via other transportation.

Most risks allow for a method of avoidance. Of course, there is no insurance for such problems as disputes over quality or loss of markets resulting from competition, but there are management instruments for three aspects of risk: not being paid, loss or damage, and foreign exchange exposure.

Avoidance of Commercial Risk

The *seller* would like to be certain that the buyer will pay on time once the goods have been shipped. The goal is to at least minimize the risk of nonpayment. On the other hand, the *buyer* wants to be certain the seller will deliver on time and that the goods are exactly what the buyer ordered.

These concerns are most often heard from anyone beginning an import/export business. Mistrust across international borders is natural; after all, there is a certain amount of mistrust even in our own culture. Two keys to risk avoidance is a check of the buyer's credit rating and reputation, as well as a well-written sales contract. In Chapter 3 you learned that an early step in the process of international trade is to gain contract agreement with your overseas business associate. This should include the method of payment.

Getting Paid

Ensuring prompt payment worries exporters more than any other factor. The truth is that the likelihood of a bad debt from an international customer is very low. In the experience of most international business people, overseas bad debts seldom exceed 0.5 percent of sales. The reason is that in overseas markets, credit is still something to be earned as a result of having a record of prompt payment. Use common sense in extending credit to overseas customers, but don't use tougher rules than you use for your domestic clients.

The methods of payment, in order of decreasing risk to the seller are: open account, consignment, bank drafts (time draft, sight draft), authority to purchase, letter of credit, and cash in advance. Table 5.1 summarizes and compares the various methods of payment in order of decreasing risk to the exporter and increasing risk to the importer. Other useful methods that enable paperless trading between companies are Electronic Data Interchange, or EDI (www.EDI.com); Swift (www.swift.com); and Bolero (www.bolero.net).

Open Account

The *open account* is a trade arrangement in which goods are shipped to a foreign buyer without guarantee of payment. Though the riskiest, many firms that have a long-standing business relationship with the same overseas firm use this method. Needless to say, the key is to know your buyer and your buyer's country. You should use an open account when the buyer has a continuing need for the seller's product or service. Some experienced exporters say that they deal only in open accounts. But they

Table 5.1 Comparison of Various Methods of Payment

(In order of decreasing risk to exporter and increasing risk to importer)

Method	Goods Available to Buyers	Usual Time of Payment	Exporter Risk	Importer Risk
Open account	Before payment	As agreed	Most: relies on importer to pay account	Least
Consignment	Before payment	After sold	Maximum: exporter retains title	Minor inventory cost
Time draft	Before payment	On maturity of draft	High: relies on importer to pay draft	Minimal check of quantity/ quality
Sight draft	After payment	On presenting draft to importer	If unpaid, goods are returned/ disposed	Little if inspection report required
Authority to purchase	After payment	On presenting draft	Be careful of recourse	Little if inspection report required
Letter of credit	After payment	When documents are available after shipment	None	None if inspection report required
Cash	After payment	Before shipment	Least	Most

always preface that statement by saying that they have close relationships and have been doing business with those overseas clients for many years. An open account can be risky unless the buyer is of unquestioned integrity and has withstood a thorough credit investigation. The advantage of this method is its ease and convenience, but with open-account sales, you bear the burden of financing the shipment. Standard practice in many countries is to defer payment until the merchandise is sold, sometimes even longer. Therefore, among the forms of payment, open-account sales require the greatest amount of working capital. In addition, you bear the exchange rate if the sales are quoted in foreign currency. Nevertheless, competitive pressures may force the use of this method.

HOT TIP

Relationships between buyer and seller make the difference by reducing mistrust. Make an effort to meet and get to know your trading partner.

Consignment
The seller (consignor) retains title to the goods during shipment and storage of the product in the warehouse or retail store. The consignee acts as a selling agent, selling the goods and remitting the net proceeds to the consignor. Like open-account sales, consignment sales can also be risky, and they lend themselves to only certain kinds of merchandise. Great care should be taken in working out this contractual arrangement. Be sure it is covered with adequate risk insurance.

Bank Drafts, Time Drafts, and Sight Drafts
Payment for many sales is arranged using one of many time-tested banking methods. *Bank drafts* (bills of exchange), *time drafts*, and *sight drafts* are each useful under certain circumstances.

   Bank Drafts   Bank drafts are simply written orders that activate payment either at sight or at "tenor," which is a future time or date. A bank draft is a check, drawn by a bank on another bank, used primarily where it is necessary for the customer to provide funds payable at a bank in some distant location. The exporter who undertakes this payment method can offer a range of payment options to the overseas customer.

Time (Date) Draft   This is an acceptance order drawn by the exporter on the importer (customer), payable a certain number of days after "sight" (presentation) to the holder. Think of it as nothing more than an IOU, or promise to pay in the future.

Documents such as negotiable bills of lading, insurance certificates, and commercial invoices accompany the draft and are submitted through the exporter's bank for collection. When presented to the importer at the bank, the importer acknowledges that the documents are acceptable and commits to pay by writing "accepted" on the draft and signing it. The importer normally has 30 to 180 days depending on the draft's term to make payments to the bank for transmittal.

Sight Draft   This is similar to the time draft except that the importer's bank holds the documents until the importer releases the funds. Sight drafts are the most common method employed by exporters throughout the world. Sight drafts are nothing more than a written order on a standardized bank format requesting money from the overseas buyer. While this method costs less than the letter of credit (defined below), it has greater risk because the importer can refuse to honor the draft.

Bill of lading. A document that provides the terms of the contract between the shipper and the transportation company to move freight between stated points at a specified charge.

Commercial or customs invoice. A bill for the goods from the seller to the buyer. It is one method used by governments to determine the value of the goods for customs valuation purposes.

At sight. Indicates that a negotiable instrument is to be paid upon presentation or demand.

Authority to Purchase

This method is occasionally used in the Far East. It specifies a bank where the exporter can draw a documentary draft on the importer's bank. The problem with this method is that if the importer fails to pay the draft, the bank has "recourse" to the exporter for settlement. If an exporter consents to this method, it is suggested that the authority to purchase specify "without recourse" and so state on drafts.

The major risk with the time, sight, and authority to purchase methods is that the buyer can refuse to pay or to pick up the goods. The method of avoidance is to require cash against documents. Unfortunately, this method is slow because banks are slow in transferring funds because they want to use the time float (short-term investment of bank money) to earn interest. Using a wire transfer can get around this.

Letters of Credit (L/C)

Ideally an exporter would deal only in cash, but in reality, few business people are initially able or willing to do business under those terms. Because of the risk of non-payment resulting from insolvency, bankruptcy, or other severe deterioration, procedures and documents have been developed that help to ensure that foreign buyers honor their agreements.

The most common form of collection is payment against a *letter of credit* (L/C). The L/C is the time-tested method in which an importer's bank guarantees that if all documents are presented in exact conformity with the terms of the L/C, it will pay the exporter. The procedure is not difficult to understand, and most cities have banks with persons familiar with L/C's mechanics.

This method is well understood by traders around the world, is simple, and is as good as your bank. Internationally the term *documentary credits* is synonymous with the term *letter of credit*. They involve thousands of transactions and billions of dollars every day in every part of the world. They are almost always operated in accordance with the Uniform Customs and Practice for Documentary Credits of the International Chamber of Commerce, a code of practice that is recognized by banking communities in 156 countries. A *Guide to Documentary Operations*, which includes all the standard forms, is available from ICC Publishing Corporation, Inc., 156 Fifth Avenue, Suite 417, New York,

NY 10010; phone: (212) 206-1150; fax: (212) 633-6025; e-mail pub@ iccwbo.org; Web address: www.iccbooks.com.

An L/C is a document issued by a bank at the importer's or buyer's request in favor of the seller. It promises to pay a specified amount of money upon receipt by the bank of certain documents within a specified time or at intervals corresponding with shipments of goods. It is a universally used method of achieving a commercially acceptable compromise. Think of a letter of credit as a loan against collateral wherein the funds are placed in an escrow account. The amount in the account depends on the relationship between the buyer and the buyer's bank.

Typically, if you don't already have an account, the bank will require 100 percent collateral. With an account, the bank will establish a line of credit against that account. For instance, if you have $5,000 in your account and the transaction is expected to cost $1,000, your account will be reduced to $4,000 and the line of credit will be established as $1,000.

Commercial letter of credit charges are competitive, so you should comparison shop. Typically they are like those shown in Table 5.2.

Table 5.2 Typical Letters of Credit Charges

Type of Credit	Typical Charges
Import and domestic	$\frac{1}{8}$ of 1% of transaction with a minimum of $75 to $100
	Amendments: $\frac{1}{8}$ of 1% flat, minimum $70
	Payment fee: $\frac{1}{4}$ of 1% flat, minimum $90 per draft
	Acceptance fee: Per annum fee (360-day basis), minimum $75 for each draft accepted
	Discrepancy fee: $40
Export	Advising: $60
	Confirmation: Subject to country risk conditions, minimum $75
	Amendments: $55
	Assignment of proceeds/transfers: $\frac{1}{8}$ of 1% of the transaction with a minimum of $75
	Discrepancy fee: $45
	Payment/negotiation: $\frac{1}{10}$ of 1%, minimum $85–$95.
Standby letters	Issuance fee: An annual percentage (360-day basis) based on credit risk considerations, minimum $250
	Amendment fee: Risk-related fee is charged, minimum $250
	Payment fee: $\frac{1}{4}$ of 1% flat, minimum $90 per draft
Collections—documentary	Incoming: sight, $75; time, $95
	Outgoing: sight, $75; time, $95

Standby L/Cs   Sometimes when dealing with an open account, the exporter requires a *standby L/C*. This means just what the name implies; the L/C is not to be executed unless payment is not made within the specified period, usually 30–60 days. Bank handling charges for standby L/Cs are usually higher than those for a commercial (import) L/C.

Issuing, Confirming, and Advising Banks   Letters of credit are payable either at *sight* or on a *time* draft basis. Under a sight L/C, the *issuing* (buyers) bank pays, with or without a draft, when it is satisfied that the presented documents conform to the conforms. An *advising* bank (most often the *confirming* or seller's bank) informs the seller or beneficiary that an L/C has been issued. Under a time (acceptance) L/C, once the associated draft is presented and found to be in exact conformity, the draft is stamped "accepted" and can then be negotiated as a "banker's acceptance" by the exporter, at a discount to reflect the cost of money advanced against the draft.

Once the buyer and the seller agree that they will use an L/C for payment and they have worked out the conditions, the buyer or importer applies for the L/C to his or her international bank. Figure 5.1 is an example of a letter of credit application.

Types of L/Cs   There are two types of letters of credit: revocable and irrevocable. *Revocable credit* means that the document can be amended or canceled at any time without prior warning or notification of the seller. *Irrevocable* simply means that the terms of the document can be amended or canceled only with the agreement of all parties.

Confirmation means that the U.S. bank guarantees payment by the foreign bank.

Using the application as its guide, the bank issues a document of credit incorporating the terms agreed to by the parties. Figure 5.2 is an example of an L/C.

Figure 5.3 shows the three phases of documentary credit in their simplest form. In Phase I, your (*issuing*) bank notifies the seller through an *advising* bank or the seller's (*confirming*) bank that a credit has been issued. In Phase II, the seller then ships the goods and presents the documents to the bank, at which time the seller is paid. Phase III is the settlement phase in which the documents are then transferred to the buyer's bank, whereupon the buyer pays the bank any remaining

Figure 5.1 Request to Open a Letter of Credit (L/C)

To: Importer's international bank

Request to open documentary
credit (commercial letter of
credit and security agreement)

Date _____

Please open for my/our account a documentary credit (letter of credit)
in accordance with the undermentioned particulars.

We agree that, except so far as otherwise expressly stated, this credit
will be subject to the Uniform Customs and Practice for Documentary
Credits, ICC Publication #290.

We undertake to execute the Bank's usual form of indemnity.

Type of Credit: Irrevocable, i.e., cannot be canceled without
beneficiary's agreement.
Revocable, i.e., subject to cancellation.

Method of Advice: [ ] Airmail   [ ] E-mail/FAX, short details
[ ] E-mail/FAX, full details

Beneficiary's bank: _____

In favor of beneficiary: Company name and address.

Amount or sum of:

Availability: Valid until_____in_____for negotiation/date
place acceptance/payment.

This credit is available by drafts drawn at _____ sight/
accompanied by the required documents.

Documents   Invoice in three copies.
required: Full set "clean on board" bills of lading to order of
shipper, blank endorsed. In case movement of goods
involves more than one mode, a "Combined
Transport Document" should be called for.

Negotiable Marine and War risk insurance for %
(usually 110%) of invoice value covering all risks.

(Continued)

Figure 5.1 (Continued)

Certificate of Inspection

Other
Documents: Certificate of origin issued by Chamber of Commerce
in three copies.

Packing List

Quantity and
description
of goods

Price per unit:

Terms and
relative port
or place: CIF/C&F/FOB/FAS/_____
Place _____

Dispatch/
Shipment   From _____ to _____

Special
Instructions
(if any):

---

monies in exchange for the documents. Thus, on arrival of the goods, the buyer or importer has the proper documents for entry.

Special Middleman Uses of Letters of Credit

There are three special uses of commercial letters of credit for the import/export middleman: transferable, assignment of proceeds, and back-to-back L/Cs. Figure 5.4 compares the risks involved with using each method.

Transferable L/C   Figure 5.5 shows pictorially how the *transferable L/C* works. The buyer opens the L/C, which states clearly that it is transferable, on behalf of the middleman as the original beneficiary who in turn transfers all or part of the L/C to the supplier(s). The transfer must be made under the same terms and conditions as those in the

Figure 5.2 Sample Letter of Credit (L/C)

Name of issuing bank	Documentary Credit No. _____
Place and date of issue	Place and date of expiration
Applicant	Amount
	Credit available with [ ] Payment [ ] Acceptance [ ] Negotiation
Shipment from _____ Shipment to _____	Against presentation of documents detailed herein [ ] Drawn on _____ Bank

Invoice in three copies

Full set "clean on board" bills of lading to order of shipper, blank endorsed. In case movement of goods involves more than one made, a "Combined Transport Document" should be called for.

Negotiable Marine and War risk insurance for _____% (usually 110%) of invoice value covering all risks.

Certificate of Inspection

Certificate of origin issued by Chamber of Commerce in three copies.

Packing List

Documents to be presented within _____ days after date of issuance of the shipping document(s) but within the validity of the credit.

We hereby issue this Documentary Credit in your favor.

                              Issuing Bank

original L/C with the following exceptions: amount, unit price, expiration date, and shipping date. In this instance the buyer and supplier are usually disclosed to each other.

Assignment of Proceeds   The *assignment of proceeds* method is shown in Figure 5.6; Figure 5.7 shows a typical letter of assignment.

Figure 5.3 The Three Phases of a Letter of Credit (L/C)

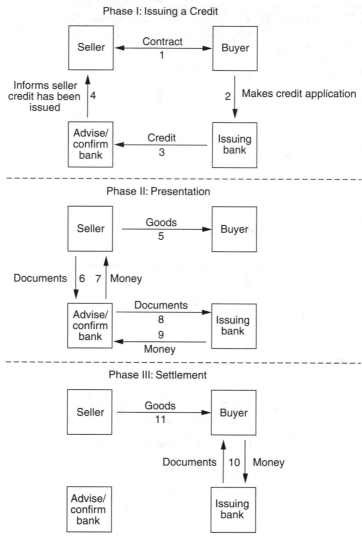

Note that the proceeds of all letters of credit may be assigned. In this instance the buyer opens the L/C as the beneficiary and relies on the middleman to comply so that the beneficiary can be paid. Any discrepancy in middleman documents will prevent payment under the L/C.

Figure 5.4 Comparison of Risks

	Assignment of Proceeds	*Transferable L/C*	*Back-to-Back L/C*
Risk to middleman	Supplier relies on middleman to comply with L/C	Middleman relies on supplier to comply with L/C	Supplier's performance must satisfy both L/Cs
Risk to middleman's bank	None	Minimal	Supplier does not comply with master L/C
Disclosure	Buyer and seller are not disclosed	Buyer and seller are disclosed	Buyer and seller are not disclosed (with third-party documents)

Figure 5.5 Transferable Letter of Credit (L/C)

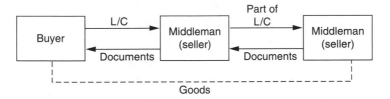

- L/C must state that it is transferable.
- Original beneficiary transfers all or part of L/C to supplier(s).
- Transfer must be made under the same terms and conditions with the following exceptions:
  Amount
  Unit price
  Expiration date
  Shipping date
- Buyer and supplier are usually disclosed to each other.

The middleman instructs the advising bank to effect payment to the supplier when the documents are negotiated. In this way, buyers and sellers are not disclosed to each other.

Back-to-Back Letters of Credit   When using the *back-to-back* method shown in Figure 5.8, the middleman must have a line of credit

Figure 5.6 Assignment of Proceeds

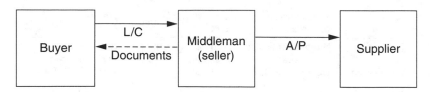

- Supplier relies on middleman to comply with L/C so that he or she can be paid. Discrepancy in middleman's documents will prevent payment under L/C.
- Middleman instructs advising bank to effect payment to supplier when documents are negotiated.
- Buyer and seller are not disclosed to each other.
- Proceeds of all letters of credit can be assigned.

because the middleman is responsible for paying the second (*backing*) L/C regardless of receipt of payment under the first (*master*) L/C. Great care should be exercised when using this method because discrepancies on the first L/C will result in non-payment, and the middleman's ability to pay could be a substantial credit risk. Back-to-back L/Cs should be issued on nearly identical terms and must allow for third-party documents.

Cash in Advance

This method of getting paid is the most desirable, but the foreign buyer usually objects to tying up his or her capital. On the grounds that seeing the merchandise is the best insurance, most foreign business people try not to pay until they actually receive the goods. Furthermore, the buyer may resent the implication that he or she may not be creditworthy.

Avoiding Bad Credit

Pick your customer carefully. Bad debts are more easily avoided than rectified. If there are payment problems, keep communicating and

Figure 5.7 Typical Letter of Assignment

ASSIGNMENT OF PROCEEDS

Gentlemen:

Here is Letter of Credit No. _____ issued by
_____ in favor of _____
_____ for an amount in excess of $ _____
expiring _____.

Our drafts and documents in terms of this credit will be presented by us to your office. We authorize and direct you to pay to
_____ the sum of $ _____ from
the proceeds of these drafts, in consideration of value received.

These instructions are irrevocable and shall continue under any ex-
tension of this Letter of Credit. Please acknowledge receipt of these
instructions directly to _____ by forwarding them
a copy of this letter.

                              Sincerely yours,

                              _____
Signature verified:

_____
     Name of Bank

_____
   Authorized Signature

The above assignment has been duly noted on our records.

_____
    International Banking Department, The Bank of San Diego
                      Authorized Signature

working with the firm until the matter is settled. Even the most valued
customers have financial problems from time to time. If nothing else
works, request that your department of industry or commerce or the
International Chamber of Commerce begin negotiations on your behalf.

Figure 5.8 Back-to-Back Letter of Credit (L/C)

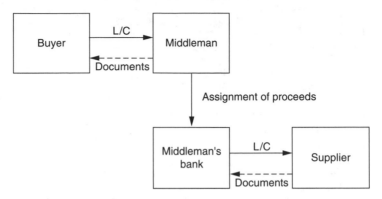

- Requires credit line for middleman.
- Middleman is responsible for paying the second (backing) L/C regardless of receipt of payment under first (master) L/C.
- Substantial credit risk in that discrepancies on the first L/C will result in nonpayment.
- L/Cs are issued on nearly identical terms.
- Middleman's ability to pay is a key consideration.
- L/C must allow third-party documents.

Information that is current and accurate is the food for good financing decisions. Basically two types of international credit information exist: (1) the ability and willingness of importing firms to make payment and (2) the ability and willingness of foreign countries to allow payment in a convertible currency.

There are several ways to obtain credit information about companies and their countries.

Information about Domestic Firms
- Commercial banks
- Commercial credit services, such as Dun & Bradstreet
- Trade associations

Information about Foreign Firms
- National Association of Credit Management (NACM)
- Foreign credit specialists in the credit departments of large exporting companies

- Commercial banks, which check buyer credit through their foreign branches and correspondents
- Commercial credit reporting services, such as Dun & Bradstreet
- Consultations with the EXIM Bank and the Foreign Credit Insurance Association (FCIA)
- The U.S. Commerce Department's *World Trade Directory Reports*

Information about Foreign Countries
- World Bank
- Chase World Information Corporation
- The magazine *Institutional Investor*
- National Association of Credit Management (NACM)

Avoiding Shipping Risks

Marine cargo insurance is an essential business tool for import/export and most startup traders are advised to work closely with a freight forwarder. Generally, coverage is sold on a warehouse-to-warehouse basis (i.e., from the sender's factory to the receiver's platform). Coverage usually ceases a specific number of days after the ship or plane is unloaded. You purchase policies on a per-shipment or "blanket" basis. Freight forwarders usually have a blanket policy to cover clients who do not have their own policy. Most insurance companies base cargo insurance on the value of all charges of the shipment including freight handling, and so on, plus 10 percent to cover unseen contingencies. Rates vary according to product, client's track record, destination, and shipping method.

Ocean cargo insurance costs about $0.50 to $1.50 per $100 of invoice value. Air cargo is usually about 25 to 30 percent less.

Avoiding Political Risk

No two national export credit systems are identical. However, there are similarities, the greatest of which is the universal involvement of government through the export credit agency concerned and of the commercial banking sector in the workings of the system.

Most countries have export/import banks. In the United States, EXIM Bank serves by providing credit support in the form of loans, guarantees, and insurance. All EXIM Banks cooperate with commercial banks in providing a number of arrangements to help exporters offer credit guarantees to commercial banks that finance export sales. The Overseas Private Investment Corporation (OPIC) and the Foreign Credit Insurance Association (FCIA) also provide insurance to exporters, enabling them to extend credit terms to their overseas buyers. Private insurers cover the normal commercial credit risks; EXIM Bank assumes all liability for political risk.

To contact the FCIA: write FCIA, Marketing Department, 11th Floor, 40 Rector Street, New York, NY 10006 or FCIA, 125 Park Avenue, New York, NY 10006; phone: (212) 885-1500; fax: (212) 885-1535.

The programs available through OPIC and FCIA are well advertised and easily available. Commercial banks are essentially intermediaries to the EXIM Bank for export guarantees on loans (beginning at loans of up to 1 year and ending at loans of up to 10–15 years). FCIA offers insurance in two basic maturities: (1) a short-term policy of up to 180 days and (2) a medium-term policy from 181 days up to 5 years. You may also obtain a combination policy of those maturities. In addition, FCIA has a master policy providing *blanket protection* (one policy designed to provide coverage for all the exporter's sales to overseas buyers).

Avoiding Foreign Exchange Risk

When the dollar is strong—as it was in the early 1980s—traders prefer to deal in the dollar. When the dollar is weak, traders begin to deal in other currencies. Of course the dollar is as good as gold because it is a politically stable currency that is traded internationally. Because of its stability, it has become the vehicle currency for most international transactions.

So long as exporters deal only in their currency, there is no foreign exchange risk. However, the strength and popularity of currencies is cyclical, and the dollar is not always the leader. Often, an exporter is faced with the prospect of pricing products or services in currencies other than dollars. Importers must buy foreign currency to pay for products and services from risk-avoiding foreign suppliers demanding payment in their own currency. In the current era of floating exchanges rates, there are risks resulting from exposure whenever there are cash flows denominated in foreign currencies.

Exposure is the effect on a firm or an individual if there is a change in exchange rates.

Hedging or *covering* is the use of the forward foreign exchange market to avoid foreign currency risk.

The *forward* or *future exchange rate* is the rate that is contracted today for the delivery of a currency at a specified date in the future at a price agreed upon today.

Successfully managing currency risk is imperative. No longer can an importer/exporter speculate by doing nothing and then pass the foreign exchange losses on to customers in the form of higher prices. The best business decision for an importer/exporter is to hedge or cover in the forward market when there is risk of exposure. To do otherwise is to be a speculator, not a business person. Use the forward rate for the date on which payment is required. This avoids all foreign exchange risk, is simple, and is reasonably inexpensive. The cost of a forward contract is small—the difference between the cost of the spot market (today's cost of money) and the cost of the forward market. Major international banks and brokerage houses can help you arrange a foreign exchange forward contract. Spot and forward markets are quoted daily in the *Journal of Commerce* and the *Wall Street Journal*.

Agency/Distributor Agreements

Chapter 3 explores your relationship with overseas distributors. A manufacturer or importer/exporter will seldom agree to meet all a distributor's conditions. Most are negotiable, and a firm that is not internationally known may have to concede to more demands than others in a more favorable position. The following five tips may help to avoid risk in doing business with distributors:

1. *Put the agency agreement in writing.* The rights and obligations resulting from a written agreement require no extraneous proof and are all that is necessary to record or prove the terms of a contract in most countries.

2. *Set forth the benefit to both parties in the agreement.* Well-balanced agreements should not place an excess of profitless burden on one of the parties. Performance of the agreement may be impossible to enforce against a party who has no apparent benefit from it.

3. *Give clear definition and meaning to all contract terms.* Many English terms that are spelled similarly in the foreign language have entirely different meanings. Require that the English version prevail when there is doubt. To avoid conflict use INCOTERMS (see Chapter 2).

4. *Expressly state the rights and obligations of the parties.* The agency contract should contain a description of the rights and duties of each party, the nature and duration of the relationship, and the reasons for which the agreement may be terminated.

5. *Specify a jurisdictional clause.* If local laws will allow, specify in the contract the jurisdiction that will handle any legal disputes that may arise. Where possible, use arbitration. Basic arbitration rules and principles are generally the same anywhere. Clauses in the contract should contain identification of the arbitration body or forum. Model arbitration clauses may be obtained from the American Arbitration Association, 140 West 51st Street, New York, NY 10020; phone: (212) 484-4000; fax: (212) 765-4874. You may also contact the U.S. Council for International Business, 1212 Avenue of the Americas, New York, NY 10036; phone: (212) 354-4480; fax: (212) 575-0327; e-mail: info@uscib.org; Web site:WWW.uscib.org.

Physical Distribution (Shipping and Packing)

Physical distribution, often referred to as *logistics*, is the means by which goods are moved from the manufacturer in one country to the customer in another. This section discusses two vital aspects for which the importer/exporter should have an appreciation: shipping and packing.

Shipping

An import/export business can directly arrange its own land, ocean, and air shipping of international cargo. Inland transportation is handled in much the same way as a domestic transaction, except that certain export marks must be added to the standard information shown on a domestic bill of lading. Also the inland carrier must be instructed to notify the ocean or air carrier.

Water Transportation

There are three types of ocean service: conference lines, independent lines, and tramp vessels. An *ocean conference* is an association of ocean carriers joined together to establish common rates and shipping conditions. Conferences have two rates: the regular tariff and a lower contract rate. You can obtain the contract rate if you sign a contract to use conference vessels exclusively during the contract period. *Independent lines* accept bookings from all shippers contingent on the availability of space. They are often less expensive than conference rates. An independent usually quotes rates at about 10 percent lower than a conference carrier in situations where the two are in competition. *Tramp vessels* usually carry only bulk cargoes and do not follow an established schedule; rather, they operate on charters.

Regardless of the type of carrier you use, the carrier will issue a booking contract, which reserves space on a specific ship. Unless you cancel in advance, you may be required to pay even if your cargo doesn't make the sailing. You must be insured with ocean marine insurance. An insurance broker or your freight forwarder can arrange this for you.

Marine insurance. Insurance that will compensate the owner of goods transported on the seas in the event of loss that would not be legally recovered from the carrier. Also covers air shipments.

Air Transportation

Air freight continues to grow as a popular and competitive method for international cargoes. The growth has been facilitated by innovation in the cargo industry. Air carriers have excellent capacity, use very efficient loading and unloading equipment, and handle standardized containers. The advantages are (1) the speed of delivery, which gets perishable cargoes to the place of destination in prime condition; (2) the ability to respond to unpredictable product demands; and (3) the rapid movement of repair parts.

Air freight moves under a general cargo rate or a commodity rate. A special unit load rate is available when approved air shipping containers are used.

Land Transportation

Transportation over land has become less regulated and, therefore, more competitive and efficient. The largest import/export market (NAFTA) can be served directly by road and rail. Importers and exporters look primarily to land transportation to move their goods to the nearest port of departure or as one leg of a sea, land, or air combination often referred to as *intermodalism*.

Intermodalism

The movement of international shipments via container using sequential transportation methods is the system of the future. The concept makes use of the most efficient and cost-effective methods to move goods.

Load Center   This concept stimulated the sophistication of today's intermodal world. As ships grew to hold more containers, they became more expensive to operate. One way to reduce costs was to hold down the number of port calls. In order to fill the ships at fewer ports, the cargo has to be funneled into these load centers. The simplification and organization of movements of cargo has become the fair-haired child of transportation specialists. An entirely new set of terms has developed around the concept.

Bridges   A *microbridge* is the routing of a container to or from anywhere in the United States to or from any port. A *minibridge* moves a container that originates or terminates in a U.S. port other than the one where it enters or leaves the country. A *land bridge* off-loads a container at any U.S. port, ships it cross-country by rail, and then reloads aboard a vessel for final movement to a foreign destination. *RO/RO* refers to the roll-on/roll-off capability of containerized cargo, which is the foundation of intermodalism.

An example of intermodalism might be a container of goods originating in Europe but destined for Japan. It could be rolled off a ship by truck and then onto a train in Newport News, Virginia (RO/RO), where it would be joined by another container trucked in from Florida, (minibridge) also destined for Japan. The containers would then be moved across the United States (land bridge) then rolled off the train and onto a ship in Long Beach, California, which would complete the movement to Tokyo. Figure 5.9 illustrates the intermodal concept.

HOT TIP

If the details of transportation and all the new-fangled ideas are not for you, then see your nearest freight forwarder (discussed in Chapter 7).

Figure 5.9 Intermodal Concept

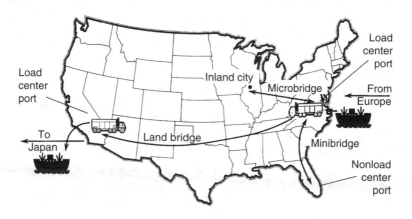

Packaging and Marking for Overseas Shipment

Whether importing or exporting, your product(s) must travel thousands of miles undamaged. Your package must be protected from breakage, dampness, careless storage, rough handling, thieves, and weather. Insurance might cover the loss, but lost time and the ill will of your overseas trading partner are a high price to pay. It has been estimated that as much as 70 percent of all cargo loss could be prevented by proper packaging and marking.

An excellent source for all aspects of packing and packaging is the *Modern Packaging Encyclopedia*, published annually by McGraw-Hill, New York.

Breakage   Ocean shipments are often roughly loaded by stevedores using forklifts, slings, nets, and conveyors. During the voyage, rough water and storms can cause loads to shift and sometimes crash into other containers. Even small packages sent through the mail can be squeezed, thrown, or crushed.

Assume the worst when packaging for overseas delivery. Use stronger and heavier materials than you would for domestic shipments. On the other hand, don't over pack—you pay by weight and volume. For large ocean shipments consider standardized containers that can be transferred from truck or rail car without being opened.

Pilferage (Theft)   Use strapping and seals and avoid trademarks or content descriptions.

Moisture and Weather   The heat and humidity of the tropics as well as rainstorms and rough weather at sea can cause moisture to seep into the holds of a ship. From that moisture comes fungal growths, sweat, and rust. Waterproofing is essential for most ocean shipments. Consider plastic shrink-wrap or waterproof inner liners, and coat any exposed metal parts with grease or other rust inhibitors.

Marking (Labeling)   Foreign customers have their needs, shippers have theirs, and terminal operators have theirs. Each will specify certain marks (port, customer identification code, package numbers, and number of packages) to appear on shipments. Other markings such as weight, dimensions, and regulations that facilitate clearing through customs can be specified. Figure 5.10 is a sample of markings.

Figure 5.10 Example of Markings

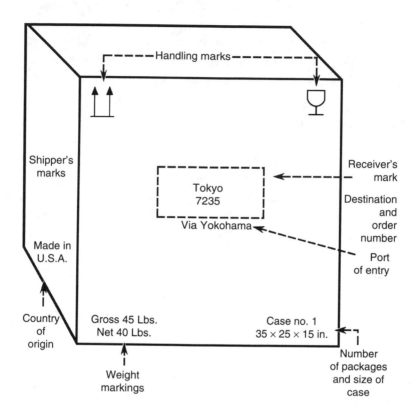

Checklist for Shipping

- Write your customer's name and address or shipping code on the package.
- Use black waterproof ink for the stencils.
- Include port of exit and port of entry on your label.
- Don't forget to include package and case number.
- Include dimensions (inches and metric).
- Mark exports "Made in U.S.A." and so on, so that the package will get through customs in most foreign countries.
- Express gross and net weight in pounds and/or kilograms.

- Don't forget cautionary markings such as, "this side up" or "handle with care" in both the language of origin and the language of destination.
- Don't use brand names or advertising slogans on packages.
- Any shipments that carry explosives or volatile liquids must conform to local law and international agreements.

Documentation

"Attention to detail" is the byword when preparing documentation. The naïve pass it off as a by-product of the transaction, but the experienced trader knows that shipments can be detained on the pier for weeks because of inattention. As ex-Yankee baseball player Yogi Berra once said, "It ain't over 'til it's over," and that's the way it is in international trade. The exporter doesn't get his or her money and the importer doesn't get his or her goods unless the paperwork is complete and accurate! Therefore, be attentive to detail.

Basically, documentation falls into two categories: *shipping* and *collecting*.

Shipping Documents

Shipping documents permit an export cargo to be moved through customs, loaded aboard a carrier, and shipped to its foreign destination. These documents are:

- Export licenses
- Packing lists
- Bills of lading
- Export declarations

Collection Documents

Collection documents are those needed for submission to the importer (in the case of a draft) or to the importer's bank (in the case of an L/C) in order to receive payment. These are:

- Commercial invoices
- Consular invoices

- Certificates of origin
- Inspection certificates
- Bills of lading

When endorsed by the shipper, you can use the bill of lading for sight draft or for L/C shipments. Other documents sometimes required for collection are manufacturing and insurance certificates and dock or warehouse receipts. Keep in mind that customs house brokers and freight forwarders are specialists in documentation as well as in physical distribution.

Collection. The procedure whereby a bank collects money for a seller against a draft drawn on a buyer abroad, usually through a correspondent bank.

The Documents

This section describes the various documents in detail and provides samples of each.

Certificate of Origin

The *certificate of origin* is a document that certifies to the buyer the country in which the goods were produced. A recognized chamber of commerce usually performs the certificate of origin of the merchandise. Some countries require a separate certificate, sometimes countersigned by a chamber of commerce and possibly even visaed by the resident consul at the port of export. These statements are required to indicate preferential rates of import duties such as "most favored nation." Often, as little as 35 percent of a nation's materials and/or labor can qualify it for favorable duties. Some nations require special forms, while others accept a certification on the shipper's own letterhead. See Figure 5.11 for an example of a certificate of origin.

Figure 5.11 Certificate of Origin

Our Company, Inc.

Hometown, Wherever

Date _____

Your Company

Hometown, Wherever

Point of Origin Declaration

For the purpose of positively identifying certain components as being manufactured in _____ and therefore qualifying for
(Country)

entry under _____.
(Tariff code identification)

Component(s) description: _____

_____

Part number: _____

_____

The manufacturer _____ warrants and repre-sents that the articles supplied to _____

_____
(Company)

and described above are articles of _____.
(Country)

The articles were manufactured at _____
(Address of location of plant)

_____.

Authorized signature and date

_____

Title

Following is a checklist for a certificate of origin that can be used as a guide:

• The letter or form should originate from the address of the manufacturer of the product.

- A responsible and knowledgeable person within the manufacturing company (an *officer* of the corporation) must sign the letter.
- The letter or form will not be accepted if it is from an outside sales office or distributor. It cannot be signed by a salesperson.
- The letter should clearly state where the product in question was manufactured.

Commercial Invoice

The *commercial invoice* is a bill that conforms in all respects to the agreement between the importer and the exporter. It could have the exact terms of the pro forma invoice first offered in response to a quotation, or it could differ in those terms that were the result of final negotiations. In any case there should be no surprises for the importer. The commercial invoice should (1) itemize the merchandise by price per unit and any charges paid by the buyer, and (2) specify the terms of payment and any marks or numbers on the packages. See Figure 5.12.

Consular Invoice

This invoice is not required by all countries. It is obtained from the commercial attaché or through the consular office of the country in question in the port of export. When required, it is in addition to a commercial invoice and must conform in every respect to that document, as well as to the bill of lading and any insurance documents. Its purpose is to allow clearance of your shipment into the country that requires it. See Figure 5.13.

Commercial attaché. The commercial expert on the diplomatic staff of his or her country's embassy or large consulate in a foreign country.

Certificate of Manufacture

This document certifies that the goods ordered by the importer have been produced and are ready for shipment. For example, it might be used in those cases in which the manufacturer has moved ahead in

Figure 5.12 Commercial Invoice

XYZ Foreign Co.
2A1 Moon River
Yokohama, Japan

Purchase Order:
Invoice Number: 00012
Invoice Date:

Sold To: Our Company, Inc.   Ship To: Our Company, Inc.
      Hometown, U.S.A.   Hometown, U.S.A.

Forwarding Agent:

Via: Country of Origin: Japan

Quantiy	Part No.	Description	Price Each	Total Price
10	A2Z	Machines	$100.00	$1,000.00

Inland freight, export packing and forwarding fees	$ 100.00
Free alongside (FAS) Yokohama	$1,100.00
Estimated ocean freight	$ 100.00
Estimated marine insurance	$ 50.00

Packed in 10 crates, 100 cubic feet   _____
Gross weight 1,000 lbs.
Net weight   900 lbs.
Payment terms: Confirmed irrevocable letter of credit confirmed by a U.S. bank. Shipment to be made two (2) weeks after receipt of firm order.
Additional conditions of sale: XYZ Foreign Co. to provide:
Certificate of Origin
Consular Invoice
Certificate of Manufacture
Insurance Certificate
Inspection Certificate

production with only a down payment, thus allowing the importer to avoid allocation of the full amount too far in advance. Generally, invoices and packing lists are forwarded to the importer with the certificate of manufacture. See Figure 5.14.

Figure 5.13 Consular Invoice

FACTURA COMERCIAL

No. de la Factura........................
(Commercial Invoice #)

Lugar (Ciudad) ....
Place (City)

Fecha: Día......... Mes......... Año...........
Date: Day   Mo.   Year

INTERVIENEN	Nombre de la Cía. o del Agente autorizado	DOMICILIO (Address)		
		Número (No.)	Calle (Street)	Ciudad (City)	Tel. (Phone)
Vendedor o remitente (Seller or shipper)					
Comprador (Buyer)					
Consig. a Destinatario (Consigned to)					
Agente o Gestor Agent-Broker					

Lugar y Puerto de Embarque Port of Loading	Lugar y Puerto de Destino Port of Unloading	Fecha de Embarque Date of Shipment	Nombre del Buque o Cía. Aérea Transp. Vessel/Airline Name

CONDICIONES DE VENTA: FOB - CIF   SEGURO (Insurance): ....

Cantidad y Número de Bultos	PESO		Detalle descriptivo de la mercadería, indicando marca, lugar de fabricación, clase o tipo del producto, series, números, etc. y cualquier otra información adicional relacionada. (Denomination and details of each article: quantity, quality, measure, merch. origin, etc.)	Precio de la Mercadería (Merchandise Price)
	Kilogramos	Libras		

(Continued)

Figure 5.13 Consular Invoice (Continued)

El agente autorizado que firma la presente, declara bajo juramento que todos los datos declarados en la presente factura, son exactos y verdaderos y que los precios pagados o por pagarse, son los reales y convenidos, que no existe convenio o arreglo alguno que permita la alteración o modificación de éstos, ni tampoco de su cantidad o calidad.

Firma del Agente, Vendedor o
Despachante autorizado. Fecha............

FACTURA COMERCIAL No.

Certifico que la firma que aparece en este

documento y dice ....

es auténtica y pertenece al funcionario des-

cripto.

Los Angeles, Calif. ....

Número de orden ....

No. del arancel ....

Der. percib. U$S. ....

Depositado en el Banco

Importe mercad. .... U$S
Merch. Price ....

Transporte .... U$S

Otros (other) .... U$S

SUB-TOTAL .... U$S

Tasa Consular, Fee U$S

IMPORTE TOTAL U$S

The............
A recognized Chamber of Commerce under the laws of the State of California has examined the manufacturer's invoice or shipper affidavit concerning the origin of the merchandise and according to the best of its knowledge and belief, finds that the products named originated in the United States of North America.

Authorized Officer............ Date............

Espacio para Certificacion Consular

Figure 5.14 Certificate of Manufacture

DATE:

REFERENCE: ACCOUNT NAME AND ADDRESS
              PURCHASE ORDER NO. AND/OR
              CONTRACT NO.

BANK NAME AND LETTER OF CREDIT NO:

MERCHANDISE DESCRIPTION:

CERTIFICATE OF RECENT MANUFACTURE

WE HEREBY CERTIFY THAT THE HEREIN DESCRIBED MER-
CHANDISE IS OF RECENT MANUFACTURE, IN THIS CASE
NOT OLDER THAN _____ YEAR(S) FROM THIS DATE.

NAME AND ADDRESS OF MANUFACTURER:

BY: _____
            (Original signature)

Export Licenses

Export licensing procedures are described in detail in Chapter 7 as one of the six topics unique to exporting. These licenses are of two basic varieties: general and validated. *Validated licenses* require careful attention because they apply to products that the government wants to control closely for either strategic or economic reasons. The commodity control list (CCL) sets forth items such as certain weapons, technologies, and high-tech products. Export administration regulations set forth all licensing requirements for commodities under the jurisdiction of the Office of Export Administration (OEA), International Trade Administration. Once it has been determined that a license is needed, the Application for Export License must be prepared and submitted to the OEA. See Figure 7.1 in Chapter 7.

Insurance Certificates

Insurance certificates provide evidence of coverage and may be a stipulation of a contract, purchase order, or commercial invoice in order to receive payment. These indicate the type and amount of coverage and identify the merchandise in terms of packages and identifying marks. You should make certain that the information on this certificate agrees exactly with invoices and bills of lading. See Figure 5.15.

Inspection Certificates

These are documents that protect the importer against fraud, error, or quality performance. The inspection is most often conducted by an independent firm, but it is sometimes accomplished by the shipper. An affidavit that certifies the inspection is often required under terms of a letter of credit. For example, a Taiwanese firm wanted to import used diesel generators from the United States. That company insisted that an independent engineer certify satisfactory operation of each generator, at specifications, prior to shipment. See Figure 5.16.

Packing Lists

A packing list accompanies the shipment and describes the cargo in detail. It includes the shipper, the consignee, measurements, serial numbers, weights, and any other data peculiar to the shipment. When correctly completed, it is placed in a waterproof bag or envelope with the words, "Packing List Enclosed" and attached to the outside of the container. See Figure 5.17.

Shippers Export Declaration

The shipper's export declaration (SED) is prepared by the exporter or freight forwarder for the U.S. government (other countries may have a similar requirement). It is a data collection document required on all exports in excess of $2,500. It is prepared for purposes of providing statistical information to the Bureau of Census and to indicate the

Figure 5.15 Certificate of Marine Insurance

CERTIFICATE OF MARINE INSURANCE

No. 573951

🌐 International Cargo & Surety Insurance Company

* $ _____
(sum insured)

This is to Certify, That on the _____ day of _____ this Company

insured under Policy No. _____ made for

for the sum of _____ Dollars,

on

(Amounts in excess of $1,000,000.00 cannot be insured under this Certificate)

Valued at sum insured. Shipped on board the S/S or M/S

at and from _____ and/or following
(Initial Point of Shipment) steamer or steamers

to _____ , via _____

(Port of Places of Destination) (Port of Shipment)

is payable to the order of
conveys the right of collecting any, such loss as fully as if the property were covered by a special policy direct to the holder hereof, and it is understood and agreed, that in case of loss, the same any liability for unpaid premiums. This certificate is issued subject to the standard International Cargo & Surety Insurance Company open cargo policy, which is incorporated herein by reference. To the extent that any terms or conditions in this certificate are inconsistent with the standard policy, the standard policy shall govern the rights and duties of all parties subject to the contract of insurance. Copies of the standard policy are available, upon request, from International Cargo & Surety Insurance Company, 1501 Woodfield Road, Schaumburg, Illinois 60173.

SPECIAL CONDITIONS

Merchandise shipped with an UNDER DECK bill of lading insured –
Against all risks of physical loss or damage from any external cause, irrespective of percentage, excepting those excluded by the
F.C & S and S-R & C.C. Warranties, arising during transportation between the points of shipment and of destination named herein.

SAMPLE

MARKS & NUMBERS

ON DECK SHIPMENTS (with an ON DECK bill of lading) and/or shipments of used merchandise insured:
Warranted free of particular average unless caused by the vessel being stranded, sunk, burnt, on fire or in collision, but including risk of jettison and/or washing overboard, irrespective of percentage.

SCHEDULE B CODE (commodity)	SCHEDULE C-E CODE (country)

TERMS AND CONDITIONS—SEE ALSO BACK HEREOF

WAREHOUSE TO WAREHOUSE. This insurance attaches from the time the goods leave the Warehouse and/or Store at the place named in the Policy for the commencement of the transit and continues during the ordinary course of transit, including customary transshipment if any, until the goods leave the Warehouse and/or Store at the place named in the Policy for the commencement of the transit and continues the goods are in transit and/or awaiting transit, until delivered to final warehouse at the destination named in the Policy or until the expiry of 15 days (or 30 days if the destination to which the goods are insured is outside the limits of the port) whichever shall first occur. The time limits referred to above to be reckoned from midnight of the day on which the discharge overside of the goods hereby insured from the overseas vessel is completed. Held covered at a premium to be arranged in the event of transhipment, if any, other than as above and/or in the event of delay in excess of the above time limits arising from circumstances beyond the control of the Assured

(Continued)

135

Figure 5.15 Certificate of Marine Insurance (Continued)

NOTE — IT IS NECESSARY FOR THE ASSURED TO GIVE PROMPT NOTICE TO THESE ASSURERS WHEN THEY BECOME AWARE OF AN EVENT FOR WHICH THEY ARE "HELD COVERED" UNDER THIS POLICY AND THE RIGHT TO SUCH COVER IS DEPENDENT ON COMPLIANCE WITH THIS OBLIGATION

PERILS CLAUSE: Touching the adventures and perils which the Company is contented to bear, and takes upon itself, they are of the seas, fires, assailing thieves, jettisons, barratry of the master and mariners, and all other like perils, losses and misfortunes (illicit or contraband trade excepted in all cases), that have or shall come to the hurt, detriment or damage of the said goods and merchandise, or any part thereof.

SHORE CLAUSE: Where this insurance by its terms covers while on docks, wharves or elsewhere on shore, and/or during land transportation, it shall include the risks of collision, derailment, overturning or other accident to the conveyance, fire, lightning, sprinkler leakage, cyclones, hurricanes, earthquakes, floods (meaning the rising of navigable waters), and/or collapse or subsidence of docks or wharves, even though the insurance be otherwise F.P.A.

BOTH TO BLAME CLAUSE: Where goods are shipped under a Bill of Lading containing the so-called "Both to Blame Collision" Clause, these Assurers agree as to all losses covered by this insurance, to indemnify the Assured for this Policy's proportion of any amount (not exceeding the amount insured) which the Assured may be legally bound to pay to the shipowners under such clause. In the event that such liability is asserted the Assured agree to notify these Assurers who shall have the right at their own cost and expense to defend the Assured against such claim.

MACHINERY CLAUSE: When the property insured under this Policy includes a machine consisting when complete for sale or use of several parts, then in case of loss or damage covered by this insurance to any part of such machine, these Assurers shall be liable only for the proportion of the insured value of the part lost or damaged, or at the Assured's option, for the cost and expense, including labor and forwarding charges, of replacing or repairing the lost or damaged part; but in no event shall these Assurers be liable for more than the insured value of the complete machine.

LABELS CLAUSE: In case of damage affecting labels, capsules or wrappers, these Assurers, if liable therefor under the terms of this policy, shall not be liable for more than an amount sufficient to pay the cost of new labels, capsules or wrappers, and the cost of reconditioning the goods, but in no event shall these Assurers be liable for more than the insured value of the damaged merchandise.

DELAY CLAUSE: Warranted free of claim for loss of market or for loss, damage or deterioration arising from delay, whether caused by a peril insured against or otherwise, unless expressly assumed in writing hereon.

AMERICAN INSTITUTE CLAUSES: This insurance, in addition to the foregoing, is also subject to the following American Institute Cargo Clauses, current forms:

1. CRAFT, ETC.	4. GENERAL AVERAGE	8. INCHMAREE	12. WAR RISK INSURANCE
2. DEVIATION	5. EXPLOSION	9. CONSTRUCTIVE TOTAL LOSS	13. SOUTH AMERICA 60 DAY CLAUSE
3. WAREHOUSING & FORWARDING CHARGES.	6. BILL OF LADING, ETC.	10. CARRIER	
PACKAGES TOTALLY LOST LOADING, ETC.	7. MARINE EXTENSION CLAUSES	11. S.R. & C.C. ENDORSEMENT	

PARAMOUNT WARRANTIES: THE FOLLOWING WARRANTIES SHALL BE PARAMOUNT AND SHALL NOT BE MODIFIED OR SUPERSEDED BY ANY OTHER PROVISION INCLUDED HEREIN OR STAMPED OR ENDORSED HEREON UNLESS SUCH OTHER PROVISION REFERS SPECIFICALLY TO THE RISKS EXCLUDED BY THESE WARRANTIES AND EXPRESSLY ASSUMES THE SAID RISKS:

F.C. & S. (a) Notwithstanding anything herein contained to the contrary, this insurance is warranted free from capture, seizure, arrest, restraint, detainment, confiscation, preemption, requisition or nationalization, and the consequences thereof or any attempt thereat, whether in time of peace or war and whether lawful or otherwise; also warranted free, whether in time of peace or war, from all loss, damage or expense caused by any weapon of war employing atomic or nuclear fission and/or fusion or other reaction or radioactive force or matter or by any mine or torpedo; also warranted free from all consequences of hostilities or warlike operations (whether there be a declaration of war or not), but this warranty shall not exclude collision or contact with aircraft, rockets or similar missiles or with any fixed or floating object (other than a mine or torpedo), stranding, heavy weather, fire or explosion unless caused directly (and independently of the nature of the voyage or service which the vessel concerned or, in the case of a collision, any other vessel involved therein, is performing) by a hostile act by or against a belligerent power; and for the purposes of this warranty "power" includes any authority maintaining naval, military or air forces in association with a power.

Further warranted free from the consequences of civil war, revolution, rebellion, insurrection, or civil strife arising therefrom, or piracy.

S.R. & C.C. (b) Warranted free of loss or damage caused by or resulting from strikes, lockouts, labor disturbances, riots, civil commotions or the acts of any person or persons taking part in any such occurrence or disorder.

This Certificate is issued in Original and Duplicate, one of which being accomplished the other to stand null and void. To support a claim local Revenue Laws may require this certificate to be stamped.

Not transferable unless countersigned

Countersigned _____

ADDITIONAL CONDITIONS AND
INSTRUCTIONS TO CLAIMANTS ON REVERSE SIDE

OM18

President

Kenneth J. Keany

Secretary

SAMPLE   ORIGINAL

Figure 5.16 Inspection Certificate

```
DATE:

REFERENCE:     ACCOUNT NAME AND ADDRESS
               PURCHASE ORDER NO. AND/OR
               CONTRACT NO.

BANK NAME AND LETTER OF CREDIT NO.

MERCHANDISE DESCRIPTION:


           INSPECTION CERTIFICATE

WE HEREBY CERTIFY THAT THE HEREIN DESCRIBED MER-
CHANDISE HAS BEEN INSPECTED AND FOUND TO BE OF
HIGHEST QUALITY AND IN GOOD WORKING ORDER.


           PORTER INTERNATIONAL INC.

       BY: _____
                 (Original signature)
```

proper authorization to export. It is the basis for measuring the volume and type of exports leaving a country. The document requires complete information about the shipment, including description, value, net and gross weights, and relevant license information, thus closing the licensing information loop back to the OEA. See Figure 5.18.

Bills of Lading

A *bill of lading* is a contract between the owner of the goods (exporter) and the carrier. It is both evidence that the shipment has been made, and the receipt for the goods that have been shipped. Figure 5.19 is a bill of lading for an air carrier, called an air waybill. Figure 5.20 is an ocean bill of lading. While e-commerce has not yet reached the bill of lading process, it is getting close and will soon be a reality. Several ship

Figure 5.17 Packing List

To XYZ Foreign Co.	Date: _____
2A1 Moon River	
Yokohama, Japan	

Gentlemen:

Under your order No. <u>123</u> the material listed below was shipped <u>1/1/18</u> via <u>Truck and vessel</u>

To <u>Yokohama</u>

Via: _____

| Shipment consists of: | | Marks: |

___ Cases ___ Packages   XYZ Foreign Co.
                          2A1 Moon River

___ Crates ___ Cartons   Yokohama, Japan

___ Bbls ___ Drums   Made in U.S.A.

___ Reels   #7235

Package Number	Weights (Lbs or Kilos)	Dimensions	Quality	Contents
	Gross Legal Net	Ht. Wth. Lth.		
7235	45 40	35 25 15		Toys

lines have already automated part of the process, and there are indications that a system to replace paper bills of lading with electronic communications will soon be marketed.

Straight Bills of Lading

These are nonnegotiable bills that consign the goods to an importer or other party named on the document. Once consummated, the seller

Figure 5.18 Shipper's Export Declaration

FORM **7525-V** (3-19-85)

U.S. DEPARTMENT OF COMMERCE — BUREAU OF THE CENSUS — INTERNATIONAL TRADE ADMINISTRATION

SHIPPER'S EXPORT DECLARATION

OMB No. 0607-0018

1a. EXPORTER (Name and address including ZIP code)

ZIP CODE

b. EXPORTER EIN NO.

c. PARTIES TO TRANSACTION

☐ Related   ☐ Non-related

4a. ULTIMATE CONSIGNEE

b. INTERMEDIATE CONSIGNEE

NONE

5. FORWARDING AGENT

Porter International, Inc.
P.O. Box 41-A
San Ysidro, California 92173

2. DATE OF EXPORTATION

3. BILL OF LADING/AIR WAYBILL NO.

6. POINT (STATE) OF ORIGIN OR FTZ NO.

7. COUNTRY OF ULTIMATE DESTINATION

MEXICO

8. LOADING PIER/TERMINAL

9. MODE OF TRANSPORT (Specify)

TRUCK

10. EXPORTING CARRIER

Truck Llc.:

11. PORT OF EXPORT

San Diego, (S.Y.), California

12. FOREIGN PORT OF UNLOADING

13. CONTAINERIZED (Vessel only)

☐ Yes   ☐ No

(Continued)

139

Figure 5.18 Shipper's Export Declaration (Continued)

14. SCHEDULE B DESCRIPTION OF COMMODITIES. *(Use columns 15—19)*

MARKS, NOS, AND KINDS OF PKGS. (15)	D/F (16)	SCHEDULE B NUMBER (17)	QUANTITY — SCHEDULE B UNIT(S) (18)	SHIPPING WEIGHT *(Pounds)* (19)	VALUE (U.S. dollars, omit cents) *(Selling price or cost if not sold)* (20)

21. VALIDATED LICENSE NO./GENERAL LICENSE SYMBOL		22. ECCN *(When required)*

23. Duly authorized officer or employee — The exporter authorizes the forwarder named above to act as forwarding agent for export control and customs purposes.

24. I certify that all statements made and all information contained herein are true and correct and that I have read and understand the instructions for preparation of this document, set forth in the **"Correct Way to Fill Out the Shipper's Export Declaration."** I understand that civil and criminal penalties, including forfeiture and sale, may be imposed for making false or fraudulent statements herein, failing to provide the requested information or for violation of U.S. laws on exportation (13 U.S.C. Sec. 305; 22 U.S.C. Sec. 401; 18 U.S.C. Sec. 1001; 50 U.S.C. App. 2410).

Signature — Confidential-For use solely for official purposes authorized by the Secretary of Commerce (13 U.S.C. 301 (g)).

Title **EXPORT CLERK** — Export shipments are subject to inspection by U.S. Customs Service and/or Office of Export Enforcement.

Date — **25.** AUTHENTICATION *(When required)*

THESE COMMODITIES LICENSED BY U.S. FOR ULTIMATE DESTINATION — MEXICO — DIVERSION CONTRARY TO U.S. LAW PROHIBITED.

Figure 5.19 Air Waybill (Bill of Lading)

Shipper's Name and Address | Shipper's Account Number

Not negotiable
Air Waybill
(Air Consignment note)
Issued by

Copies 1, 2 and 3 of this Air Waybill are originals and have the same validity

Consignee's Name and Address

It is agreed that the goods described herein are accepted in apparent good order and condition (except as noted) for carriage SUBJECT TO THE CONDITIONS OF CONTRACT ON THE REVERSE HEREOF. THE SHIPPER'S ATTENTION IS DRAWN TO THE NOTICE CONCERNING CARRIERS' LIMITATION OF LIABILITY. Shipper may increase such limitation of liability by declaring a higher value for carriage and paying a supplemental charge if required.

To expedite movement, shipment may be diverted to motor or other carrier unless shipper gives other instructions hereon.

Issuing Carrier's Agent Name and City

Accounting Information

SEE WARSAW NOTICE AND CONDITIONS OF CONTRACT ON REVERSE SIDE.

Agent's IATA Code | Account No.

Airport of Departure (Addr of first Carrier) and requested Routing

By first Carrier | Routing and Destination | | Currency | WT/VAL PPD COLL | Other PPD COLL | Declared Value for Carriage | Declared Value for Customs

Airport of Destination | Flight/Date | For Carrier Use only | Flight/Date | Amount of Insurance | INSURANCE - If Carrier offers insurance, and such insurance is requested in accordance with conditions on reverse hereof, indicate amount to be insured in figures in box marked amount of insurance.

Handling Information

These commodities licensed by the United States for ultimate destination .... Diversion contrary to United States law prohibited.

(Continued)

Figure 5.19 Air Waybill (Continued)

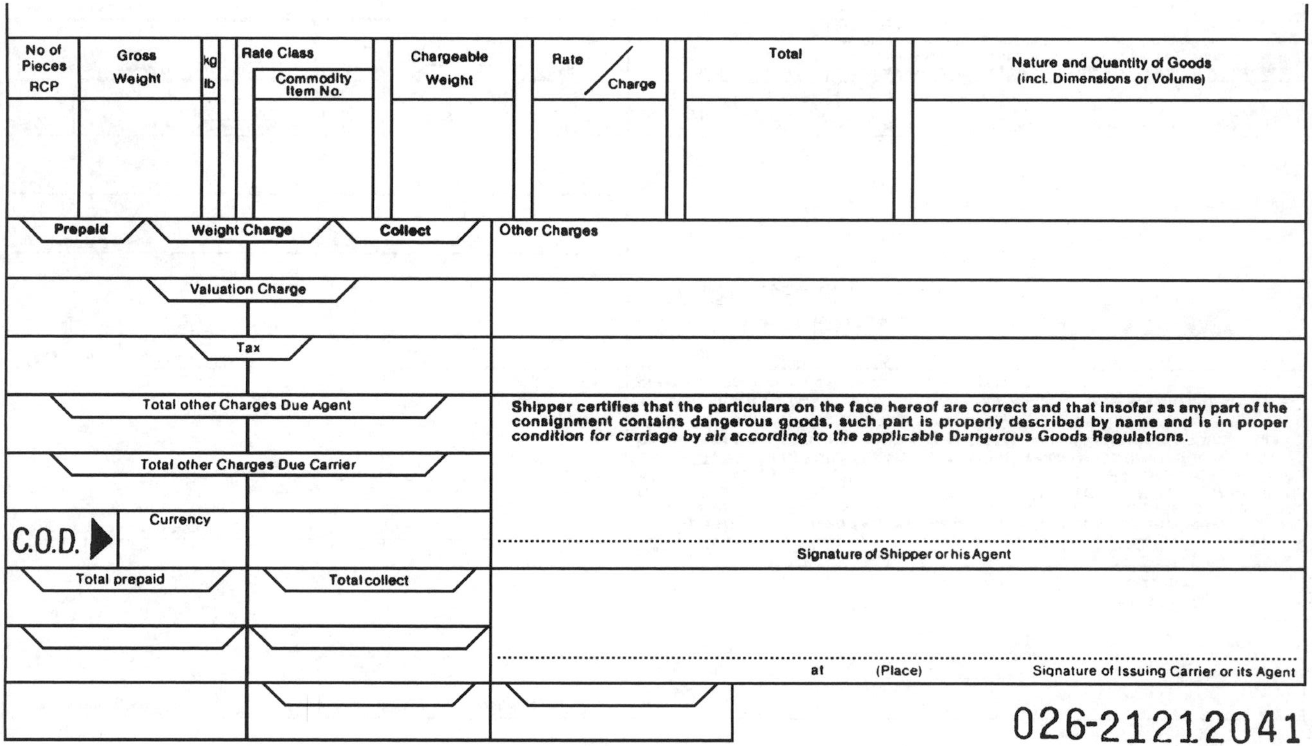

No of Pieces RCP	Gross Weight	kg lb	Rate Class / Commodity Item No.	Chargeable Weight	Rate / Charge	Total	Nature and Quantity of Goods (incl. Dimensions or Volume)

Prepaid	Weight Charge	Collect	Other Charges
	Valuation Charge		
	Tax		
	Total other Charges Due Agent		Shipper certifies that the particulars on the face hereof are correct and that insofar as any part of the consignment contains dangerous goods, such part is properly described by name and is in proper condition *for carriage by air according to the applicable* Dangerous Goods Regulations.
	Total other Charges Due Carrier		
C.O.D. ▶ Currency			Signature of Shipper or his Agent
Total prepaid		Total collect	
			at (Place) Signature of Issuing Carrier or its Agent

026-21212041

Figure 5.20 Ocean Bill of Lading

Shipper		B/L No. M132-11156
Consignee		BILL OF LADING

COPY

NON-NEGOTIABLE

Notify party		ALL TERMS, CONDITIONS AND EXCEPTIONS AS PER ORIGINAL BILL OF LADING

Pre-carriage by	Place of receipt KAOHSIUNG CY	"SUBJECT TO ALL THE TERMS AND CONDITIONS OF THE APPLICABLE TARIFF"
Ocean vessel Voy. No. AMERICA MARU 55227B	Port of loading KAOHSIUNG	
Port of discharge LOS ANGELES	Place of delivery TIJUANA CY	Final destination for the Merchant's reference

Container No. Seal No. Marks and Numbers	No. of Cont- Kind of packages; description of goods ainers or pkgs.	Gross weight	Measurement
	''SHIPPER'S LOAD & COUNT''		
△ 3 CONTAINERS (677 CTNS)		9,014 KGS	120.32 M3
TIJUANA B.C. MEXICO VIA LOS ANGELES CA. MODEL: H260 C/NO. 1-235 MADE IN TAIWAN REPUBLIC OF CHINA -DO-BUT H667 C/NO.1	vvvvvvvvvvvvvvv △ MODEL: C/NO. 1-441 MADE IN TAIWAN REPUBLIC OF CHINA	MODEL:H260,H670,H667 MODEL: JOB NO. & CODE NO. MODEL: JOB NO. CODE NO. MODEL: JOB NO. & CODE NO. ''FREIGHT COLLECT''	
	GSTU-8135538	C/S-480409 HS-41019 (192 C/T)	
	GSTU-8135939	C/S-480410 HS-41014 (192 C/T)	
	MOLU-2021646	C/S-480411 HS-41015 (293 C/T)	

*Total number of Containers or other packages or units received by the Carrier (in words)   THREE CONTAINERS ONLY

Freight and charges	Revenue tons	Rate	per	Prepaid	Collect
BOX RATE		(40'x3)	US $2,100.00/VAN (INCLUDING D.D.C.)		US$6,300.00 vvvvvvvvvvvv
+ CY RECEIVING CHARGE			NT$900.00/VAN	NT$2,700.00 vvvvvvvvvvv	

Exchange rate	Prepaid at	Payable at TIJUANA	Place and date of issue TAIPEI TAIWAN
	Total prepaid in national currency	No. of original H/L THREE/3	by

LADEN ON BOARD THE VESSEL
Date   Signature

and/or the seller's bank loses title control because the goods will be delivered to anyone who can be identified as the consignee.

Order Bill of Lading

This is a negotiable bill; unlike the straight bill, it represents the title to the goods in transit, and the original copy must be endorsed before it is presented to the bank for collection. In other words, the order bill can be used as collateral in financing—as documentation to discount or sell a draft. L/C transactions specify to whom the endorsement is to be made. Typically, they are made "in blank" or to the order of a third party, a bank, or a broker. *Air bills of lading* are usually "straight" (i.e., non-negotiable). Ocean shipping companies can issue "straight" or "to order."

Clean on Board

To verify shipping performance, the carrier indicates the condition of the goods upon acceptance. You should prefer to ship on a bill of lading marked *clean on board*. That means that the carrier accepted the cargo and loaded it on board the vessel without exception.

Foul Bill

A foul bill indicates an exception—that some damage is noted on the bill of lading. Discuss this with your carrier or freight forwarder to make sure that you have an opportunity to exchange any damaged goods and obtain a "clean" bill.

The next chapter explains, from A to Z, how to set up and build your company. It discusses how to decide on a name, how to go about getting start-up funds, and most importantly how to think through and write a business plan.

CHAPTER 6

HOW TO SET UP YOUR OWN IMPORT/EXPORT BUSINESS

"How do I start my own import/export business?"

That question is universal. The language might be different, but in any country in the world you will hear the same words. The answer depends on these questions: Have you done your homework? What is your product? Who will buy it? Is it profitable? Do you have contacts? Do you have a marketing plan?

By incorporating what you've learned in Chapters 2 through 5 about the fundamentals of import/export with the methods to be explained in this chapter, you should be ready to start your own import/export business.

The first part of this chapter describes the mechanics of start-up. The second part shows you how to develop a business plan so that you can raise capital and grow.

The Mechanics of Start-Up

The process for starting a small business is the same in any country in the world. You need capital, know-how, and management skills, but you do not need a fancy college degree. Anyone can operate a business.

Start-Up Capital

In the initial stages of starting your own import/export business, the funds needed to support expenses will most likely come from your own pocket. While it is possible to begin an import/export business with as little as a few thousand dollars, many people underestimate the amount of capital needed to sustain the business through the early tough times.

Sources of Financial Capital

When your personal finances will not sustain the expenses of start-up until you reach breakeven and begin to show a profit, you must look for outside financial assistance. Unfortunately, banks are seldom the source of start-up capital. Why? Because banks seldom take risks. They generally expect a track record and collateral. Catch 22? Where can you go for financing? Most often, the best sources are relatives and/or friends—people who know you and believe in you. Even they may want a description of your intended business, so from the beginning you should develop a written plan for your business. It is not unusual that some people use their credit cards for initial funds. You may want to skip to the second part of this chapter immediately to learn how to write that plan. You can return to this section when you complete your business plan.

Business Name/Logo

Think of a name for your business. The company's name should reflect what your business does and be easily advertised by letter, fax, or over the Internet. For example, you can easily visualize the nature of the business called the "Southeast U.S.A. Furniture Import." It gives a more accurate picture of the company than would, "Kim Yee and Son." If the name you choose does not contain the owner's surname, a request to use a fictitious name, or DBA (doing business as) is required in most places. If the name of your business includes your last name, you might not be required to file a fictitious name approval. The cost for registering your fictitious name varies from country-to-country. In the United States, it is about $20.00. There is also a requirement to publish that name in a newspaper for several days. The U.S. cost for this is usually about $30 to $40.

Business Organization

Next, decide how your business will be organized. The three common legal forms are sole proprietorship, partnership, and corporation. Most start-up import/export businesses begin as proprietorships or partnerships. They find little need to take on the extra paperwork and reporting requirements of a corporation in the beginning. Select the form of your business based on the intent, complexity, tax implications, and liability requirements of the business. If you're in doubt, consult a lawyer. Partnership agreements and incorporation papers can be expensive, ranging from as little as a few hundred dollars to several thousand.

Business License

Some countries require licenses to do international trade, but in the United States there is no licensing requirement; that is, there is no regulatory body that requires you to show special qualifications in order to present yourself as an importer or exporter. However, like any other business, you probably must meet local and state business licensing requirements. It is possible that the foreign country you are doing business with will require a license as well. Check with your freight forwarder.

Seller's Permit

Most nations and states have a sales tax. In order to ensure collection, a seller's permit is often required. These permits are usually state controlled, so as you begin your own import/export business, you should investigate your local laws.

Financial Records

Open a separate bank account in the name of your business. Keep accurate records, and pass all business income and expenses through your business account. Do not pay personal expenses from this account or otherwise mix personal income or expenses with business income and expenses. You may list personal "capital contributions" and "capital withdrawals," but keep these infrequent and in reasonably large sums—don't take out money in dribs and drabs.

Accounting

From the beginning, learn to keep a simple set of books to feed into your Internal Revenue Service (IRS) forms at tax time. Keep a careful record (and all receipts) of all business expenses, and invoice all work on your company letterhead. At a minimum, you will need a general ledger organized into four sections: expenses, income, receivables (sales invoiced), and payables (bills received). For example, your expenses, like the cost of your trip to Hong Kong or Paris, should be listed chronologically, by month, down the left margin of the expense section. Across the page, the categories should correspond to tax categories. Check current IRS publications and tax software.

What kind of expenses should you expect in your own import/export business? Here are the most common ones:

- Stationery and business cards
- Telephone, answering machines, computer, calculator, copier, facsimile
- Internet Web site
- Rent, utilities, office furniture
- Inventory
- Business checking account
- Salaries and other staff expenses
- Travel

Table 6.1 offers an example of the categories of expenses shown in the expense section of your general ledger. The other sections of your ledger should be set up similarly.

Table 6.1 Categories of Expenses

Date	Utilities	Telephone/ Fax	Travel Air	Travel Auto	Office Expense
January					
February					
March					

The Office

You can set up an office in your home or elsewhere. The location and outfitting will be determined by the volume and complexity of your firm. In the beginning, you may do business by letter and/or use e-mail and fax and part-time employees only occasionally. However, as your import/export business grows, you may need warehouse space for inventory and a larger office for a growing staff.

Employees

As your office and trading staff grows, the complexity of paperwork and record keeping will also grow. Prior to hiring anyone, you must obtain an employer ID number from the IRS. You should also consider worker's compensation and benefits insurance.

Business Insurance

Other kinds of business insurance that you should consider on a case-by-case basis are liability, disability, an FCIA (Foreign Credit Insurance Association) umbrella policy, and a customs bond.

Support Team

Early in the establishment of your import/export business, you should develop a relationship with your international support team. After a brief period of shopping around, settle on a long-term relationship with

(1) an international banker, (2) a freight forwarder, (3) a customs house broker, (4) an international accountant, and (5) an international attorney. Also, consider contacting the Small Business Administration (SBA) if you run into problems. Members of the SBA's Service Corps of Retired Executives (SCORE) are often available to provide free advice.

The 10 Commandments of Starting an Overseas Business

1. Limit the primary participants to people who not only can collaborate and contribute directly, but also are experienced in some form of international business.
2. Define your import/export market in terms of what is to be bought, precisely by whom, and why.
3. Concentrate all available resources on two or three products or objectives within a given time period.
4. Obtain the best information through your own industry.
5. Write down your business plan and work from it.
6. "Walk on two legs." Pick a good freight forwarder or customs house broker to walk alongside your banker.
7. Translate your literature into the language(s) of the country(ies) in which you will do business.
8. Use the services of the Departments of Commerce and Treasury.
9. Limit the effects of your inevitable mistakes by starting slowly.
10. Communicate frequently and well with your international contacts, and visit the overseas markets and manufacturers.

The Business Plan

In the beginning you may have only a notion of your plan tucked away in your head. As the concept of your business grows, it will be necessary to formalize your plan and stick to it. Putting out brush fires in order to maintain marginal survival is hardly a wise use of anyone's time.

The underlying concept of a business plan is to write out your thoughts. By raising and then systematically answering basic operational questions, you force self-criticism. Once it's on paper, others can read it and you can invite their opinions. Don't let your ego get in your way. Ask for constructive criticism from the most experienced people you can find. Often it is better to ask strangers because friends and relatives tend to want to shield you from hurt. Explain to your readers that you want to hear both the bad news and the good news. The more eyes that see the plan, the more likely you will (1) identify hazards while you still can act or avoid them and (2) spot opportunities while you can easily act to maximize them.

The plan is nothing; planning is everything.

—President (General) Dwight Eisenhower

A business plan can be as brief as 10 pages and as long as 50. On average, they run about 20 pages. Every outline is usually about the same. Figure 6.1 suggests an outline format for your business plan.

How to Begin the Business Plan

Stop everything and begin writing. The first draft of your plan will contain about 80 percent of the finished draft and can be finished in less than two days. One measure of the success of the process is the amount of pain it causes you. By looking at your business as an onlooker would, you may find that some of your vision, a pet project for instance, may have to be abandoned. Often, the process is done in eight steps:

1. Define long-term objectives
2. State short-term goals
3. Set marketing strategies
4. Analyze available resources (personnel, material, etc.)
5. Assemble financial data
6. Review for realism
7. Rewrite
8. Implement

Figure 6.1 Business Plan Outline

Cover Sheet: Name, principals, address, etc.

International Costumes, Inc.
Business Plan
Fiscal Year 20XX

Statement of Purpose:

Table of Contents: (corresponds to each exhibit)

A. Executive summary
B. Description of the business
C. Product-line plan
D. Sales and marketing plan
E. Operations plan
F. Organization plan
G. Financial plan
H. Supporting documents
I. Summary

Exhibits:
Exhibit A Executive Summary
   1. Written last, summarizes in global terms the entire plan; succinct expression of long- and short-term goals

Exhibit B Description of the Business
   1. Long- and short-term goals
     Financial
     Nonfinancial

   2. Strategies
     Product line
     Sales and marketing
     Product development
     Operations
     Organizational
     Financial

   3. Location
     Reasons

Exhibit C Product-Line Plan
   1. Product line and products
     Description

(Continued)

Figure 6.1 (Continued)

Price
Costs
Historical volume
Future expectations

2. Competition's product line and product position
   Pricing
   Advertising and promotion

Exhibit D   Sales and Marketing Plan
   1. Person(s) responsible for generating product line and product sales
   2. Competition's approach to sales and marketing

Exhibit E   Operations Plan
   1. Production and operations function
      Production scheduling
      Inventory (product line and product)
   2. Capital expenditures (if required)

Exhibit F   Organization Plan
   1. Organization's structure
      Organization chart
      Résumés of key personnel
      Managerial style

Exhibit G   Financial Plan
   1. Summary of operating and financial schedules
   2. Schedules*
      Capital equipment
      Balance sheet
      Cash flow (breakeven analysis)
      Income projections
      Pro forma cash flow
      Historical financial reports for existing business
      (Balance sheets for past three years; income statements
      for past three years; tax returns)

Exhibit H   Supporting Documents
   1. Personal résumés
   2. Cost of living budget
   3. Letters of reference
   4. Copies of leases
   5. Anything else of relevance to the plan
Exhibit I   Summary

*See Figures 6-2 to 6-5.

Defining Long-Term Objectives

Start with the objectives of your import/export business. Think ahead. What do I want the business to be like in three years? Five years? Twenty years? How big a business do you want?

Stating Short-Term Goals

Define your import/export business in terms of sales volume and assets. Be precise; state them in measurable units of time and dollars.

Setting Marketing Strategies

If you have done your homework as explained in Chapter 2 and applied the marketing concepts offered in Chapter 3, this part of the business plan should be simple.

If not, go back and review the marketing section of Chapter 3, because nothing will happen with your business until you make a sale. If sales aren't made, projections and other plans fall apart. Profitable sales support the business, so be prepared to spend 75 percent of your planning time on marketing efforts. Ultimately, the best marketing information comes through your own industry, here or overseas. Talk to those with experience. Talk to manufacturers as well as other importers/exporters. Don't overlook the data that can be found in libraries and over the Internet.

Make your market plan precise. Describe your competitive advantage. Outline your geographical and product line priorities. Write down your sales goals. List your alternatives for market penetration. Will you sell direct or through agents? What is the advertising budget? Travel in an import/export business is a must. What is the travel budget? How much will it cost to expand your markets? What will be the cost of communications? Don't minimize your cost projections. It is not unusual to underestimate expenses. They are often three times more than you think they will be.

Analyzing Available Resources

Now for the pain. You must ask yourself whether you have the resources to make the plan work. Take a management inventory. Do you have the skills to market your products? Do you need administrative or accounting skills? Will you need warehouse space? Will you need translators? How much cash will you need?

Assembling Financial Data

After all the dreaming and reality testing of the first four steps, you must now express them in terms of cash flow, profit and loss projections, and balance sheets. Figure 6.2 shows a pro forma sales projection (three-year summary, detailed by month for the first year; detailed by quarter for the second and third years). Figure 6.3 is a pro forma income (profit and loss) statement (detailed by month for the first year; detailed by quarter for the second and third years), Figure 6.4 is a pro forma balance sheet, and Figure 6.5 is a pro forma cash flow statement (detailed by month for first year; detailed by quarter for the second and third years). This use of *pro forma* here means estimating information in advance in a prescribed form.

The cash flow and the profit and loss projections serve double duty. They quantify the sales and operating goals, including use of personnel and other resources expressed in dollars and time. As a guide to the future, they can be used as control documents and measure progress toward goals. The balance sheet shows what your business owns, what it owes, and how those assets and liabilities are distributed.

Reviewing for Realism

Your plan must not set contradictory goals. A coherent plan fits together. You cannot be expanding the introduction of goose liver from China at the same time you are getting out of animal products and into irrigation machinery. Look at your plan as a whole and ask, "Does this make good business sense?"

Rewrite

Now that the first draft is complete, let at least 10 experienced people look at it. Ask them to be critical and to tell you the truth. Let them know up

Figure 6.2 Pro Forma Sales Projections

Pro Forma Sales (Shipments) Projections
Fiscal Year 20xx

Product Line(s) Product(s)	Jan	Feb	March	April	May	June	July	Aug	Sept	Oct	Nov	Dec	Year
A. Product Line A													
1. Product 1													
Shipments (Units)													
× Avg. Price/Unit													
Gross Sales	$	$	$	$	$	$	$	$	$	$	$	$	$
2. Product 2													
3. Product 3													
— — —													
n. Product N													
Product Line A—													
Gross Sales	$	$	$	$	$	$	$	$	$	$	$	$	$

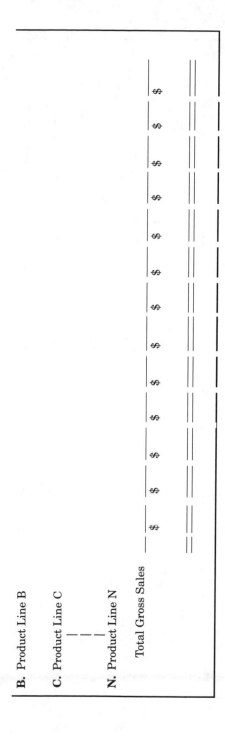

B. Product Line B

C. Product Line C

N. Product Line N

Total Gross Sales

$ $ $ $ $ $ $ $ $ $ $

Figure 6.3 Pro Forma Income Statement (Profit and Loss)

Pro Forma Income Statement
Fiscal Year 20xx

	Jan	Feb	March	April	May	June	July	Aug	Sept	Oct	Nov	Dec	Year
Gross Sales													
less: Discounts, allowances, etc.													
Net Sales													
less: Variable costs													
Manufacturing:													
Material													
Labor													
Variable overhead													
Other													
Variable costs (manufacturing)													
Operating:													
Commissions													
Other													
Variable costs (operating)													
Variable costs (total)													
Contribution													
Percent of net sales	(%)												

less: Fixed costs										
Manufacturing	—	—	—	—	—	—	—	—	—	—
Engineering	—	—	—	—	—	—	—	—	—	—
Selling	—	—	—	—	—	—	—	—	—	—
General and	—	—	—	—	—	—	—	—	—	—
Administrative	—	—	—	—	—	—	—	—	—	—
Financial	—	—	—	—	—	—	—	—	—	—
Fixed costs (total)	—	—	—	—	—	—	—	—	—	—
Profit before taxes	—	—	—	—	—	—	—	—	—	—
less: Taxes	—	—	—	—	—	—	—	—	—	—
Net income	—	—	—	—	—	—	—	—	—	—

159

Figure 6.4 Pro Forma Balance Sheet

Pro Forma Balance Sheet Fiscal Year 20xx	Actual Dec	Jan	Feb	March	April	May	June	July	Aug	Sept	Oct	Nov	Dec
A. Assets Employed													
1. Current Assets													
Cash													
Accounts receivable (net)													
Inventory													
Prepaids													
Other													
Subtotal													
2. Current Liabilities (excluding debt)													
Accounts payable													
Accrued liabilities													
Taxes payable													
Other													
Subtotal													
Working capital (1 − 2)													
3. Property, Plant, and Equipment													
Land													
Building													

Equipment
Less: Accumulated
    depreciation

    Subtotal

4. *Other Assets*
Investments
Other

    Subtotal

Assets Employed

B. *Capital Structure*
1. *Debt*

Short-term Notes
Long-term (current
    portion)
Long-term Debt
Other

    Subtotal

2. *Deferred Taxes*

3. *Shareholders Equity*
Paid-in Capital
Retained Earnings

    Subtotal

Capital Structure

Figure 6.5 Pro Forma Cash Flow Statement

Pro Forma Cash Flow Statement (Operational)
Fiscal Year 20xx

	Jan	Feb	March	April	May	June	July	Aug	Sept	Oct	Nov	Dec	Year
Cash Receipts													
Collection of accounts receivable													
Sale of assets													
Borrowings													
Equity financing													
Other													
Cash receipts													
Cash Expenditures													
Material													
Freight													
Wages and salaries													
Commissions													
Fringe benefits													
Manufacturing expenses													
Selling expenses													
General and administrative expenses													
Financial expenses													
Subtotal													

Capital expenditures							
Debt repayment							
Dividends							
Other							
Cash expenditures							
Cash flows							
Cumulative cash flows							

front that you have a lot of ego in this project, but that because you want to be a success, you want their criticism, no matter how much it hurts.

Implementation

Your business plan provides a road map, but the acid test is whether it will work. Like a map, you may have to detour to get where you are going, so don't put the map on the shelf and forget about it. Use it as an operating document. Review it and revise it as experience dictates.

Now you're ready to go. You've done your homework and written your business plan. If you've gotten this far, you have the style and determination to make it work.

By now, you have written your first letter and made your first contact. As an importer, you've asked for literature and samples; as an exporter you've sent them. You want early orders, and if you have done your homework, they should start rolling in, but be patient. Everything takes a little longer than you would expect or would like in international business.

As you have learned in the previous five chapters, most of the fundamentals of international trade are common to both importing and exporting, but some major elements are specific to one or the other. The next part of the book explains those things that are unique to exporting or to importing, such as government support systems, information systems, tax considerations, tariffs, and private sector support organizations.

PART 2

THE DIFFERENCES

CHAPTER 7

EXPORTING FROM THE UNITED STATES

The figure presented in the introduction to this book (Figure I.1) demonstrates that gross global merchandise trade has risen dramatically since the end of World War II. However Figure 1.1, in Chapter 1, shows that since about 1975, the United States has been in serious chronic trade deficit.

This chapter explores the processes that are unique to exporting from the United States and how you can take advantage of them to export your products and services, thus assisting in the reduction of the nation's deficits. Among other things, you will learn which public and private organizations support the export function and where to go for export information. The topics specific to export are:

- Government support
- Information sources
- Freight forwarding
- Export controls
- "Made in USA"
- Tax incentives for exporting
- How to gain relief from unfair import practices
- Export cities

Government Support

All governments promote exporting because it brings needed foreign
exchange and stimulates job expansion. Therefore, every nation and
many states and provincial governments provide a wide range of export
counseling and assistance programs.

International Trade Administration (ITA)

Most countries have an organization similar to the U.S. International
Trade Administration (ITA), which is a division of the Department of
Commerce. Its importance to the nation is emphasized by the fact that
it gets a dominant share of that department's budget. The ITA is organized basically into three arms: overseas, headquarters, and domestic
covering the territorial boundaries of the United States. To make
contact and find the office nearest you go to: www.export.gov or
www.ita.doc.gov; phone: 800-USA-TRAD(E) (800-872-8723); e-mail:
TIC@ITA.GOV

Overseas Offices

The *overseas* function of the ITA is called the Foreign Commercial
Service (FCS). It maintains offices in more than 108 domestic offices
and 140 overseas posts in major foreign cities in the 80 countries that
are the principal trading partners of the United States. ITA offers
export solutions to help smaller firms increase profits and lower risk. To
help U.S. firms compete, these offices provide a full range of business
services, trade leads, and financial counseling services, which include
political and credit risk analysis, advice on market entry strategy, sources
of financing, and major project identification, tracking, and assistance.
Commercial Service officers identify and evaluate importers, buyers,
agents, distributors, and joint-venture partners. Through their local
Commercial Service centers, they can introduce you to local business
and government leaders and assist in trade disputes. These services are
available to U.S. companies that either produce or have the export rights
to a product or service that is composed of 51 percent or more U.S.
content. All you have to do is call or write either your local Export

Assistance Center within the U.S. Commerce Department Office or check the list of offices found at www.ita.doc.gov

The senior Commercial Service officer in each country is a principal advisor to the U.S. Ambassador. Commercial Service staff members gather data on specific export opportunities, country trends affecting trade and investment, and prospects for specific industries. They also monitor and analyze local laws and practices that affect business conditions.

Headquarters Offices (Washington, DC)

The International Trade Administration of the U.S. Department of Commerce also has approximately 165 country and regional desk officers at its headquarters in Washington, DC. Their job is to be experts in assigned countries, from Afghanistan to Zimbabwe. These desk officers provide specific information about the laws and products of their assigned countries to U.S. business people. Desk officers are organized into two groups: (1) market access and commercial policy and (2) trade information/trade development.

The desk officers are specialists who assess the needs of an individual firm wishing to sell in a particular country in the full context of that country's economy, trade policies, and political situation. Trade development officers are industry specialists who work with manufacturing and service industry associations and firms to identify trade opportunities and obstacles by product or service, industry sector, and market.

Exporters who are planning to visit Washington, DC and would like to schedule appointments with either desk officers or program specialists within the Commerce Department (and/or other agencies involved in international marketing) should contact the nearest Export Assistance Center; phone: 800-USA-TRAD(E); Web site: www.export.gov.

Domestic Offices

The United States offers a broad range of trade-related information, as well as one-on-one counseling from experienced trade specialists located in more than 50 Export Assistance Centers (EACs) in industrial and commercial centers throughout the United States. These are customer-focused offices designed to streamline export marketing and trade finance assistance by integrating in a single location the counselors and services of the Commercial Service, Export-Import (EXIM) Bank, the Small Business Administration (SBA), and in some cities, the U.S. Agency for International Development. To contact call 800-USA-TRAD(E) or see the local Commercial Service office addresses listed at www.ita.doc.gov; or e-mail at tic@da.doc.gov.

The EACs can help exporters and other prospective businesses with:

- Market research
- Trade and investment opportunities abroad
- Foreign markets for U.S. products and services
- Possible grant opportunities
- Insurance from the FCIA
- Tax advantages of exporting
- International trade exhibitions
- Export documentation requirements
- Economic facts on foreign countries
- Export licensing requirements
- Promotion of products and services
- Locating export prospects

District Export Councils

District Export Councils (DECs) are organizations of leaders from the local business community, appointed by successive Secretaries of Commerce, whose knowledge of international business provides a source of professional advice for local firms.

In order to help small businesses succeed in the world economy, DECs volunteer their time to sponsor and participate in numerous trade promotion activities, as well as to supply specialized expertise and mentoring programs to small- and medium-sized businesses that are interested in exporting. They run seminars on export basics and trade finance, host international buyer delegations, design breakthrough guides to help firms export, and put exporters on the Internet to help build export assistance partnerships to strengthen the support given to local businesses in exporting.

The Commercial Service's Export Assistance Centers work closely with these experienced regional international business people through 56 District Export Councils. The 1,700 volunteer DEC members are available to counsel prospective exporters on:

- The how-tos of international trade
- Co-sponsoring seminars and workshops with the EACs
- Addressing business groups on international business opportunities
- Promote awareness of the trade-assistance programs of the Department of Commerce

Small Business Development Centers (SBDCs)
SBDCs provide a full range of export assistance services to small businesses, particularly those new to export, and offer counseling, training, managerial, and trade finance assistance. To contact, phone: 800-UASK-SBA, 800-827-5722, or 202-606-4000; Web site: www.sba.gov; address: SBA Answer Desk, 6302 Fairview Road, Suite 300, Charlotte, North Carolina, 28210.

Service Corps of Retired Executives (SCORE)
The Service Corps of Retired Executives (SCORE), usually co-located with your local SBA office, provides one-on-one counseling and training seminars. For the office nearest you, phone: 800-634-0245; 202-205-6762; fax: 202-205-7636; Web site: www.score.org.

**Office of Export Trading Company
Affairs (OETCA)**
The Office of Export Trading Company Affairs (OETCA), a part of USITA Trade Development, is designed to promote the team concept of exporting through the formation and use of export trading companies (ETCs), export management companies (EMCs), and, in general, the intermediary industry. Office of Export Trading Company Affairs administers the Export Trade Certificate of Review program which permits an antitrust "insurance policy" under the Export Trading Company Act (ETCA). This law permits bankers' banks and holding

companies to invest in ETCs, reduces the restrictions on export financing provided by financial institutions, and modifies the application of the antitrust laws to certain export trade.

Export joint ventures offer firms the opportunity to reduce economies of scale and spread the risks. Specific areas in which gains can be obtained are:

- Market research
- Market development
- Overseas bidding
- Non-tariff barriers
- Transportation and shipping
- Joint bidding and selling arrangements
- Pricing policies
- Service and promotional activities

For information, phone: 202-482-5131; fax: 202-482-1790; Web site: www.ita.doc.gov.

Information Sources

Information needed for exporting is easier to obtain than is information needed for domestic sales. Why? Because most governments subsidize the gathering and analysis of international trade data. A wealth of information, both on paper and electronic, exists to promote exporting. More information is available than one could digest in a lifetime, and the U.S. Department of Commerce has made it easy to acquire. For example, the Trade Opportunities Program (TOP) and the Export Contact List Service files are available in both printed form and up-to-the minute computer-resident databases.

Your nearest Export Assistance Center offers the following information services to U.S. exporters:

- *Trade Information Center (TIC).* The TIC is the most comprehensive resource for information on all government export assistance programs. The center's staff advises exporters on how to locate and use government programs, guides exporters through the export process, supplies general market information, and provides basic export counseling. To contact, phone: 800-USA-TRAD(E) or 202-482-5131; e-mail: tic@ita.doc.gov; fax: 202-482-1790; Web site: tradeinfo.doc.gov. A special phone line is available for those who are hearing impaired using a TDD machine: 800-TDD-TRAD(E). Ask for a free copy of the excellent pamphlets *Export Programs: A Business Directory of U.S. Government Services*, *Export Programs Guide*, and *A Basic Guide to Exporting.*

- *National Trade Data Bank (NTDB).* The NTDB is a one stop source for export promotion and international trade data collected by 17 U.S. government agencies. Updated each month and released on two CD-ROMs, the NTDB enables IBM-compatible personal computers equipped with CD-ROM readers to access over 100,000 trade-related documents. To contact, phone: 800-STAT-USA; Web site: www.stat-usa.gov or tradeport.org. You may wish to visit www.buyusa.com, a site that matches U.S. suppliers with international buyers, the Yellow Pages of foreign countries, and www.globaledge.msu.edu.

- *Economic Bulletin Board (EBB).* The EBB, a personal computer–based electronic bulletin board, is your online source for trade leads as well as for the latest statistical releases from the Bureau of the Census, the Bureau of Economic Analysis, the Bureau of Labor Statistics, the Federal Reserve Board, and other federal agencies. To contact, phone: 800-STAT-USA, 800-782-8872, 202-482-3870, or 202-482-1986. You may use your fax machine to receive trade leads and the latest trade and economic information from the federal government. You can access this by dialing 900-RUN-A-FAX. Contact EBB/FAX help line, phone: 202-482-1986; fax: 202-482-2164.

- *Industry Sector Analysis (ISA).* This organization produces market research reports on location in leading overseas markets. The reports cover market size and outlook, characteristics, and competitive and end-user analysis for a selected industry sector in a particular country. Selected analyses are available on the National Trade Data Bank (NTDB).

- *International Market Insights (IMI).* Market insights are short profiles of specific foreign market conditions or opportunities prepared in overseas markets and at multilateral development banks. These non-formatted reports include information and updates on dynamic sectors of a particular country and could profile new major projects or trade events. These are also available on the NTDB.

Export Prospects

Most governments have programs to help exporters make cross-border contacts. The U.S. government is no exception. As a matter of fact, you should take advantage of its full range of programs. For basic information go to www.trade.gov/td/tic.

- *Agent Distributor Service (ADS).* ADS performs a custom overseas "search" for interested and qualified foreign representatives on behalf of a U.S. client. Commercial Services (CS) staff abroad conduct the search and prepare a report identifying up to six foreign prospects that have personally examined the U.S. firm's product literature and have expressed interest in representing the firm. ADS charges a fee per market or specific area. Contact your local EAC, phone: 800-USA-TRAD(E); Web site: www.ita.doc.gov.
- *Trade Opportunities Program (TOP).* Commercial specialists around the world collect TOP leads at trade shows, through conversation, and through market research. Individual sales lead messages are then sent directly to subscribers and the EACs nationwide. They can be sent via computer or facsimile, or sent as a printed hard copy. Each message contains detailed information regarding a current foreign trade lead, typically including the specifications, quantities, end use, delivery and bid deadlines for the product or service desired by the foreign customer. A fee is required to set up the subscribers interest file and for each block of 50 leads up to five blocks. To contact, phone: 800-STAT-USA or 202-482-1986; e-mail: statmail@PSA.doc.gov.

HOT TIP

The Trade Opportunities Program (TOP) matches product interests of foreign buyers with those of U.S. subscribers.

- *International Company Profile (ICP).* Information provided in an international company profile includes type of organization, year established, size, general reputation, territory covered, sales, product lines, principal owners, financial information, and trade references, with recommendations from on-site commercial officers as to the company's suitability as a trading partner.
- *Commercial Service International Contacts (CSIC).* CSIC provides the name and contact information for directories of importers, agents, trade association, government agencies, and the like on a country-by-country basis. Available on the NTDB.

Overseas Promotion

The ITA, U.S. Department of State offices within U.S. embassies, and consulates worldwide collaborate to assist in the promotion of products and services.

Services and Programs

- *Agent/Distributor Services.* Discussed earlier, these services are often used in conjunction with the Gold Key Service. They assist with issues of industrial property rights, territory covered (exclusive and nonexclusive contracts) the problems of terminating the contract, possibility of host country of switching from contract laws to labor laws according of the comparative size of the principal's company and distributor's company.
- *Gold Key Service.* A custom-tailored service that combines orientation briefings, market research, appointments with potential

partners, interpreter service for meetings, and assistance in developing follow-up strategies. Gold Key Service is offered by the Commercial Service in export markets around the world. Prices and conditions vary by country.

- *Matchmaker Trade Delegations.* "Matches" U.S. firms with prospective agents, distributors, and joint-venture or licensing partners abroad. For each "matchmaker" the Commercial Service staff evaluates the marketing potential of U.S. firms' products and services, finds and screens contacts, and handles all event logistics. U.S. firms visit the designated countries with the delegation and, in each country, receive a schedule of business meetings and in-depth market and finance briefings.

- *International Buyer Program (IBP).* Supports selected leading U.S. trade shows in industries with high export potential. The Department of Commerce offices abroad recruit delegations of foreign buyers and distributors to attend the U.S. shows, while program staff members help exhibiting firms make contact with international visitors at the show. The International Buyer Program achieves direct export sales and international representation for interested U.S. exhibitors.

- *Multistate/Catalog Exhibitions.* The exhibitions showcase U.S. company product literature in fast-growing markets within a geographic region. During multi-state/catalog exhibitions, the U.S. Department of Commerce staff and representatives from state development agencies present product literature to hundreds of interested business prospects abroad and send the trade leads directly to participants.

- *Trade Fair Certification.* Supports major international industry trade shows, thereby providing high-profile promotion of U.S. products. Trade fair certification encourages private organizers to recruit new-to-market, new-to-export U.S. exhibitors to maintain Department of Commerce standards for events and to provide services ranging from advance promotion to on-site assistance for U.S. exhibitors.

Publications and Reports

- *The Overseas Trade Promotions Calendar.* Revised quarterly, this calendar provides a 12-month schedule of U.S. Trade Center exhibitions and international trade fairs in which U.S. participation is planned. It also includes other overseas promotional activities that are planned and to be organized by the U.S. Department of Commerce.
- *How to Get the Most from Overseas Exhibitions.* Contains helpful planning tips and details the steps to be taken to participate in an overseas exhibition. Write to the Office of Export Development, International Trade Administration, U.S. Department of Commerce, Washington, DC 20230. No charge.
- *Export Statistics Profile.* Provides a variety of export statistics by product and arrays the data in ways that make market analysis easy. It provides multiyear coverage, percentage of market shares, and top markets for products in rank order. The price ranges from $30 to $70 depending on the depth and specification. Go to www.trade.gov/td/tic.
- *Customs Service Statistics.* This statistical service provides customs statistics in four export and/or import tables. Prices for these statistical reports range from $50 to $150 depending on complexity:

  1. For up to 10 selected products showing trade to 9 major world market areas.
  2. For up to 10 selected products showing trade to every country worldwide in rank order.
  3. For up to 10 selected countries showing trade in individually specified products in rank order.
  4. For the top 30 countries showing trade in up to 10 individually specified products in rank order.

- *Understanding U.S. Foreign Trade Data.* Explains the different foreign trade classifications and valuation systems and other factors that complicate the understanding of U.S. foreign trade data.

Price: $7.50. Contact Superintendent of Documents at,
phone: 866-512-1800; fax: 202-512-2250; e-mail:
Orders@gpo.gov; Web site: www.gpoaccess.gov.

- *U.S. Government Information: Publications, Periodicals, and
  Electronic Products.* Popular government publications are
  organized into subject areas and can be ordered from the online
  bookstore operated by the Government Printing Office (GPO)
  Web site: www.gpoaccess.gov; e-mail orders@gpo.gov.
- *A Basic Guide to Exporting.* Published by the U.S. Department
  of Commerce, it can be obtained by writing the Superintendent of
  Documents, U.S. Government Printing Office, Washington, DC
  20402; phone: 202-783-3238; or available online on NTDB's
  "International Trade Library" at www.stat-usa.gov.

This booklet is designed to show step by step how to expand an existing
manufacturing business into the international marketplace. It is also an
excellent resource for the small importer/exporter. The cost is about $16.

- *The EMC—Your Export Department.* Describes the services
  provided to exporters by export management companies as well as
  how to go about selecting a suitable EMC. Write to the Office of
  Export Development, International Trade Administration, U.S.
  Department of Commerce, Washington, DC 20230.
- *Exporter Yellow Pages.* A public/private partnership that features
  over 13,000 providers, trading companies, and manufacturers who
  have registered their export interest with EACS. It can be found at
  www.myexports.com; phone: 877-390-2629.
- *The U.S. Export Management Companies (EMCs) Directory.*
  Emphasizes the marketing capability of EMCs. This is the
  international trade import/export portal and is the source
  for international trade business-to-business leads and news about
  international trade. Visit the Web site at http://fita.org/emc.html.
- *Exporter's Encyclopedia (Annual).* A valuable publication for the
  serious trader's library. It's chock full of fingertip information and
  can be found in most libraries. Costs about $450. Order from
  Dun & Bradstreet International, 103 JFK Parkway, Short Hills,

NJ 07078. Phone: 800-234-3867 or 800-932-0025 (international); Web site: www.dnb.com/prods_svcs/allprods.htm.

- ***An Introduction to the Overseas Private Investment Corporation (OPIC).*** Reviews how OPIC can assist firms interested in investing in developing nations. Order from Overseas Private Investment Corporation, 1100 New York Avenue, NW, Washington, DC 20527. Phone: 202-336-8400; fax: 202-408-9859; e-mail: info@opic.gov.
- ***Export–Import Bank of the United States.*** Explains U.S. export financing programs. No charge. Order from Export-Import Bank of the United States, 811 Vermont Avenue, NW, Washington, DC 20571. E-mail: www.exim.gov.
- ***Carnet.*** Explains what a carnet is and how it can benefit exporters. Contains application forms for applying for a carnet. No charge. Order from U.S. Council for International Business, 1212 Avenue of the Americas, New York, NY 10036. Phone: 212-354-4480; fax: 212-575-0327; e-mail: info@uscib.org; Web site: www.uscib.org.

Freight Forwarding

A *freight forwarder* is a private service company licensed to support shippers and the movement of their goods. These specialists in international physical distribution act as agents for the exporter (shipper) in moving cargo to an overseas destination. They are familiar with:

- The import rules and regulations of foreign countries
- Methods of shipping
- U.S. government export regulations
- The documents connected with foreign trade

From the beginning, freight forwarders can assist with an order by advising on such things as freight costs, consular fees, and insurance costs. They can recommend the degree of packing, arrange for an inland carrier, find the right airline, and even arrange for the containerization of the cargo. They quote shipping rates, provide information, and book cargo space. These firms are invaluable because they can handle everything from the factory to the final destination, including all documentation, storage, and shipping insurance, and they will route your cargo at the lowest customs charges.

Shipper

Any person whose primary business is the sale of merchandise may, without a license, dispatch and perform freight forwarding services on behalf of his or her own shipments, or on behalf of shipments or consolidated shipments of a parent, subsidiary, affiliate, or associated company. The shipper may not, however, receive compensation from the common carrier.

A large manufacturer usually has its own shipping department that serves as its own freight forwarder, but smaller manufacturing firms and small import/export businesses seldom have either the staff or the time to make their own arrangements. Often freight forwarders are called upon to help an exporter put together the final price quotation to a distributor. For example, when quoting CIF, in addition to the manufacturer's price and the commission, the forwarder can provide information on dock and cartage fees, forwarder's fees, marine insurance, ocean freight costs, duty charges, consular invoice fees, and packing charges. It's not unusual (and it may be quite prudent) to review a price quotation with the freight forwarder before sending it on the telex.

How to Become a Freight Forwarder

Their are two types of freight forwarders—ocean and air—but most freight forwarding businesses can do both.

An *ocean freight forwarder* must be licensed by the Federal Maritime Commission (FMC). The criteria to become eligible for a freight forwarding license are:

- Three years' experience in ocean freight forwarding duties
- Necessary character to render forwarding services
- Possession of a valid surety bond

For more information on how to submit an application, contact the Office of Freight Forwarders, Bureau of Tariffs, Federal Maritime Commission, Washington, DC 20573.

Air cargo agents are administered by the International Air Transportation Association (IATA), headquartered in Montreal, Quebec, Canada. This organization through its subsidiary Cargo Network Services, Inc., administers the qualifications and certification of agents in the United States. Additional information can be obtained by writing CNS, 300 Garden City Plaza, Suite 400, Garden City, NY 11530.

HOT TIP

You can become a licensed freight forwarder, but you do not have to be one to arrange movement of goods on behalf of your own shipments. Caution: Don't act as a forwarder for someone else before being issued a license.

Export Controls

Another area in which exporting differs from importing is the licensing required to control exports. The history of export controls in the United States is based on the presumption that all exported goods and technical documentation are subject to regulation by the government. This presumption is fundamentally different from that of most nations, which often presume the freedom to export unless there is an explicit statement of a need to control.

The exercise of controls by the United States varies from minimal (as is the case of Canada) to embargoes (as in the case of North Korea and Cuba). Several departments have legal authority to control exports. Arms, ammunition, implements of war, technical data relating thereto, and certain classified information are licensed by the Department of State. Narcotics and dangerous drugs are licensed by the Department of Justice. Nuclear material is licensed by the Nuclear Regulatory Commission.

There are other exceptions, but in general, the Bureau of Industry and Security (BIS)/Department of Commerce administers the control system that affects most exporters. The BIS provides assistance on exporting licensing requirements through its Office of Exporter Services (OEXS). OEXS interprets the Export Administration Regulations (EAR). Section 15 Federal Regulations 730–774 published in 1996, as amended, are designed to promote the foreign policy of the United States, protect national security, and protect the domestic economy from the excessive drain of scarce materials. Phone: 202-482-4811; fax: 202-482-2927; Web site: www.bis.doc.gov

An export license is a grant of authority from the government issued to a particular exporter to export a designated item to a specific destination. An export license is granted on a case-by-case basis for either a single transaction or for several transactions within a specified period of time. If an export license from BIS is required, the exporter must prepare a Form BIS-748P (Multipurpose Application Form) and submit it to the BIS. The applicant must be sure to follow the instructions on the form carefully. In some instances, technical manuals and support documentation must also be included. The BIS also gives the applicant the option of filing the license application electronically.

If the application is approved, an export license is sent to the applicant. The license contains an export authorization number and expiration date that must be placed on the shipper's export declaration (SED). The SED is used to indicate to U.S. Customs the type of export authorization being used, and serves as an export control document for BIS. The SED is also used by the Department of Commerce's Bureau of Census to compile statistics on U.S. trade. Unlike some goods exported under NLR (no license required) or a license exception, all exports under an export license must be accompanied by an SED.

Export controls are organized on the Commodity Control List (CCL) by country or by item. Some, however, have a more general focus, such as those that advance the human rights cause or those prohibiting doing business with business entities that boycott for ethnic or political reasons.

With few exceptions, an exporter must complete a shipper's export declaration (Commerce Form 7525-V) and deposit it with the exporting carrier regardless of whether a shipment is exported under a validated license or a "license exception."

The vast majority of all exports *do not* require a validated export license and require only the appropriate "license exception" notation on the SED. The symbol NLR is used in specific instances where (1) an item is subject to the EAR but is not listed on the CCL under a specific ECCN, or (2) is listed on the CCL but does not require a license to the destination in question. Virtually all shipments to Canada and the majority of exports to most other destinations are exported from the United States under NLR. Currently, less than 4 percent of U.S. manufactured exports require an export license.

Exporter Obligations

There are five questions that you need to ask to determine your obligations under the EAR:

1. *What is being exported?* The item's classification needs to be determined according to the CCL.
2. *Where is it going?* The country of ultimate destination is a factor in determining export licensing requirements using the country chart.
3. *Who will receive it?* There are restrictions on certain end users, such as persons denied export privileges.
4. *What will they do with it?* The ultimate end use of your item will affect the licensing requirements related to the proliferation of nuclear, chemical, or biological weapons and missile delivery systems.
5. *What else is involved in your transaction?* You may be restricted from engaging in a transaction based on conduct such as contracting, financing, and freight forwarding in support of a proliferation project.

Once you determine that you require a validated license for a specific export, you should submit an application for a license to the Bureau of Industry and Security (BIS), PO Box 273, Washington, DC 20044. An application consists of a completed Form BIS-748P (Multipurpose Application Form) and required supporting information. Figure 7.1 is the application form for an export license.

Figure 7.1 Export License Application Form

B	U.S. DEPARTMENT OF COMMERCE Bureau of Export Administration	DATE RECEIVED (Leave Blank)	X
FORM BXA-748P FORM APPROVED OMB NO. 0694-0088, 0694-0089	**MULTIPURPOSE APPLICATION**		

1. CONTACT PERSON	Information furnished herewith is subject to the provisions of Section 12(c) of the Export Administration Act of 1979, as amended, 50 U.S.C. app. 2411(c), and its unauthorized disclosure is prohibited by law.
2. TELEPHONE	APPLICATION CONTROL NUMBER **This is NOT an export license number**
3. FACSIMILE	**Z181053**

3. DATE OF APPLICATION

5. TYPE OF APPLICATION	6. DOCUMENTS SUBMITTED WITH APPLICATION		7. DOCUMENTS ON FILE WITH APPLICANT	8. SPECIAL COMPREHENSIVE LICENSE
☐ EXPORT	☐ BXA-748P-A	☐ LETTER OF EXPLANATION	☐ BXA-711	☐ BXA-752 OR BXA-752-A
☐ REEXPORT	☐ BXA-748P-B	☐ FOREIGN AVAILABILITY	☐ LETTER OF ASSURANCE	☐ INTERNAL CONTROL PROGRAM
☐ CLASSIFICATION REQUEST	☐ BXA-711	☐ OTHER	☐ IMPORT/END-USER CERTIFICATE	☐ COMPREHENSIVE NARRATIVE
☐ SPECIAL COMPREHENSIVE LICENSE	☐ IMPORT/END-USER CERTIFICATE		☐ NUCLEAR CERTIFICATION	☐ CERTIFICATIONS
☐ OTHER	☐ TECH. SPECS		☐ OTHER	☐ OTHER

9. SPECIAL PURPOSE

10. RESUBMISSION APPLICATION CONTROL NUMBER	11. REPLACEMENT LICENSE NUMBER	12. FOR ITEM(S) PREVIOUSLY EXPORTED, PROVIDE LICENSE EXCEPTION SYMBOL OR LICENSE NUMBER

13. IMPORT/END-USER CERTIFICATE COUNTRY	**NUMBER:**	

14. APPLICANT	15. OTHER PARTY AUTHORIZED TO RECEIVE LICENSE		
ADDRESS LINE 1	ADDRESS LINE 1		
ADDRESS LINE 2	ADDRESS LINE 2		
CITY	POSTAL CODE	CITY	POSTAL CODE
STATE/COUNTRY	EMPLOYER IDENTIFICATION NUMBER	STATE/COUNTRY	TELEPHONE OR FAX

17. PURCHASER	17. INTERMEDIATE CONSIGNEE		
ADDRESS LINE 1	ADDRESS LINE 1		
ADDRESS LINE 2	ADDRESS LINE 2		
CITY	POSTAL CODE	CITY	POSTAL CODE
COUNTRY	TELEPHONE OR FAX	COUNTRY	TELEPHONE OR FAX

24. ADDITIONAL INFORMATION

For all applications: I certify that to the best of my knowledge, all the information on this form is true and correct, and that it conforms to the instructions accompanying this form and the Export Administration Regulations. For license applications: I certify or agree as appropriate that (a) to the best of my knowledge all statements in this application, includin the description of the commodities, software or technology and their end-uses, and any documents submitted in support of this application are correct and complete and that they fully and accurately disclose all the terms of the order and other facts of the transaction: (b) I will retain records pertaining to this transaction and make them available as required by the Export Administration Regulations: (c) I will report promptly to the Bureau of Export Administration any material changes in the terms of the order or other facts or intentions of the transaction as reflected in this application and supporting documents, whether the application is still under consideration or a license has been granted: and (d) if the license is granted, I will be strictly accountable for its use in accordance with the Export Administration Regulations and all the terms and conditions of the license. A number of the parts of this form include certifications based on a person's knowledge. As defined in Part 772 of the Export Administration Regulations, "Knowledge" of a circumstance includes not only positive knowledge that the circumstance exists or is substantially certain to occur, but also an awareness of a high probability of its existance or future occurrence. Such awareness is inferred from evidence of the conscious disregard of facts known to a person and is also inferred from a persons willful avoidance of facts.

25. SIGNATURE (of person authorized to execute this application)	NAME OF SIGNER	TITLE OF SIGNER

This license application and any license issued pursuant thereto are expressly subject to all rules and regulations of the Bureau of Export Administration. Making any false statement or concealing any material fact in connection with this application or altering in any way the license issued is punishable by imprisonment or fine, or both, and by denial of export privileges under the Export Administration Act of 1979, as amended, and any other applicable Federal statutes. No license will be issued unless this form is completed and submitted in accordance with Export Administration Regulation.

X	X	B

USCOMM-DC 96-24024

Within 10 days after the date the OEXS receives the application, the office issues the license or denies it, sends the application to the next step in the license process, or, if the application is improperly completed or additional information is required, returns the application without action. Once the approved license is received, the exporter keeps the validated license on file. All the applicant must submit is the SED; however, all information on the SED must conform to that found in the validated license.

The Internet-based simplified network application process (SNAP) provides a secure environment for the electronic submission of license applications, commodity classification requests, and high-performance computer notices.

To avoid export control violations and shipping delays, applicants should contact their local ITA district office or the Exporter's Service staff, Office of Export Administration, International Trade Administration, for assistance.

HOT TIPS

How to Avoid Export Control Violations

- Determine whether a validated export license is required. When in doubt, contact the Export License Application and Information Network for assistance.
- Fully describe commodities or technical data on export shipping documents.
- Use the applicable destination control statement on commercial invoices, air waybills, and bills of lading, as required by Section 386.6 of the Export Administration Regulations.
- Avoid overshipments by maintaining an accurate account of the quantity and value of goods shipped against a validated export license.
- Be mindful of the expiration date on validated export licenses to avoid shipments after the applicable license has expired.
- Enter the applicable validated export license number or general license symbol on the shipper's export declaration (SED).
- Make certain that shipping documents clearly identify the exporter, intermediate consignee, and ultimate consignee.
- Mail the completed Form BIS-748P.

Where to Get Assistance

In addition to obtaining the applicable export license, U.S. exporters should be careful to meet all other international trade regulations established by specific legislation, regulation, or other authority of the U.S. government. The import laws and regulations of foreign countries must also be taken into account. The exporter should keep in mind that even if help is received with the license and documentation from others, such as banks, freight forwarders, or consultants, the exporter remains responsible for ensuring that all statements are true and accurate.

To avoid confusion, the exporter is strongly advised to seek assistance in determining the proper licensing requirements. The best source is the Bureau of Export Administration's Office of Exporter Services at 14th Street and Constitution Avenue, NW, U.S. Department of Commerce, Washington DC 20230. Telephone or write to the Exporter Counseling Division, Room 1099C, U.S. Department of Commerce, Washington, DC 20230; phone: 202-482-3825; fax: 202-482-0751. Exporters may also contact one of the western regional office locations at 3300 Irvine Avenue, Suite 345, Newport Beach, CA 92660; phone: 949-660-0144; fax: 949-660-9347; or the BIS Western Regional Office at 152 North Third Street, Suite 550, San Jose, CA 95112; phone: 408-998-7402.

The BIS also has a Web site (www.BIS.doc.gov) from which you can access a variety of information related to exports, such as seminars, up-to-date regulations, policy issues, and lists of countries, government agencies, companies, and individuals for whom specific controls apply. Whenever there is any doubt about how to comply with the BIS's Export Administration Regulations, Department of Commerce officials should be contacted for guidance.

"Made in USA"

Buyers have the right to know the true origin of the product they are purchasing. The coveted label "Made in USA" or "Made in America" cannot be randomly used. There are rules, and the rules are becoming more and more important in an international marketplace where U.S.

manufacturers scour the globe for the right components at the best price, using input made in foreign countries.

The Federal Trade Commission (FTC) has a voluntary requirement that "all or virtually all" of a product be made in the United States, and it has issued a guide book, titled *Complying with the Made in the USA Standard*, that spells out the guidelines. The three essential rules are noted below:

- Origin of the products significant parts
- Dominant value (must be U.S. dollars)
- Final assembly location (must be in the United States)

When in doubt, check the FTC guide book, which can be ordered by calling 877-FTC-HELP (382-4357) or by e-mailing via the Web site at www.ftc.gov. The mailing address is 600 Pennsylvania Avenue, NW, Washington, DC 20580.

Tax Incentives for Exporting

A prominent tax attorney once said, "Business in America? It's all about taxes." International business is no exception.

Taxes on income derived from international trade are in accordance with current laws for other income except that tax incentives for exporting are substantial. There are no tax incentives for importing. See www.ncseonline.org and www.irs.gov/tax.

Tax incentives for exporters amount to approximately 15 percent exclusion of the combined taxable income earned on international sales. The tax law provides for a system of tax deferrals for domestic international sales corporations (DISCs) and foreign sales corporations (FSCs).

Prior to December 31, 1984, the DISC was the only medium for distributing export earnings. DISCs don't require a foreign presence and, in fact, are legal entities established only on paper. The DISC incentive was created by the Revenue Act of 1971 and provides for deferral of federal income tax on 50 percent of the export earnings allocated to the DISC with the balance treated as dividends to the parent company. Since its enactment, the DISC had been the subject of an ongoing dispute between the United States and certain other signatories of the General Agreement on Tariffs and Trade (GATT). Other nations contended that the DISC amounted to an illegal export subsidy because it allowed indefinite deferral of direct taxes on income from exports earned in the United States.

Under new rules put into effect on January 1, 1985, to receive a tax benefit that is designed to equal the tax deferral provided by the DISC, exporters must establish an office abroad. The FSC must also be a foreign corporation, maintain a summary of its permanent books of account at the foreign office, and have at least one director resident outside the United States.

Meeting the requirement of the new regulations isn't difficult for big U.S.-based multinationals with overseas offices and ample resources, but thousands of small businesses involved in international commerce are concerned about administrative costs and other overhead. Actually small exporters have several options for their foreign sales operations. They may continue to export through a DISC, paying an interest charge on the deferred income, or they may join together with other exporters to own an FSC. Another alternative is that they may individually take advantage of relaxed, small FSC rules, under which they need not meet all the tests required of large FSCs. A small FSC, one with up to $5 million of gross receipts during the taxable year, is excused from the foreign management and foreign economic process requirements.

The mechanics of setting up a DISC or an FSC are somewhat complex but are within the capability of most accountants. Some 23 foreign countries that have an agreement to exchange tax information with the United States, and U.S. possessions such as the Virgin Islands, Guam, and Saipan have established offices that are capable of providing direct assistance in setting up an FSC.

Exporters with up to $10 million of annual exports may continue to operate through DISCs, generally under the present rules. But they must pay an annual interest charge on the amount of tax that would be due if the post-1984 accumulated DISC income were included in the shareholder's income. This interest is imposed on the shareholders and paid to the Treasury of the United States.

Multiple exporters, up to 25 of them, may jointly own an FSC, and through the use of several classes of common stock divide the profits of an FSC among the shareholders.

How to Gain Relief from Unfair Import Practices

Remaining competitive in world markets is an internal management problem. The underlying elements are quantity, quality, and price. Nevertheless, government intervention is sometimes necessary when you learn about foreign firms that are not competing on what has become known as a "level playing field."

The Department of Commerce's Import Administration (IA) division participates with the U.S. trade representative in monitoring and negotiating fair and transparent international rules. The IA enforces laws and agreements to prevent unfairly traded imports and to safeguard jobs and the competitive strength of U.S. industry.

Copies of the U.S. International Trade Committee's (ITC) *Rules of Practice and Procedure*, which set forth the procedures for the filing and conduct of investigations, are available from the Docket Section, U.S. International Trade Commission, 500 East Street SW, Washington, DC 20436; phone: 202-205-2000; Web site: www.USITC.gov.

The IA, ITC, Congress, and/or the U.S. trade representative can investigate the following allegations:

- Countervailing duties imposed by a foreign country
- Antidumping
- General investigations of trade and tariff matters
- Investigations of costs of production
- Alleged unfair practices in import trade
- Investigations of injury from increased imports
- Workers adjustment assistance
- Firms adjustment assistance
- Enforcement of U.S. rights under trade agreements and response to certain foreign trade practices

- U.S. response to foreign trade practices which restrict or discriminate against U.S. commerce
- Investigations of market disruptions by imports from communist countries

The point of contact for instituting investigations is Import Administration (IA), International Trade Administration, U.S. Department of Commerce,1401 Constitution Avenue, NW, Washington, DC 20230; phone: 202-482-5497 or 1-800-USA-TRAD(E); Web site: www.ita.doc.gov; e-mail: TIC@ita.doc.gov.

Export Cities

To combat America's enormous imbalances, cities are rolling up their sleeves. Mayors are becoming more and more involved and are holding their city councils accountable for methods that contribute to international trade. Cities are calculating their contributions to gross national exports. International trade is too important not to seek solutions from the bottom up. One innovative American idea is the formation of export city clusters.

What Are Export Cities?

Export cities organize clusters that are public–private partnerships to serve the unique products of their region. Export city clusters participate in international trade exporting by displaying the city or regional products year round. Some provide buildings, rooms, or space on the city's Web site.

How Do Export City Clusters Work?

Most exporters travel to foreign buyers, but since the events of 9/11, such travel has been reduced. The export city cluster not only provides a method for displaying products, but it also includes a travel company with an import/export marketing company, a bank, and hotels and restaurants, thus attracting buyers to the export city. Sister cities are being factored into the cluster equation.

The export cluster concept shows a city's involvement in trade and requires vision and creativity by leadership for the long term. You can become a part of this effort.

The next chapter explains those things that are unique to importing, such as customs, tariffs, and quotas.

CHAPTER 8

HOW TO IMPORT INTO THE UNITED STATES

Importing is simply the flip side of exporting, but some aspects of exporting don't apply to importing. For example, the tariff schedule applies only to importing and the Customs Service is concerned only with goods coming into a country.

The following basics unique to importing are discussed in this chapter:

- World Customs Organization
- Homeland Security
- Government support
- Information sources
- Customs house brokers
- Getting through the customs maze
- How to use the tariff schedule
- Import quotas
- Special import regulations
- Free trade zones
- Customs bonded warehouses

World Customs Organization (WCO)

For more than 50 years, the World Customs Organization (WCO) has provided leadership in expanding the avenues of international trade. The organization's success has been driven by a clear-minded adherence to a principle: the more simple and harmonized the world's customs procedures, the more prosperity for international trade and the world at large. The WCO has scored many triumphs across the entire spectrum of customs-based issues. For example, it created and administers several international agreements that facilitate world trade. The major international conventions created or administered by the WCO include:

- Harmonized System Convention (the basis for the U.S. import and export schedules)
- GATT Customs Valuation Agreement
- Nairobi and Johannesburg Conventions, both dealing with sharing of information
- 1973 Kyoto Convention on customs procedures
- 1999 Revised Kyoto Convention, formally known as the International Convention on the Harmonization and Simplification of Customs Procedures

In June 2002, the WCO council unanimously adopted a resolution on the security and facilitation of the international trade supply chain proposed by the United States that has resulted in the development of numerous guidelines, benchmarks, and best practices.

Together with the WCO, U.S. Customs and Border Protection (CBP) has been actively drafting and writing best practices, guidelines, and standards relating to the security of international supply chains. While much has been accomplished, the work continues both at the CBP and the WCO. To know more about the WCO go to www.cbp. gov/xp/cgov/border_security/international_activities/international_ agreements/wco/ wco.xml.

Homeland Security

The National Strategy for Homeland Security and the Homeland Security Act of 2002 served to mobilize and organize the United States to secure itself from terrorist attacks. The department's organization chart is shown in Figure 8.1. The vision and mission statements, strategic goals, and objectives provide the framework that guides the actions that make up the daily operations of the department.

Everything you wish to know—the department's mission, goals, operations, prevention measures, and means of protection—can be found on its Web site at www.dhs.gov.

Government Support

Immigration and Customs Enforcement (ICE)

When created in March 2003, Immigration and Customs Enforcement (ICE) became the largest investigative branch of the Department of Homeland Security (DHS). The agency was created after the events of 9/11 by combining the law enforcement arms of the former Immigration and Naturalization Service (INS) and the former U.S. Customs Service to more effectively enforce our immigration and customs laws and to protect the United States from terrorist attacks. ICE is a key component of the DHS "layered defense" approach to protecting the nation.

To further understand ICE, its mission and processes, go to its Web site at www.ice.gov/about/index.htm or call 202-344-2370.

Before the events of 9/11, immigration and customs authorities were not widely recognized as an effective counterterrorism tool in the United States. ICE changed this by creating a host of new systems to better address national security threats and to detect potential terrorist activities in the United States. ICE:

- Targets the people, money, and materials that support terrorist and criminal activity.
- Is the second largest federal law enforcement contributor to the Joint Terrorism Task Force.
- Dismantled gang organizations by targeting their members, seizing their financial assets, and disrupting their criminal operations through Operation Community Shield.

Figure 8.1 Homeland Security Organization Chart

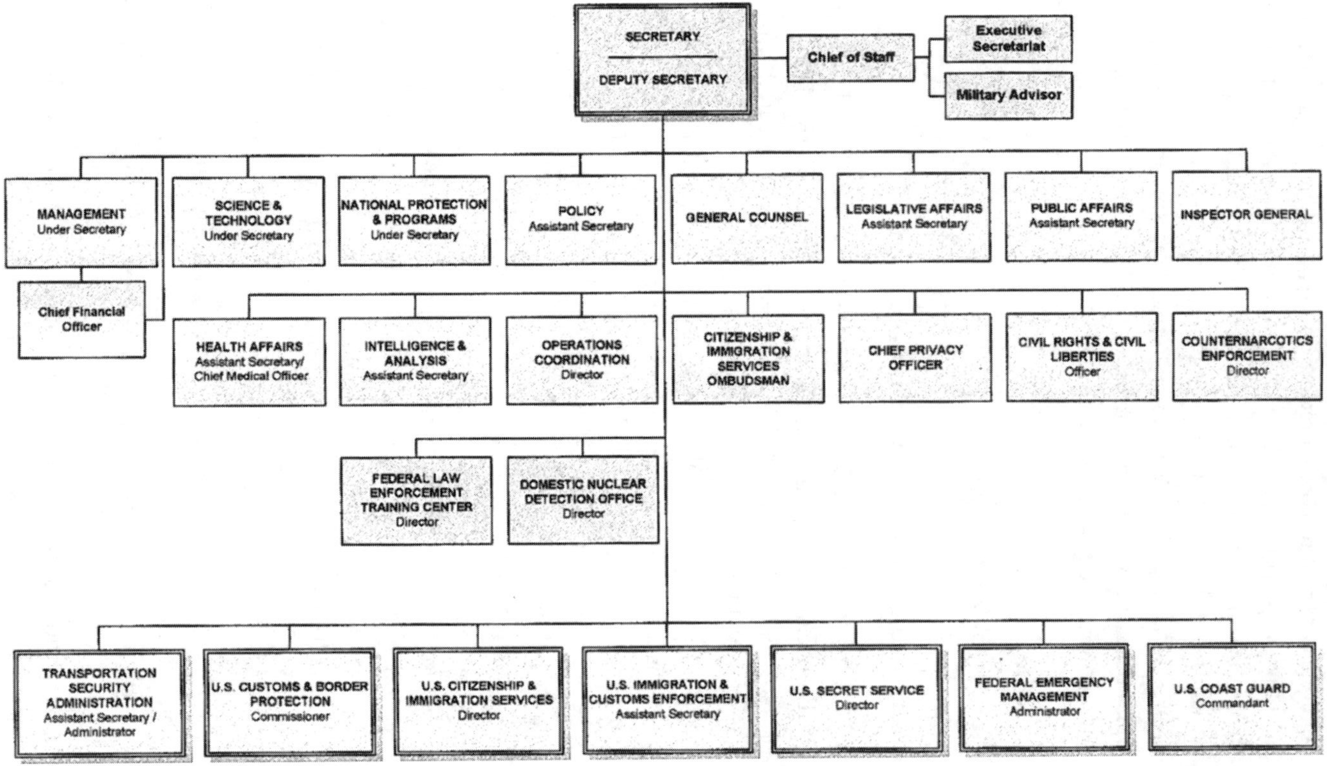

- Investigates employers and targets illegal workers who have gained access to critical infrastructure worksites (like nuclear and chemical plants, military installations, seaports, and airports) through its Worksite Enforcement Initiative.
- Helps to identify fraudulent immigration benefit applications and fraudulent illegal document manufacture, and targets violators through its Identity and Benefit Fraud Program.
- Investigates the illegal export of U.S. munitions and sensitive technology through its Project Shield America Initiative.
- Helps combat criminal organizations that smuggle and traffic in humans across U.S. borders through its Human Smuggling and Trafficking Initiative.
- Ensures that every alien who has been ordered removed departs the United States as quickly as possible. It works to reduce the number of fugitive aliens in the United States through its National Fugitive Operations Program.
- Aggressively seeks to destroy the financial infrastructure that criminal organizations use to earn, move, and store illicit funds through its Cornerstone Initiative.
- Provides law enforcement and security services to more than 8,800 federal buildings that receive nearly 1 million visitors and tenants daily through its Federal Protective Service.
- Plays a leading role in targeting criminal organizations responsible for producing, smuggling, and distributing counterfeit products through its National Intellectual Property Rights Coordination Center.
- Supports the law enforcement community through three units dedicated to sharing information and providing investigative support: the Law Enforcement Support Center, Forensic Document Laboratory, and the Cyber Crimes Center.

Customs and Border Protection Service (CBP)

The U.S. Customs and Border Protection Service (CBP) cannot be thought of as supporting importing in the way the Department of

Commerce encourages exports. Nevertheless it is responsible for enforcement of relevant trade. To obtain more information about its functions, methods, and operations, see its Web site at www.cbp.gov or www.customs.gov.

One of the nation's oldest public institutions, the Customs Service was probably the second thing the First Congress saw to after forming the new nation. Created in 1789, it provided most of the federal government's revenue for almost 130 years. After the income tax became the federal government's primary revenue source, the major responsibility of the Customs Service shifted to the administration of the Tariff Act of 1930, as amended. These duties include: (1) enforcing laws against smuggling and (2) collecting all duties, taxes, and fees due on the volumes of goods moved through the more than 300 ports of entry of the United States. A Customs Court, consisting of nine judges appointed by the U.S. President, reviews and settles disputes between importers and exporters and those who collect duties for the Bureau of Customs.

The CBP is organized with a domestic arm as well as an overseas arm. For additional information, call 202-344-2370.

Domestic Offices

The CBP's domestic offices are organized into five strategic trade centers (STC), 20 customs management centers (CMCs), and 317-plus ports of entry offices.

The 20 CMCs are responsible for oversight of operations within their area of jurisdiction and exercise line authority over the ports. They provide technical assistance and work with the ports in addressing operational problems. They oversee the execution of the core business processes—trade compliance, passenger operations, and outbound operations. They also coordinate with counterpart special agent-in-charge (SAIC) offices in executing anti-smuggling/K-9 and other enforcement strategies. CMCs are the point of contact for providing the answers to questions that concern the following issues:

- Release, classification, and valuation of imported merchandise
- Processing and entry of passengers into the United States
- Exported merchandise

- Fines, penalties, and forfeitures
- Seized properties
- Other activities engaging the trade and travel communities

Ports of entry are responsible for all daily operational aspects of the Customs Service. They are responsible for maintaining a focus on trade compliance (imports/cargo), passenger operations, outbound operations (exports), and antismuggling/K-9 strategies. Figure 8.2 illustrates the Customs Service organization.

Overseas Offices

Although not as extensive as Commerce's Foreign Commercial Service (FCS), Customs attachés (Customs' *overseas arm*) are attached to the embassies or missions in the following countries:Belgium, Italy, Thailand,

Figure 8.2 Organization of U.S. Customs Service

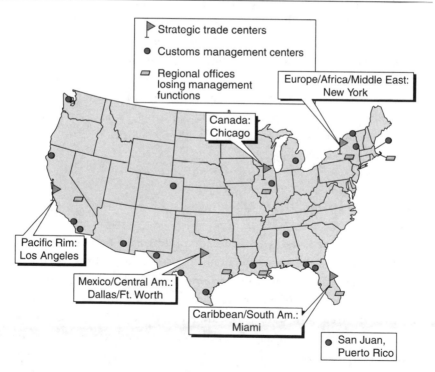

Canada, Japan, West Germany, England, Korea, France, Mexico, Hong Kong, China, and Pakistan.

Import Information Sources

The Customs Service does provide considerable information related to the importing function in the form of booklets, newsletters, and seminars available through the management centers or the Government Printing Office (GPO). Most of this information amounts to extractions from and simplification of customs regulations. Information about how to make contacts and/or perform the import function must be obtained through private sector publishers and organizations such as chambers of commerce or trade associations. Two sources are helpful for learning more about importing:

- *Importing into the United States.* This excellent booklet published by the Treasury Department through the GPO outlines the requirements that must be met by the importer to enter goods. It costs about $20. See www.gpoaccess.gov.
- *Thomas Register of American Manufacturers.* A compilation of manufacturers in the United States and where they are located. This publication may be used as a source for marketing in the United States. Published through the Thomas Publishing Company, 5 Penn Plaza, New York, NY 10001, it is easily found in most libraries. You may also call 800-699-9822 or go to www.thomaspublishing.com.

Customs House Brokers

The *customs house broker* is a private, for-profit liaison between the Customs Service and the importing public. Customs house brokers will be needed as long as there are legal requirements and regulations pertaining to the movement of merchandise.

Like the freight forwarder for exporting, the customs house broker is a private service company licensed to assist importers in the movement of their goods.

Formal entries of foreign-made goods representing many billions of dollars in duty collections are filed each year with the Customs Service, and virtually all of them are prepared by customs house brokers on behalf of importers. Some brokers are sole proprietors with a single office at one port of entry, while others are large corporations with branches in many ports throughout the country, but all are licensed and regulated by the Treasury Department. Some even have offices throughout the world.

Importers employ the customs broker as their agent, who is frequently their only point of contact with the Customs Service. It is not necessary for importers to employ a broker to enter goods on their behalf; however, a bond is required if they do not.

Most experienced importers will recommend the services of a broker because of the extras, such as the comfort in knowing that a professional is supporting their project and answering the many technical questions. Another good reason is that at some point, importers' time will become more valuable to them in managing their companies and marketing their product(s) than it might be in handling the paperwork of an entry.

A broker advises on the technical requirements of importing, preparing, and filing entry documents; obtaining the necessary bonds; depositing U.S. import duties; securing release of the product(s); arranging delivery to the importer's premises or warehouse; and obtaining "drawback" refunds (see below). The broker often consults with customs to determine the proper rate of duty or bases of appraisement and, on many occasions, if dissatisfied with either rate or value, will pursue appropriate administrative remedies on behalf of the importer.

Consult the Yellow Pages of the local phone book for a listing of customs brokers in your area.

Surety Bonds

Importers must post a *surety bond* with the customs service to ensure payment of the proper amounts of duties, taxes, and other charges associated with entry. Bonds can be for single entry or continuous (term). Based on the value of the shipment, customs determines the value of the required bond. Often a bond three times the value of the shipment is required. A surety company usually requires 100 percent collateral in the form of an irrevocable letter of credit (L/C), trust deed, or cashiers check. Bond premiums are about 2 percent of the value with a minimum of about $100. The premium for a term bond is usually higher (5 percent). Collateral depends on the financial condition of the importer.

Drawback

Drawback is the refunding of duties paid on imported goods and their derivatives if they are subsequently exported. Suppose, for example, that you simply re-export goods that were originally imported, or you export items that contain imported merchandise or that contain whole imported components. For each of these you might claim a drawback of tariffs paid when imported. The key to drawback is good inventory tracking and record-keeping procedures. Apply for drawback with your local customs port of entry office.

Automated Brokerage Interface (ABI)

The automated brokerage interface (ABI) is for those large-volume importers who file many simple entries and wish to avoid the cost of a broker. ABI permits importers (and brokers) to electronically file preliminary entry data in advance of the arrival of cargo.

How to Become a Customs Broker

Customs brokers are private individuals, partnerships, associations, or corporations licensed, regulated, and empowered by U.S. Customs and Border Protection (CBP) to assist importers and exporters in meeting federal requirements governing imports and exports. Brokers submit necessary information and appropriate payments to CBP on behalf of their clients and charge the clients a fee for this service.

Corporations, partnerships, and associations must have a broker license to transact customs business. Each of these businesses must have at least one individually licensed officer, partner, or associate to qualify the company's license. Failure to have a qualifying officer or member (of a partnership) for more than 120 days will result in the revocation of the broker license.

You can become a customs broker by (1) studying the Customs Service regulations and learning the application of the tariff schedules and then (2) passing an examination given several times a year. This license is not necessary for you to act on your own behalf, but it is needed if you act as an agent for others. Details about the examination and costs involved can be obtained from any Customs Service office. Figure 8.3 shows the application form required to obtain a license.

Figure 8.3 Application for Customs Broker License

Form Approved: O.M.B. No. 1515-0076

Privacy Act Statement on Reverse of Form

DEPARTMENT OF THE TREASURY
UNITED STATES CUSTOMS SERVICE

APPLICATION FOR CUSTOMHOUSE BROKER'S LICENSE
19 U.S.C. 1641; 111.12 C.R.

1. APPLICANT'S NAME AND ADDRESS *(Principal Office OR Home Address)*

INSTRUCTIONS: Applicants must be United States citizens. Submit application in duplicate to the District Director of the District named in Block 3. All additional continuation sheets, if required, and attachments should also be in duplicate

2. TYPE OF LICENSE APPLIED FOR
☐ Individual ☐ Corporation ☐ Partnership ☐ Association

3. CUSTOMS DISTRICT FOR WHICH LICENSE IS APPLIED

4. HAVE YOU EVER APPLIED FOR A CUSTOMHOUSE BROKER'S LICENSE? ☐ NO ☐ YES *(Explain in item 17)*

5. HAS THE APPLICANT *(OR ANY OFFICER OR MEMBER THEREOF)* EVER HAD A LICENSE SUSPENDED, REFUSED, REVOKED, OR CANCELED? ☐ NO ☐ YES *(Explain in item 17)*

6. IF APPLICANT HAS A CURRENT LICENSE, STATE WHEN AND FOR WHAT DISTRICT ISSUED.

7. IS THE APPLICANT *(OR ANY OFFICER OR MEMBER THEREOF)* AN OFFICER OR EMPLOYEE OF THE UNITED STATES? ☐ NO ☐ YES *(Explain in item 17)*

SECTION I — INDIVIDUALS ONLY

8. DATE OF BIRTH	9. BIRTHPLACE *(City & State)*	10. SOCIAL SECURITY NO.	11. HOME PHONE NO.	12. BUSINESS PHONE NO.

13. U.S. CITIZENSHIP
☐ NATURAL-BORN ☐ NATURALIZED-*Give Date & Place*→

14. HAVE YOU EVER BEEN A DEFENDANT IN A CRIMINAL PROSECUTION? *(You may exclude minor traffic violations where the fine was $50 or less.)* ☐ NO ☐ YES *(Explain in item 17)*

15. DO YOU PROPOSE TO ENGAGE IN THE BUSINESS OF A CUSTOMHOUSE BROKER:

(More than one may apply. Explain answer(s) in Item 17.)

(a) ☐ ON YOUR OWN INDIVIDUAL ACCOUNT? *(State name in which business is to be conducted; if trade name, state authority for use of the name and attach evidence of such authority.)*

(b) ☐ AS A MEMBER OF A PARTNERSHIP? *(State name of partnership and list names of all the partners.)*

(c) ☐ AS AN OFFICER OF AN ASSOCIATION? *(State name of the association, the title of the office you hold, and the general nature of your duties.)*

(d) ☐ AS AN OFFICER OF A CORPORATION? *(State name of the corporation, the title of the office you hold, and the general nature of your duties.)*

(e) ☐ AS AN EMPLOYEE? *(State name and address of your employer (if different than item 1) and the nature of your employment.)*

16. LIST THE NAMES AND ADDRESSES OF SIX REFERENCES.

SECTION III — CERTIFICATION *(ALL APPLICANTS)*

INDIVIDUAL	ASSOCIATION, CORPORATION, OR PARTNERSHIP
I, ______________, certify that the statements contained in the foregoing application and supporting attachments thereto are true and correct to the best of my knowledge and belief. Written notice of any change in my mailing address, any business connection, or the name and style under which I conduct my business will be given to the Commissioner of Customs.	I, ______________, certify that I am an officer or partner of the applicant that I am a licensed customhouse broker; and that the statements contained in the foregoing application and supporting attachments thereto are true and correct to the best of my knowledge and belief. The officers or partners who are licensed customhouse brokers are aware of the requirements for the exercise by them of responsible supervision and control of the transaction of the customs business of the applicant. Written notice of any change in the applicant's mailing address, name, licensed officers or partners, or the charter, certificate, articles, or other instrument of organization of the applicant will be given to the Commissioner of Customs.

23. SIGNATURE	24. DATE

Customs Form 3124 (03-03-81)

Brokers must have expertise in entry procedures, admissibility requirements, classification, valuation, and rates of duty and applicable taxes and fees for imported merchandise. Contact U.S. Customs and Border Protection, Trade Enforcement and Facilitation, Broker Management Branch, 1300 Pennsylvania Avenue, NW, Room 5.2C, Washington, DC 20229; phone: 202-344-2580.

Additional information on this profession may be obtained from local brokers or the National Customs Brokers and Forwarders Association of America (NCBFAA), which has its own Web site at www.NCBFAA.org.

Getting through the Customs Maze

A *tariff* is a schedule of duties. It is also the duty or tax imposed by a country and the duty or tax within the tariff schedule. As a tax, it is placed on goods as they cross the border between two countries.

At one time, tariffs were the primary means by which the United States raised funds to support the federal government. However, in the early 1900s, when the income tax was introduced, tariffs for the purpose of raising revenue took on less importance. Since then, tariffs have been predominantly used to protect home industries.

HISTORICAL NOTE

The word *tariff* presumably comes from the Arabic term for inventory, which is *ta'rif*. The French word *tariff*, as well as the Spanish word *tarifa*, means price list or rate book. An alternate version has it that the word originated sometime after 700 AD. At that time, near Gibraltar, there was a village called Tarifa, where a small band of thieves lived. The thieves stopped every merchant ship and forced the captain to pay a handsome sum of money before the vessel could proceed through the strait. Seamen began calling the money they were forced to pay a tariff.

The Four-Step Entry Process

When a shipment of goods intended for commercial use reaches the United States, it may not be legally entered until after (1) it enters the port of entry, (2) estimated duties have been paid, and (3) customs authorizes delivery of the merchandise. During this process only the owner (or the owner's agent) is responsible for the entry—the Customs Service simply checks each step to ensure correctness. Table 8.1 compares the steps of the commercial entry process.

Table 8.1 Commercial Entry Process

Who Is Responsible?	What Does Customs Do?
Owner; agent; purchaser	
Step	Step
1. Entry: Shipment arrives within port a. Decide consumption or bonded warehouse/FTZ	1. Check and verify. Store in general warehouse?
b. If consumption, file entry documents	
c. Documents required	Check
1. Entry manifest	
2. Right to make entry	
3. Invoices	
4. Packing lists	
5. Entry summary	
6. Evidence of bond	Verify
2. Valuation	
3. Classify/appraise	
4. Estimate and pay tariff (check or cash)	2. Examine
	3. Validate
	a. Classification
	b. Appraisement
	4. Authorize entry
	5. Liquidate transaction

• If pay more than required tariff: refund (90 days)
• If pay less: billed to pay or protest (90 days)
• Protest: U.S. Court of International Trade (180 days)
• If re-export: Drawback

The process, in its simplest form has four basic steps: entry, valuation, classification, and payment.

Step One: Entry

Within twenty-four hours of arrival of a shipment at a U.S. port of entry, the owner/agent must decide whether to *enter* the goods for consumption or place them into a bonded warehouse or free (foreign) trade zone (explained in detail later in this chapter). This can be done electronically. If the decision is made to enter for consumption, the following entry documents must be filed:

- Entry manifest, customs form 7533, or application and special permit for immediate delivery, customs form 3461
- Evidence of right to make entry
- Commercial invoice or pro forma invoice
- Packing list(s) if appropriate
- Entry summary, form 7501, and other documents necessary to determine merchandise admissibility
- Evidence of bond

Form 3461 is a special permit for immediate delivery and is an alternative procedure that provides for the immediate release of a shipment. Figure 8.4 shows the form used for land shipments, and Figure 8.5 the form used for ocean and air shipments. Application should be made before the arrival of the goods, and if approved, the goods won't have to sit on the dock or in a warehouse. They are released on arrival. You are allowed 10 working days to file a proper entry summary (form 7501) and to deposit estimated duties. Release under this provision is limited to:

- Merchandise arriving from Canada or Mexico
- Fresh fruits and vegetables for human consumption arriving from Canada or Mexico
- Articles for a trade fair
- Tariff-rate quota merchandise and, under certain circumstances, merchandise subject to an absolute quota

Figure 8.4 Special Immediate Entry Permit (Land)

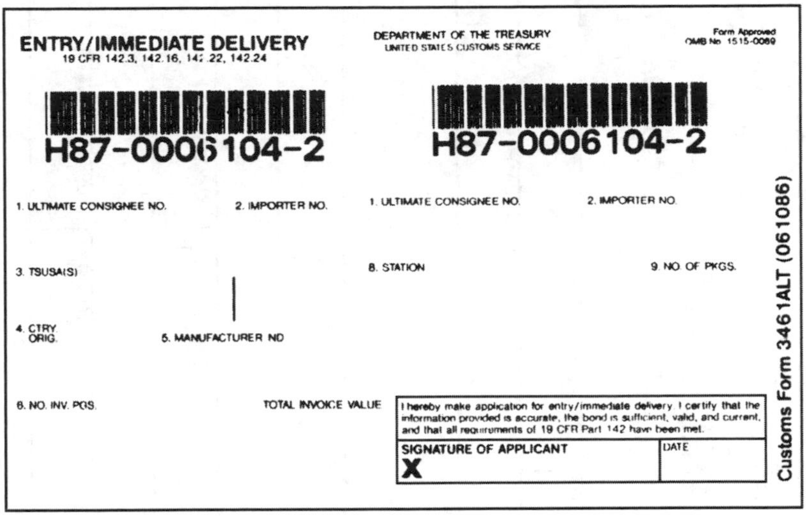

- Merchandise specifically authorized by customs because of perishability or inconvenience to the importer, carrier, or agent

Step Two: Valuation

This step determines the *value* of the goods for purposes of applying any tariffs or duties. Generally, the customs value will be the transaction value or the price actually paid or payable for the merchandise when sold for exportation to the United States, plus amounts for the following items if they are not included in the price:

- The packing costs incurred by the buyer
- Any selling commission paid by the buyer
- The value of any assist (Note: An example of an assist would be tools, dies, molds, engineering, artwork, etc.)
- Any royalty or license fee that is required from the buyer as a condition of the sale
- The proceeds from the sale of the imported goods that accrue to the seller

Figure 8.5 Special Immediate Entry Permit (Ocean and Air)

Form Approved
OMB No. 1515-0069

DEPARTMENT OF THE TREASURY
UNITED STATES CUSTOMS SERVICE

ENTRY/IMMEDIATE DELIVERY

19 CFR 142.3, 142.16, 142.22, 142.24

1. ARRIVAL DATE	2. ELECTED ENTRY DATE	3. ENTRY TYPE CODE/NAME	4. ENTRY NUMBER
5. PORT	6. SINGLE TRANS. BOND	7. BROKER/IMPORTER FILE NUMBER	
	8. CONSIGNEE NUMBER		9. IMPORTER NUMBER
10. ULTIMATE CONSIGNEE NAME		11. IMPORTER OF RECORD NAME	
12. CARRIER CODE	13. VOYAGE/FLIGHT/TRIP	14. LOCATION OF GOODS—CODE(S)/NAME(S)	
15. VESSEL CODE/NAME			
16. U.S. PORT OF UNLADING	17. MANIFEST NUMBER	18. G O NUMBER	19. TOTAL VALUE
20. DESCRIPTION OF MERCHANDISE			

21. IT/BL/AWB CODE	22. IT/BL/AWB NO.	23. MANIFEST QUANTITY	24. TSUSA NUMBER	25. COUNTRY OF ORIGIN	26. MANUFACTURER NO.

27. CERTIFICATION

I hereby make application for entry/immediate delivery. I certify that the above information is accurate, the bond is sufficient, valid, and current, and that all requirements of 19 CFR Part 142 have been met.

SIGNATURE OF APPLICANT

X

PHONE NO.   DATE

29. BROKER OR OTHER GOVT. AGENCY USE

28. CUSTOMS USE ONLY

☐ OTHER AGENCY ACTION REQUIRED, NAMELY:

☐ CUSTOMS EXAMINATION REQUIRED.

☐ ENTRY REJECTED, BECAUSE:

DELIVERY AUTHORIZED: | SIGNATURE   DATE

Paperwork Reduction Act Notice: This information is needed to determine the admissibility of imports into the United States and to provide the necessary information for the examination of the cargo and to establish the liability for payment of duties and taxes. Your response is necessary.

Customs Form 3461 (112085)

If the transaction value for the goods cannot be used, then secondary bases are used in the following order of precedence:

- Transaction value of identical merchandise
- Transaction value of similar merchandise
- Deductive value
- Computed value

Step Three: Classification

The responsibility for *classification* rests with the importer, customs house broker, or other person preparing the entry papers. The importance of this step cannot be overemphasized because it determines the ad valorem (percentage) tariff rate that should be applied to the valuation of the goods. Familiarity with the Tariff Schedule of the United States of America (TSUSA) and the Harmonized Tariff Schedule of the United States facilitates the process.

HOT TIP

The first rule of importing is this: *always* get advance ruling from customs.

Step Four: Payment

Payment of duties is made by check or cash to the Treasurer of the United States.

Customs Service Responsibilities

The Customs Service involvement in the entry process can be characterized by five steps: check and verify, examine, validate, authorize entry, and liquidate.

Step One: Check and Verify

For this step, customs officers *check* the entry documents and *verify* evidence of a bond. Of course, on arrival of the goods at the port of entry, the owner or agent is responsible to immediately make arrangements for the shipment and storage of the goods. Those goods that are not claimed are stored in a general warehouse. Storage is billed to the owner when the goods are retrieved, or they are sold at auction.

Step Two: Examine

This step, which is the customs officer's *examination* to determine the value of the goods and their suitability for entering, has five substeps:

- Valuation of the goods for customs purposes and their dutiable status
- Checking the proper markings of the goods with the country of origin
- Determining whether the shipment contains prohibited items
- Determining whether the goods are correctly invoiced
- Taking inventory to determine whether there are excesses or shortages of the invoiced quantities

Step Three: Validate

The *validation* step consists of checking the classification of the goods and appraising them to ensure correct valuation.

Step Four: Authorize Entry

After the classification and valuation, and after other required import information has been reviewed for correctness, proper appraisement, and agreement of the submitted data, the merchandise may be *authorized* for actual import.

Step Five: Liquidation

If the goods are accepted without changes, they are *liquidated* "as entered." This step is finalized in the traditional way of posting a notice on the public bulletin board at the customs house. The bulletin board is now a computer printout. After the liquidation, an importer may pursue claims for adjustment or refund by filing, within 90 days, a protest on customs form 19. Time limits do not begin to run until the date of posting. If, after further review, the importer is still not satisfied, a summons may be filed with the U.S. Customs Court of International Trade.

The Harmonized System

The Harmonized System (HS) is an international multipurpose, classification system designed to improve the collection of import and export statistics as well as to serve customs purposes. Intended as a core for national systems, it promotes a high degree of international uniformity in the presentation of customs tariffs and foreign trade statistics.

The U.S. Harmonized Tariff Schedule (often referred to as HTSUS) is about the size of a major city's telephone book and is available through the GPO in three-hole, loose-leaf form for about $99 or as a CD from www.Boskage.com for about $89.00. It can also be downloaded from the International Trade Commission's Web site at www.usitc.gov. It can also be ordered from the government bookstore.

The HS is a complete product classification system, which is organized in a framework that employs a numbering system. To assist the user, a section in the front of the book gives instructions known as General Notes and General Rules of Interpretation (GRI), which explain the use and interpretation of the schedule.

At the international level, about 5,000 article descriptions are grouped into 21 sections and arranged into 97 chapters. The U.S. version has 22 sections and 99 chapters. Chapter 98 includes information from the "old" TSUSA Schedule 8 (articles 806.20, 806.30, and 807) related to offshore assembly. Chapter 99 contains information transformed from the TSUSA Schedule 9. The 22 sections and their chapter headings are listed in a table of contents in the front of the book.

HISTORICAL NOTE

For decades, the international trading community was confronted with problems caused by the number of differing classification systems covering the movement of goods in international trade. In 1970, representatives of the Customs Cooperation Council (CCC), formerly known as the Brussels Tariff Nomenclature (BTN), undertook a study of commodity description and coding with a view to developing a system capable of meeting the principal requirements of customs authorities, statisticians, carriers, and producers. The result of the study was that the development of such a system was not only feasible but imperative. Some 13 years later the "Harmonized Commodity Description and Coding System" and a convention for its implementation were completed. Forty-eight countries and more than a dozen private and public organizations participated in its development.

HOT TIP

Reading the Harmonized Tariff Schedule
CHAPTER: FIRST TWO DIGITS, Example: 44
HEADING: FIRST FOUR DIGITS, Example: 4409
SUBHEADING: FIRST SIX DIGITS, Example: 4409.10
ITEM: FIRST EIGHT DIGITS, Example: 4409.10.10

Case Study: Guitars

Let's hypothesize that you are an importer of "guitars valued at less than $100." Your order from Germany arrives. Assuming that you wish to enter the guitars immediately into commerce, within five working days you must present the documents listed in step one of the entry process to customs.

Note: If the guitars were perishable or if you had a special scheduling problem, you could have applied (in advance) for their immediate delivery using special entry permit form 3461.

In this case, let us assume there was no need for immediate entry, so we proceed as a normal, formal entry. Let's further assume that you used an L/C to make payment, so you can pick up your entry documents only after you square your account with your banker. The invoice shows 1,000 guitars at $89 each, for a total of $8,900. This is the transaction value for purposes of valuation. Because the value is over $1,250, you must make a formal entry. Had the value been under $1,250, the informal entry process would have been much simpler; you could very easily do your own paperwork, and a bond would not have been required. Figure 8.6 shows an entry summary, the basic form used for both formal and informal entry. Table 8.2 shows the difference between a formal and an informal entry.

Had the goods been for your personal use and you had been out of the country for more than 48 hours, the first $400 ($800 when returning from a U.S. insular possession) would have been exempt, the next $1,000 dutied at 10 percent, and the remainder at the ad valorem rate from the TSUSA.

Beginners sometimes ask, "What if I entered the goods for personal use in small quantities and then sold them?" One customs agent responded, "You may get away with it the first time, but we (the computers) remember, and sooner or later, we'll catch you. The penalty is at least a $5,000 fine."

Full, complete, and honest disclosure is the responsibility of the importer. The penalties are severe and not worth the gamble. Make your money and pay your duties.

In the guitar example, because the value is $1,250 or greater ($8,900), a formal entry is required. For the formal or informal entry process, you need to classify the product. Begin by scanning the table

Table 8.2 Formal versus Informal Entry

	Informal	Formal
Value	Less than $2,000*	$1,250 or greater
Bond	No	Yes
Duties	Pay on entry	Pay within 10 days†
Liquidation	On the spot	Liquidation notice
Forms required	7501, invoice, B/L, check ($$$ duties), packing list	7501, entry invoice, B/L, packing list, check ($$$ duties), other agency, documents, bond

*For some articles, formal entry is specified regardless of value (check your local Customs Service office or customs house broker).
†An example of a good that might require immediate payment is an item under quota.

Figure 8.6 Sample Entry Summary

DEPARTMENT OF THE TREASURY
UNITED STATES CUSTOMS SERVICE

ENTRY SUMMARY

1. Entry No.	2. Entry Type Code	3. Entry Summary Date
4. Entry Date	5. Port Code	
6. Bond No.	7. Bond Type Code	8. Broker/Importer File No.
10. Consignee No.	11. Importer of Record Name and Address	12. Importer No.

9. Ultimate Consignee Name and Address

State

	13. Exporting Country	14. Export Date
	15. Country of Origin	16. Missing Documents
	17. I.T. No.	18. I.T. Date
20. Mode of Transportation	21. Manufacturer I.D.	22. Reference No.
24. Foreign Port of Lading	25. Location of Goods/G.O. No.	
27. Import Date		

19. B/L or AWB No.

23. Importing Carrier

26. U.S. Port of Unlading

(Continued)

Figure 8.6 Sample Entry Summary (Continued)

(28) Line No.	(30) (A) T.S.U.S.A. No. (B) ADA CVD Case No.	(29) Description of Merchandise			(33) (A) Entered Value (B) CHGS (C) Relationship	34. (A) T.S.U.S.A. Rate (B) ADA/CVD Rate (C) I.R.C. Rate (D) Visa No.	(35) Duty and I.R. Tax	
		31. (A) Gross Weight (B) Manifest Qty.	(32) Net Quantity in T.S.U.S.A. Units				Dollars	Cents

---

(36) Declaration of Importer of Record (Owner or Purchaser) or Authorized Agent

I declare that I am the

☐ importer of record and that the actual owner, purchaser, or consignee for customs purposes is as shown above.

OR

☐ owner or purchaser or agent thereof.

I further declare that the merchandise

☐ was obtained pursuant to a purchase or agreement to purchase and that the prices set forth in the invoice are true.

OR

☐ was not obtained pursuant to a purchase or agreement to purchase and the statements in the invoice as to value or price are true to the best of my knowledge and belief.

I also declare that the statements in the documents herein filed fully disclose to the best of my knowledge and belief the true prices, values, quantities, rebates, drawbacks, fees, commissions, and royalties and are true and correct, and that all goods or services provided to the seller of the merchandise either free or at reduced cost are fully disclosed. I will immediately furnish to the appropriate customs officer any information showing a different state of facts.

Notice required by Paperwork Reduction Act of 1980. This information is needed to ensure that importers/exporters are complying with U.S. Customs laws, to allow us to compute and collect and collect the right amount of money, to enforce other agency requirements, and to collect accurate statistical information on imports. Your response is mandatory.

↓ U.S. CUSTOMS USE ↓		TOTALS	
A. Liq. Code	B. Ascertained Duty	(37) Duty	
	C. Ascertained Tax	(38) Tax	
	D. Ascertained Other	(39) Other	
	E. Ascertained Total	(40) Total	

(41) Signature of Declarant, Title, and Date

Customs Form 7501 (030984)

of contents for the general category within which your product fits. In this case "Musical instruments" is in Section XVIII, Chapter 92.

If you have a copy of the HS available, turn to page 92-2. If not, refer to Figure 8.7, which is a replication of page 92-2 from the Harmonized Tariff Schedule related to our case study about guitars.

Run your finger down the page until you find "Guitars: Valued not over $100." In this case, the classification of guitars is straightforward, but keep in mind that classifying a product is usually the most difficult part of using any tariff schedule. The correct classification can save you money and heartache. Consult the Customs Service or your customs house broker if you have any doubts.

The heading for this product is 9202.90.20. The first two digits refer to the chapter number, in this case Chapter 92. The next two refer to the heading, the next two to the international subdivision or subhead, then the U.S. subdivision or item, and finally the U.S. statistical subdivision or item.

Now, draw your finger across the page. Note that there are three columns with an ad valorem duty rate. In column 1 "general," the rate is 6.8 percent. This is the rate for most favored nations (MFNs) such as England, France, or Germany. Thus, because your guitars came from Germany, you will pay 6.8 percent of $8,900, or $605.20 ad valorem duty.

Note that the duty rate shown in column 1, "special," is *free* (pay no tariff) for country groups A, E, IL, and J and only 3.4 percent for CA. The countries in these groups are listed in the "special" category programs in the front of the Harmonized Tariff Schedule under head notes. Table 8.3 shows these special programs.

The column labeled "2" shows a rate of 40 percent for guitars valued under $100. This column shows the ad valorem duty rate for countries under "Communist domination or control," such as North Korea, Cuba, and the like. If the guitars had come from North Korea instead of Germany, the ad valorem duty paid to the U.S. Treasury would be 40 percent of $8,900 or $3,560.

Having estimated your duties as $605.20, the next step is to fill out the required entry documents and post surety in the form of cash or evidence of having a bond (minimum of $10,000). If a customs broker

Figure 8.7 Sample Page from Harmonized Tariff Schedule

HARMONIZED TARIFF SCHEDULE of the United States (1993)
Annotated for Statistical Reporting Purposes

Heading/ Subheading	Stat. Suf- fix	Article Description	Units of Quantity	Rates of Duty — 1 General	Rates of Duty — 1 Special	Rates of Duty — 2
9201		Pianos, including player pianos; harpsichords and other keyboard stringed instruments:				
9201.10.00	00	Upright pianos	No.	5.3%	Free (A, E, IL, J) 2.6% (CA)	40%
9201.20.00	00	Grand pianos	No.	5.3%	Free (A, E, IL, J) 2.6% (CA)	40%
9201.90.00	00	Other	No.	5.3%	Free (A, E, IL, J) 2.6% (CA)	40%
9202		Other string musical instruments (for example, guitars, violins, harps):				
9202.10.00 37.5%	00	Played with a bow	No.	4.9%	Free (A, E, IL, J) 2.4% (CA)	
9202.90		Other: Guitars:				
9202.90.20	00	Valued not over $100 each, excluding the value of the case	No.	6.8%	Free (A, E, IL, J) 3.4% (CA)	40%
9202.90.40	00	Other	No.	13%	Free (A, E, IL, J) 6.5% (CA)	40%
9202.90.60	00	Other	No.	7%	Free (A, E, IL, J) 3.5% (CA)	40%
9203.00		Keyboard pipe organs; harmoniums and similar keyboard instruments with free metal reeds:				
9203.00.40	00	Keyboard pipe organs	No.	Free		35%
9203.00.80	00	Other	No.	5.3%	Free (A, CA, E, IL, J)	40%

Heading/ Subheading	Stat. Suffix	Article Description	Unit of Quantity	General	Special	2
9204		Accordions and similar instruments; mouth organs;				
		Accordions and similar instruments:				
9204.10		Piano accordions				
9204.10.40	00	Piano accordions	No.	4.7%	Free (A, CA, E, IL, J)	40%
9204.10.80	00	Other	No.	5.1%	Free (A, CA, E, IL, J)	40%
9240.20.00	00	Mouth organs	Doz.	4.7%	Free (A, E, IL, J) 2.3% (CA)	40%
9205		Other wind musical instruments (for example, clarinets, trumpets, bagpipes):				
9205.10.00		Brass-wind instruments		5.8%	Free (A, E, IL, J) 2.9% (CA)	40%
	40	Valued not over $10 each	No.			
	80	Valued over $10 each	No.			
9205.90		Other:				
		Woodwind instruments:				
9205.90.20	00	Bagpipes	No	Free	Free (A, E, IL, J) 1/	40%
9205.90.40		Other		4.9%	2.4% (CA) 1/	40%
	20	Clarinets	No.			
	40	Saxophones	No.			
	60	Flutes and piccolos (except bamboo)	No.			
9205.90.60	80	Other	No.	3.4%	Free (A, E, IL, J) 1.7% (CA)	40%
	00	Other	No.			
9206.00		Percussion musical instruments (for example, drums, xylophones, cymbals, castanets, maracas):				
9206.00.20	00	Drums	No.	4.8%	Free (A, CA, E, IL, J)	40%
9206.00.40	00	Cymbals	No.	Free	Free (A, CA, E, IL, J)	40%
9206.00.60	00	Sets of tuned bells known as chimes, peals or carillons	No.	2.5%	Free (A, CA, E, IL, J)	50%
9206.00.80	00	Other	No.	5.3%	Free (A, CA, E, IL, J)	40%

1/ See subheading 9905.92.10.

219

Table 8.3 Special Tariff Treatment Programs

General System of Preferences	A or A*
Automotive Products Tade Act	B
Agreement on Trade in Civil Aircraft	C
North American Free Trade Agreement:	
Goods of Canada, under the terms of general note 12 of this schedule.	CA
Goods of Mexico, under the terms of general note 12 of this schedule.	MX
Caribbean Basin Economic Recovery Act	E or E*
United States–Israel Free Trade Area	IL
Andean Trade Preference Act	J or J*

*Extracted from the Harmonized Tariff Schedule of the United States.

makes the entry for you, the broker may use its own bond. This is not automatic. In many cases brokers will assist you to obtain your own bond. There are three types of bonds:

- Term bonds cover only one port of entry
- General bonds cover all U.S. ports
- Continuous bonds can substitute for both

After filling out the commercial customs invoice, the special (consular) customs invoice, the bill of lading, and the entry form, the goods may now be picked up from the carrier.

Remember that you or your agent (customs broker) originally classified and estimated the duties owed. Final liquidation of this transaction by the Customs Service could take as much as several months but must be finalized (with exceptions) within one year. You will receive notice of the date of liquidation and what amounts are due, if any.

Generalized systems of preference (GSP). GSP countries are those designated by the United Nations as "developing." To assist in their economic growth, they receive special preference and therefore pay no tariff.

Import Quotas

The importation of certain products is controlled by quantity. *Quotas* for this control are established by specific legislation, usually to protect infant industries or established industries under marketing pressure from foreign countries. Most textiles and apparel are subject to these quotas country by country and product by product. Most of the quotas have fixed ceilings for the amount that can be imported in a calendar year. The status of quotas is maintained by a central Customs Service computer in Washington, DC. Access to current quota status country by country can be obtained by calling 202-927-5850, the "Quota Watch" column in the *Journal of Commerce*, or accessing www.customs.gov.

United States import quotas are divided into two types: absolute and tariff rate.

Absolute Quotas

Absolute quotas are *quantitative quotas*, that is, no more than the amount specified may be permitted during the quota period. Some are global, while others apply only to certain countries. When an absolute quota is filled, further entries are prohibited during the remainder of the quota period.

Tariff-Rate Quotas

Tariff-rate quotas provide for the entry of a specified quantity at a reduced rate of duty during a given period. Quantities entered in excess of the quota for the period are subject to higher duty rates.

Special Import Regulations

Many countries require a license to import, but the United States does not. Thousands of products are imported freely with no restrictions. Although the importation of goods does not require a license from the Customs Service, certain classes of merchandise might be prohibited or restricted by other agencies (1) to protect the economy and the security of the country, (2) to safeguard health, or (3) to preserve domestic plant and animal life. The importer is wise to inquire (complete with samples and specifications) with the regulatory body involved well before entering into any business arrangements. There are cases in which the importer ended up with a warehouse full of products unfit or prohibited from entering the United States. For more information go to www.customs.gov/impoexpo/impoexpo.htm.

Agricultural Commodities

The U.S. Food and Drug Administration and the Department of Agriculture control or regulate the importation of most animals, animal foods, insects, plants, and poultry products.

Arms, Ammunition, and Radioactive Materials

The Bureau of Alcohol, Tobacco, and Firearms of the Department of the Treasury, Washington, DC 20226, prohibits the importation of implements of war except when it issues a license. Even temporary importation, movement, and exportation are prohibited unless licensed by the Office of Munitions Control, Department of State, Washington, DC 20520. Of course, the Nuclear Regulatory Commission controls all forms of radioactive materials and nuclear reactors. To contact the bureau, e-mail ATFMail@atf.gov. Their Web address is www.atf.treas.gov.

Consumer Products—Safety and Energy Conservation

Consumer products such as refrigerators, freezers, dishwashers, water heaters, television sets, and furnaces, as well as other energy-using products, are regulated by the Consumer Products Efficiency Branch of the Department of Energy. The Consumer Product Safety Commission (CPSC) overseas safety issues.

Electronic Products

Radiation-producing products, including sonic radiation such as cathode ray tubes and the like, are regulated by the FDA, Center for

Devices and Radiological Health, Rockville, MD 20850 and the FCC, Washington, DC 20554.

Food, Drugs, Cosmetics, and Medical Devices

The Federal Food, Drug, and Cosmetic Act governs the importation of food, beverages, drugs, medical devices, and cosmetics. This act is administered by the Food and Drug Administration of the Department of Health and Human Services, Rockville, MD 20857.

Gold, Silver, Currency, and Stamps

Provisions of the National Stamping Act, enforced by the Department of Justice, Washington, DC 20530, regulate some aspects of importing silver and gold.

Pesticides and Toxic and Hazardous Substances

Three acts control the importation of these substances: the Insecticide, Fungicide, and Rodenticide Act of 1947; the Toxic Substances Control Act of 1977; and the Hazardous Substances Act. Further information can be obtained from the Environmental Protection Agency, Washington, DC 20460.

Textile, Wool, and Fur Products

Textile fiber products must be stamped, tagged, and labeled as required by the Textile Fiber Products Identification Act. Similarly, wool products must be clearly marked in accordance with the Wool Products Labeling Act of 1939. Fur, not to be left out, must be labeled as required by the Fur Products Labeling Act. Regulations and pamphlets containing the text of these labeling acts may be obtained from the Federal Trade Commission, Washington, DC 20580.

Trademarks, Trade Names, and Copyrights

The Customs Reform and Simplification Act of 1979 strengthened the protection afforded trademark owners against the importation of articles bearing counterfeit marks. In general, articles bearing trade-marks or marks that copy or simulate a registered trademark of a United States or foreign corporation are prohibited importation. Similarly, the Copyright Revision Act of 1976 provides that the importation into the United States of copies of a work acquired outside the United States without authorization of the copyright owner is an infringement of the copyright.

Wildlife and Pets

The U.S. Fish and Wildlife Service, Department of Interior, Washington, DC 20240, controls the importation of (1) wild or game animals, birds, and other wildlife, or any part or product made therefrom and (2) the eggs of wild or game birds. The importation of birds, cats, dogs, monkeys, and turtles is subject to the requirements of the U.S. Public Health Service, Centers for Disease Control, Quarantine Division, Atlanta, GA 30333.

Customs Container Security Initiative

About 90 percent of all world cargo moves by container. Almost half of incoming trade (by value) arrives in the United States by sea containers.

The primary purpose of the Container Security Initiative (CSI) is to protect the global trading system and the trade lanes between CSI ports and the United States. First announced in 2002, the CSI deploys a team of officers with host nation counterparts to target all containers that pose a potential threat. Phone: 202-344-2990; Web site: www.cbp.gov.

Free Trade Zones

Special zones for free trade, sometimes called *in-bond regions*, did not develop in any significant way until the nineteenth century. Some of the more notable zones worldwide are the port regions of Hamburg, Hong Kong, Koushieng in Taiwan, and Jurong Port in Singapore.

Inland free trade zones also exist, most notable of which are the in-bond, free zones surrounding the Mexican Maquiladoras. Even Russia is establishing free zones to promote interchange of business with market economies.

Free trade zones, under legislation of the sovereign nation where they are located, are considered outside the customs territory of that country. The concept is an ancient one, dating back to Egyptian times. Goods entering the zone pay no tariff or other taxes, under a guarantee (bond) that they will not be entered into the domestic market. Should they enter the domestic market, all duties must be routinely paid. While in these free zones, typically goods can be altered, assembled, manufactured, and manipulated. Thus the zones become areas where barriers to free trade are circumvented.

U.S. Foreign Trade Zones

Every where else in the world they are called free zones, but in the United States they are called foreign trade zones (FTZs). In the United States like elsewhere, they are restricted areas considered outside the territory under the supervision of the Customs Service.

Typically an FTZ is a large warehouse, fenced and alarmed for security reasons, which tenants lease in order to bring in merchandise, foreign or domestic, to be stored, exhibited, assembled, manufactured, or processed in some way. They are usually located in or near customs ports of entry, usually in industrial parks or in terminal warehouse facilities. The usual customs entry procedures and payment of duties are not required on foreign merchandise in the zone unless it enters the customs territory for domestic consumption. The importer has a choice of paying duties either on the original foreign material or the finished product. Quota restrictions do not normally apply to foreign merchandise in a zone.

From the point of view of the local governments in the United States that build them, the purpose of FTZs is to stimulate international trade and thus contribute to the economic growth of a region by creating jobs and income. But from the point of view of an import/exporter, it's all about *profits*.

HISTORICAL NOTE

The success of free zones like the "free port of Hamburg" stimulated American interest that culminated in the passage of the Foreign Trade Zones Act of 1934 and its amendment in 1950. The early history of American foreign trade zones is not glamorous. Growth was slow and profits modest. Until the early 1970s there were fewer than 25 authorized foreign trade zones in operation in the United States; that number had not changed appreciably from the time the enabling legislation was passed in 1934. However, since 1975 the number of FTZs has grown to more than 110 with 56 special subzones. See www.cbp.gov/xp/cgov/home.xml.

Advantages of Using an FTZ

Actually, perceived advantages of FTZs are limitless; unfortunately, there are many cases of firms that have begun operations in FTZs and lost money. Each operation in the zone must make business and profit sense and must be individually analyzed. Here is a list of the regulatory advantages:

- Customs procedural requirements are minimal.
- Merchandise may remain in a zone indefinitely, regardless of whether it is subject to duty.
- Customs security requirements provide protection against theft.
- Customs duty and internal revenue tax, if applicable, are paid when merchandise is transferred from a foreign trade zone to the customs territory for consumption.
- While in a zone, merchandise is not subject to U.S. duty or excise tax. Tangible personal property is generally exempt from state and local ad valorem taxes.
- Goods may be exported from a zone free of duty and tax.
- The zone user who plans to enter merchandise for consumption in the customs territory may elect to pay the duty and taxes

on the foreign material placed in the zone or on the article transferred from the zone. The rate of duty and tax and the value of the merchandise may change as a result of manipulation or manufacture in the zone. Therefore, the importer may pay the lowest duty possible on the imported merchandise.

- Merchandise under bond may be transferred to a foreign trade zone from the customs territory for the purpose of satisfying a legal requirement to export or destroy the merchandise. For instance, merchandise may be taken into a zone in order to satisfy any exportation requirement of the Tariff Act of 1930 or an exportation requirement of any other federal law insofar as the agency charged with its enforcement deems it advisable. Exportation or destruction may also fulfill requirements of certain state laws.

The Role of the Customs Service

The director of the Customs Service district office is responsible for controlling the admission of merchandise into the FTZ, the handling and disposition of merchandise within the FTZ, and the removal of merchandise from it.

Operations that May Be Performed in an FTZ

All businesses may not benefit from FTZ operations, and those contemplating leasing a zone must analyze their market potential and economic potential. Some businesses that might benefit are:

- Automotive parts—repack, remark, and distribute
- Clothing—cut and sew imported fabric for import and export
- Food stuffs—label, sample, and repack for shipment
- Liquor—affix stamps, destroy broken bottles, defer duty
- Machinery—inspect, repair, clean, and paint
- Office equipment—inspect and distribute
- Sporting goods—sort and repackage for shipment
- Televisions and other electronics—repackage for shipment

Money-Saving Reasons to Use an FTZ

The uses of an FTZ for money-saving reasons are only limited by the creativity of the user and the trade-off of the costs of leasing space in an FTZ versus storing goods in a commercial warehouse. Here are several standard reasons:

- *Cost of money.* The drawback is the recovery of duty already paid and is a costly and time-consuming process. The Treasury Department does not expedite the repayment of duties already paid, and if it finally does, it pays only 99 percent of the original amount, keeping 1 percent to cover administrative costs. If the duty had not been paid in the first place, that sum of money could have been earning interest. The interest and administrative costs result in a cost of money that for companies with high inventories could have been avoided by using an FTZ.
- *Cash flow.* The money paid to the Customs Service under the tariff schedule is money no longer available for other uses, even if that money is later recovered under drawback procedures. Using an FTZ to defer duty or taxes improves a cash flow position.
- *Reclamation.* There are many examples of reclamation within an FTZ that can provide a cost savings; in fact, the possibilities are limited only by the imagination of the user and the legality of the operation. Consider this example: A computer manufacturer imports chips from offshore (Asia or Mexico). Before importing them into the United States, the manufacturer conducts the quality assurance (QA) check within the FTZ. The firm reclaims the gold and other materials from the failed boards, sends the recovered material back to the offshore plant, and imports only the chips that pass QA, thus avoiding duty on the failed units.
- *Inverted tariff.* An FTZ is the only method under U.S. law whereby an importer can choose between paying the duty rate of material parts or the rate of a finished product. The importer would of course make the choice that provided the greatest cost savings.
- *Lower insurance costs.* An FTZ is required to be a secure area. It is fenced and alarmed and often guarded. For that reason, and

because the value of an inventory is not increased by the value added in the FTZ, the inventory stored within a zone is often charged at lower insurance rates.

- *Transportation time savings.* Goods destined for an FTZ are not delayed on the dock for customs, but rather, because they are considered in-bond, are usually given priority for pierside movement. Therefore, those items that have some manipulations or reclamation or that need to be broken into smaller shipping amounts can be expedited by using the FTZ.
- *Reduced pierside pilferage and/or damage.* Because there are no dockside delays, there is less risk of theft, pilferage, and damage to the incoming goods.
- *Fine avoidance.* Goods imported into the United States with improper or incorrect labels are subject to fines. By checking the labels within an FTZ, the fines can be avoided.
- *Advantage over a bonded warehouse.* Users of FTZs can avoid the cost of a bond; the zone operator buys the bond.
- *Environmental protection.* Reclamation activities within an FTZ are centered within an enclosed area, using special machines, and can be carefully controlled.
- *General system of preferences (GSP).* The duty-free advantage of this multilateral trade agreement can be combined with the benefits of FTZs.
- *Customs item 9802.00.8050.* Duty reduction can be obtained through the use of this method of incorporating this item of customs law (relates to labor content) in offshore assembly.
- *Customs item 9801.00.10108.* This item offers duty-free treatment of goods of U.S. origin that are improved or advanced in condition or value while abroad. (Relates to packaging material content.)
- *State and local taxes.* Under federal law, tangible personal property imported into an FTZ, and tangible personal property produced in the United States and held in an FTZ for export, is exempt from state and local ad valorem taxes.
- *Quota allocations.* Duty and charges against quota allocations can be avoided if shipments are rejected.

- ***Duty elimination.*** Duty on merchandise that is re-exported or destroyed in the zone is eliminated.
- ***Duty deferral.*** Duty on foreign goods will be deferred until they leave the zone.
- ***Indefinite storage.*** Goods may be stored indefinitely while awaiting a receptive market or favorable sales conditions.

Customs Bonded Warehouse

A *bonded warehouse* is a building or other secure area within the customs territory where dutiable foreign merchandise may be placed for a period of up to five years without payment of duty. Only cleaning, repacking, and sorting may take place. The owner of the bonded warehouse incurs liability and must post a bond with the U.S. Customs Service and abide by those regulations that pertain to control and declaration of tariffs for goods on departure. The liability is canceled when the goods are removed.

Types of Bonded Warehouses

U.S. customs regulations authorize eight different types of bonded warehouses:

1. Storage areas owned or leased by the government to store merchandise undergoing customs inspection or that is under seizure; these areas may also be used for unclaimed goods.
2. Privately owned warehouses used exclusively for the storage of merchandise belonging or consigned to the proprietor.
3. Publicly bonded warehouses used exclusively to store imported goods.
4. Bonded yards or sheds for the storage of heavy and bulky imported merchandise such as pens for animals—stables and corrals—and tanks for the storage of imported fluids.
5. Bonded grain storage bins or elevators.

6. Warehouses used for the manufacture in bond, solely for exportation, of imported articles.
7. Warehouses bonded for smelting and refining imported metal-bearing materials.
8. Bonded warehouses created for sorting, cleaning, repacking, or otherwise changing the condition of imported merchandise, but not for manufacturing.

How to Establish a Bonded Warehouse

Your local Customs Service district office has all the needed information on how to get started, but in general, the following five requirements must be fulfilled:

1. Submit an application to the district office giving the location and stating the class of warehouse to be established. Such application should describe the general character of the merchandise, the estimated maximum duties and taxes that could become due at any one time, and whether the warehouse will be used for private storage or treatment or as a public warehouse.
2. A fee of about $80.
3. A certificate that the building is acceptable for fire insurance purposes.
4. A blueprint of the building or space to be bonded.
5. A bond of $5,000 or greater on each building, depending on the class of the bonded area.

Bonded Warehouse or FTZ?

Table 8.4 shows a comparison of an FTZ and a bonded warehouse.

Awareness of all the possibilities is a vital part of competing and winning the trade game. Not every importer/exporter will need countertrade or make use of an FTZ or a customs bonded warehouse, but proper and advance planning is essential in order to take advantage

Table 8.4 Comparison of an FTZ and Bonded Warehouse

Function	Bonded Warehouse	Zone
Customs entry	A bonded warehouse is within U.S. customs territory; therefore a customs entry must be filed to enter goods into the warehouse.	A zone is not considered within customs territory. Customs entry is, therefore, not required until merchandise is removed from a zone.
Permissible cargo	Only foreign merchandise may be placed in a bonded warehouse.	All merchandise, whether domestic or foreign, may be placed in a zone.
Customs bonds	Each entry must be covered by either a single-entry term bond or a general term bond.	No bond is required for merchandise in a zone.
Payment of duty	Duties are due prior to release from bonded warehouses.	Duties are due only upon entry into U.S. territory.
Manufacture of goods	Manufacturing is prohibited.	Manufacturing is permitted with duty payable at the time the goods leave the zone for U.S. consumption. Duty is payable on either the imported components or the finished product, whichever carries a lower rate.
Appraisal and classification	Immediately.	Tariff rate and value may be determined either at the time goods are admitted into a zone or when goods leave a zone, at the importer's discretion.
Storage periods	Not to exceed 5 years.	Unlimited.
Operations on merchandise destined for domestic consumption	Only cleaning, repackaging, and sorting may take place and under customs supervision.	Zone operations include sort, destroy, clean, grade, mix with foreign or domestic goods, label, assemble, manufacture, exhibit, sell, and repack.
Customs entry regulations	Apply fully.	Applicable only to goods actually removed from a zone for U.S. consumption.

of the subtleties of the trade laws. An appreciation of the capabilities of each of the business tools presented in this chapter could lead to the recognition of a winning opportunity.

The next part of the book is dedicated to understanding the basics of doing business in the globalized world and covers such things as world trade centers, integrated economies like NAFTA, the European Union, and specific nations.

PART 3

DOING BUSINESS IN THE GLOBALIZED WORLD

CHAPTER 9

DOING BUSINESS THROUGH WORLD TRADE CENTERS

The World Trade Centers Association (WTCA) is a not-for-profit, nonpolitical association dedicated to the establishment and effective operation of world trade centers as instruments for trade expansion.

Background

Founded in 1970, the World Trade Centers Association has become the world's largest, apolitical, private, international organization that is dedicated to providing services to those who develop and facilitate international trade. With its unique global mission and membership, the WTCA has been a world leader in creating innovative service for international business.

WTCA membership comprises 282 centers in 85 countries. Its centers are located in over 170 cities with about 100 more in the planning stages. Over 750,000 companies are affiliated with WTCA members worldwide. In other words, the organization is in virtually every major trading city in the world.

Over the WTCA's 36-year history, its purpose has not changed. Its principal goals are to:

- Foster increased participation in world trade.
- Encourage and support the establishment of world trade centers in every region of the world.
- Stimulate mutual assistance and a cooperative exchange of services and information among members.
- Develop special programs to meet the needs of the world's developing regions.

Headquarters

The headquarters of the WTCA are located in New York City, one of the world's major centers for international trade. Address: World Trade Centers Association, 420 Lexington Avenue, Suite 518, New York, NY 10170; phone: 212-432-2626; fax: 212-488-0064; e-mail: wtca@wtca.org.

What Is a World Trade Center?

A world trade center (WTC) is a shopping center that puts all the services associated with international trade under one roof. It is the first stop for your import/export venture. WTCs complement and support the existing services of private and government agencies. Some of the services you will find at a WTC are:

- *Trade information.* WTCs provide up-to-date information about their respective regions, including local products and services, market conditions, government regulations, and business culture. They also furnish detailed profiles of local business contacts, including manufacturers, distributors, and service providers. They also perform market research tailored to specific needs.

- *WTCA OnLine services.* The WTCA's Web site (www.wtca.org) is a one-stop source for global business information. Through strategic alliances with leading information and service providers, WTCA OnLine offers quality products representing the best international trade information and services at discount prices. These include:

  > WTCA OnLine trade opportunities
  > Trade flow pricing system
  > STAT-USA's national Trade Data Bank
  > WTCA OnLine catalog
  > World Trade Library
  > Directory of World Trade Center services
  > Port Import/Export Reporting Services (PIERS)
  > World trade center events

- *World trade center clubs.* World trade center clubs feature comfortable lounge and dining services for members and their guests at an impressive, centrally located address.
- *Trade education programs.* These are practical workshops, seminars, and courses for credit on key local and global business issues conducted or sponsored by the local WTC.
- *Trade mission assistance.* WTCs help businesses explore new markets by working together with other WTCs to promote their products and services.
- *Display and exhibit services.* Many WTCs have world-class exhibition facilities with a full range of support services.

WTCA Services and Member Benefits

Every WTC is a member of the WTCA and therefore enjoys the following:

- Exclusive rights to use the WTCA's service marks and logo
- Exclusive rights to market WTCA OnLine in the member's region
- Access to information and services available through other WTCs

- Reciprocal privileges for local members at all operating WTCs and world trade center clubs
- Seminars on how to establish a successful WTC
- Manuals on planning and operating specific WTC services
- A monthly newsletter and many other useful publications
- Annual general assemblies and regular committee meetings to promote a variety of special projects and mutual assistance programs

Trade Card was originally the WTCA's electronic commerce system. It now operates as an independent company and offers an electronic solution for fulfillment and settlement operations in international trade transactions.

To learn more about the WTCA, contact the World Trade Centers Association, 420 Lexington Avenue, Suite 518, New York, NY 10170; phone: 212-432-2626; fax: 212-488-0064; Web site: www.wtca.org; e-mail: wtca@wtca.org.

CHAPTER 10

DOING BUSINESS IN THE INTEGRATED AMERICAS

Contemporary nations have learned that economic boundaries often transcend geographical borders and stimulate international trade. Negotiated economic integration such as the North American Free Trade Agreement (NAFTA) and the European Union (EU) fuel the exchange of economic wealth within regions and blocs and is the primary method used to harmonize international trade and investment in the globalized world.

There is strong evidence that trade tends to increase within a region of trading nations when interstate controls such as tariffs are reduced. Enterprises are thus encouraged to expand their operations into other markets within the region. Economic integration tends to have an overall positive effect on trade by providing increased understanding within trading blocs and more cooperation among nations. On the other hand, most forms of regional economic cooperation are highly preferential and, in the views of some, serve as barriers to outsiders and are in opposition to multilateral trade concepts.

Economic integration is not new. The United States was one of the earliest nations to employ economic integration when, in 1776, visionary leadership established an economic union of the original 13 states wherein people, goods, services, and money were free to move across state boundaries. Today that union has expanded to 50 states, and over time that form of economic cooperation proved to be of great value to the growth of North America.

> *Outsourcing* is the practice in which companies move or contract out some or all of their manufacturing or service operations to other companies that specialize in those operations or to companies in other countries. In these cases outsourcing is usually done to take advantage of lower-cost labor or other efficiencies. Other names for outsourcing are *offshoring* or *production sharing*.

Free Trade Areas

Trade among the nations of the Americas (see Table 10.1) has always been brisk, but tariffs and other barriers have often stifled profitability and therefore economic growth. Incentives have been put in place to stimulate the potential market (see Table 10.2) that could bring increased wealth to the hemisphere. Most notable among these efforts have been the Caribbean Basin Initiative (CBI) instituted in 1984 and expanded in 2000, the U.S./Canadian Free Trade Agreement of 1989, and the North American Free Trade Agreement (NAFTA) of 1994. NAFTA is currently a single market composed of three North American countries (the United States, Canada, and Mexico); however, integration of the other 31 (not including Cuba) is being considered. At a meeting called the "Miami Summit" held in December 1994, the leaders of 34 of the 35 democratic nations of the Americas signed a declaration to negotiate by the year 2005 a Free Trade Area of the Americas (FTAA). This area of no trade barriers would embrace a market of

Table 10.1   The Americas

Antigua and Barbuda	Dominican Republic	Paraguay
Argentina	Ecuador	Peru
Bahamas	El Salvador	St. Kitts-Nevis
Barbados	Grenada	St. Lucia
Belize	Guatemala	St. Vincent and the
Bolivia	Guyana	Grenadines
Brazil	Haiti	Surinam
Canada	Honduras	Trinidad and Tobago
Chile	Jamaica	United States of America
Colombia	Mexico	Uruguay
Costa Rica	Nicaragua	Venezuela
Cuba	Panama	
Dominica		

almost a billion people and stretch from Alaska to the tip of Argentina. However FTAA negotiations have stalled amid discussions leading to new approaches and as of this writing, little progress has been made. One method of achieving the FTAA would be through the expansion of NAFTA; another route being considered might be the merger and linking the other subregional trade arrangements with the FTAA.

Table 10.2 shows the potential of the total Americas market. Central and Latin American markets, although having smaller gross domestic

Table 10.2   The Americas Trade Potential

		Purchasing Power Parity	
Country	Population (Millions)	National Income ($ in Trillions)	National per Capita Income ($)
Canada	33.3	1.274	35,200
United States	301	13.86	46,000
Mexico	108.7	1.35	12,500
NAFTA totals	443	Average 3.0	31,233
Central/Latin America totals	620	Average 3.78	7,332

Source: CIA Factbook, 2008 (www.cia.gov).

products, nevertheless have a growing middle class and offer excellent trade potential.

Each nation of the Americas has its own tariff schedule, and each belongs to one or more regional trade arrangements that dictate the bloc tariff.

This chapter deals with three major elements of doing business in the Americas:

- NAFTA and NAFTA expansion
- Maquiladora implications
- Other existing trade arrangements

Expanded NAFTA

The North American Free Trade Area (NAFTA) is composed of Canada, the United Mexican States, and the United States of America. With their combined 440 million people and high average per capita incomes of over $29,000 a year (about $7,332 in Mexico), it is the richest market in the world and has always been the first target for anyone doing international business.

NAFTA offers preferential tariff treatment for businesses trading within the single market and is a major step toward stimulating regional trade. NAFTA rules are clear and understandable but require thought as they apply to a given firm's products. The tactical implications of NAFTA depend on a product-by-product analysis as well as whether a firm is an insider or outsider.

Key Provisions

The NAFTA document is over 1,000 pages, and its companion tariff schedule is even longer. Changes are the result of users (exporters and importers) shoring up loopholes and finding better ways of doing business. The intent of the basic document remains as follows:

- Phase-out of all tariffs from applied rates. This went into effect on July 1, 1991. It includes the U.S. General System of

Preferences (GSP) and the Canadian General Preference
Treatment (GPT) rates.
- Eliminated of all tariffs between the United States and Canada.
- Phase out and elimination of duties on U.S. and Canadian trade
  with Mexico.
- Certificates of origin are used to prevent third country intrusion.
- Elimination of customs user fees and duty drawback.
- Elimination of quotas unless grandfathered.
- Prohibition of product standards as a barrier to trade.
- Elimination of agriculture tariffs and subsidies.
- Elimination of Mexican tariffs on all U.S. exports.
- Expansion of government procurement markets.
- Elimination of discrimination on laws related to service
  providers.

National Treatment

NAFTA incorporates the fundamental "national treatment" obligation
of the General Agreement on Tariffs and Trade (GATT). This commitment means that goods of other parties will be treated, in terms of
tariffs and laws, as if they were domestic goods and extends to provincial and state measures.

Temporary Entry of Business People

Taking into account the preferential trading relationship between the
NAFTA countries, on a reciprocal basis, the agreement commits to
temporary entry into their respective territories of business people who
are citizens of Canada, Mexico, or the United States.

Each country will grant temporary entry to four categories of business people:

- *Business visitors* engaged in international business activities for
  the purpose of conducting activities related to research and
  design, growth, manufacture and production, marketing,
  sales, distribution, after-sales service, and other general services.

- *Traders and investors* who carry on substantial trade in goods or services between their own country and the country they wish to enter, provided that such persons are employed or operate in a supervisory or executive capacity or one that involves essential skills.
- *Intracompany transfers* employed by company in a managerial or executive capacity or one that involves specialized knowledge and who are transferred within that company to another NAFTA country.
- *Certain categories of professionals* who meet minimum educational requirements or who possess alternative credentials and who seek to engage in business activities at a professional level in that country.

HOT TIP: TEMPORARY ENTRY RULES

Ordinary business (non-NAFTA):

- U.S. citizens: No papers up to 72 hours and 48 miles
- Longer: Tourist card or visa
- Mexican citizens: Valid border crossing card (USINS) up to 72 hours and 25 miles
- Longer: Visa

NAFTA business visitors:

- Proof of citizenship
- Purpose documentation (i.e., must be international in scope)
- Employment outside territory of grantor
- Each party grants temporary entry visa .

Duty-Free Temporary Admission of Goods

The agreement allows business people covered by NAFTA's "temporary entry" provisions to bring into a NAFTA country "professional equipment" and "tools of the trade" on a duty-free, temporary basis. These rules also cover the importation of commercial samples, certain types of advertising films, and goods imported for sports purposes or for display and demonstration.

Other rules provide that all goods that are returned after repair or alteration in another NAFTA country will re-enter duty-free.

Country-of-Origin Marking

Under NAFTA, country-of-origin marking is designed to minimize unnecessary costs, and to this end the following rules apply:

- Any reasonable method may be used (e.g., stickers, labels, tags, paint)
- Markings must be conspicuous and permanent

HOT TIP: MARKING EXEMPTIONS

- Item incapable of being marked
- Item cannot be marked prior to exportation without injury to goods
- Item cannot be marked except at great expense, which would discourage exportation
- A crude substance
- An original work of art

Certificates of Origin

Each of the three countries in NAFTA has its own certificates for goods entering from non-NAFTA countries; however, there is a common NAFTA *certificate of origin* as shown in Figures 10.1 to 10.3. Note that the key elements of the certificate are:

Item 5—description of goods

Item 6—HS tariff classification number

Item 7—preference

Item 8—producer

Item 9—net cost

Item 10—country of origin

Figure 10.1 NAFTA Certificate of Origin

DEPARTMENT OF THE TREASURY
UNITED STATES CUSTOMS SERVICE

NORTH AMERICAN FREE TRADE AGREEMENT
CERTIFICATE OF ORIGIN

Aproved through 12/31/96
OMB No. 1515-0204
See back of form for Paper-
work Reduction Act Notice

Please print or type   19 CFR 181.11, 181.22

1. EXPORTER NAME AND ADDRESS	2. BLANKET PERIOD *(DD/MM/YY)*
	FROM
	TO
TAX IDENTIFICATION NUMBER:	
3. PRODUCER NAME AND ADDRESS	4. IMPORTER NAME AND ADDRESS
TAX IDENTIFICATION NUMBER:	TAX IDENTIFICATION NUMBER:

5. DESCRIPTION OF GOOD(S)	6. HS TARIFF CLASSIFICATION NUMBER	7. PREFERENCE CRITERION	8. PRODUCER	9. NET COST	10. COUNTRY OF ORIGIN

I CERTIFY THAT:

• THE INFORMATION ON THIS DOCUMENT IS TRUE AND ACCURATE AND I ASSUME THE RESPONSIBILITY FOR PROVING SUCH REP-RESENTATIONS. I UNDERSTAND THAT I AM LIABLE FOR ANY FALSE STATEMENTS OR MATERIAL OMISSIONS MADE ON OR IN CON-NECTION WITH THIS DOCUMENT;

• I AGREE TO MAINTAIN, AND PRESENT UPON REQUEST, DOCUMENTATION NECESSARY TO SUPPORT THIS CERTIFICATE, AND TO INFORM, IN WRITING, ALL PERSONS TO WHOM THE CERTIFICATE WAS GIVEN OF ANY CHANGES THAT COULD AFFECT THE ACCU-RACY OR VALIDITY OF THIS CERTIFICATE;

• THE GOODS ORIGINATED IN THE TERRITORY OF ONE OR MORE OF THE PARTIES, AND COMPLY WITH THE ORIGIN REQUIREMENTS SPECIFIED FOR THOSE GOODS IN THE NORTH AMERICAN FREE TRADE AGREEMENT, AND UNLESS SPECIFICALLY EXEMPTED IN ARTICLE 411 OR ANNEX 401, THERE HAS BEEN NO FURTHER PRODUCTION OR ANY OTHER OPERATION OUTSIDE THE TERRITORIES OF THE PARTIES; AND

• THIS CERTIFICATE CONSISTS OF [   ] PAGES, INCLUDING ALL ATTACHMENTS.

11a. AUTHORIZED SIGNATURE	11b. COMPANY
11c. NAME *(Print or Type)*	11d. TITLE
11e. DATE *(DD/MM/YY)*	11f. TELEPHONE NUMBER ▷ : *(Voice)* : *(Facsimile)*

11.

Customs Form 434 (121793)

Figure 10.2 NAFTA Certificate of Origin (Continuation Sheet)

DEPARTMENT OF THE TREASURY
UNITED STATES CUSTOMS SERVICE

Aproved through 12/31/96,
OMB No. 1515-0204. See
Customs Form 434 for Paper-
work Reduction Act Notice.

NORTH AMERICAN FREE TRADE AGREEMENT
CERTIFICATE OF ORIGIN CONTINUATION SHEET

19 CFR 181.11, 181.22

5. DESCRIPTION OF GOOD(S)	6. HS TARIFF CLASSIFICATION NUMBER	7. PREFERENCE CRITERION	8. PRODUCER	9. NET COST	10. COUNTRY OF ORIGIN

Customs Form 434A (121793)

Figure 10.3 NAFTA Certificate of Origin (Instruction Sheet)

Instructions for the CF 434, as found on the form:

PAPERWORK REDUCTION ACT NOTICE: This information is needed to carry out the terms of the North American Free Trade Agreement (NAFTA). NAFTA requires that, upon request, an importer must provide Customs with proof of the exporter's written certification of the origin of the goods. The certification is essential to substantiate compliance with the rules of origin under the Agreement. You are required to give us this information to obtain a benefit.

Statement Required by 5 CFR 1320.21: The estimated average burden associated with this collection of information is 15 minutes per respondent or recordkeeper depending on individual circumstances. Comments concerning the accuracy of this burden estimate and suggestions for reducing this burden should be directed to U.S. Customs Service, Paperwork Management Branch, Washington DC 20229, and to the Office of Management and Budget, Paperwork Reduction Project (1515-0204), Washington DC 20503.

NORTH AMERICAN FREE TRADE AGREEMENT CERTIFICATE OF ORIGIN INSTRUCTIONS

For purposes of obtaining preferential tariff treatment, this document must be completed legibly and in full by the exporter and be in the possession of the importer at the time the declaration is made. This document may also be completed voluntarily by the producer for use by the exporter. Please print or type:

FIELD 1: State the full legal name, address (including country) and legal tax identification number of the exporter. Legal taxation number is: in Canada, employer number or importer/exporter number assigned by Revenue Canada; in Mexico, federal taxpayer's registry number (RFC); and in the United States, employer's identification number or Social Security Number.

FIELD 2: Complete field if the Certificate covers multiple shipments of identical goods as described in Field # 5 that are imported into a NAFTA country for a specified period of up to one year (the blanket period). "FROM" is the date upon which the Certificate becomes applicable to the good covered by the blanket Certificate (it may be prior to the date of signing this Certificate). "TO" is the date upon which the blanket period expires. The importation of a good for which preferential treatment is claimed based on this Certificate must occur between these dates.

FIELD 3: State the full legal name, address (including country) and legal tax identification number, as defined in Field #1, of the producer. If more than one producer's good is included on the Certificate, attach a list of additional producers, including the legal name, address (including country) and legal tax identification number, cross-referenced to the good described in Field #5. If you wish this information to be confidential, it is acceptable to state "Available to Customs upon request". If the producer and the exporter are the same, complete field with "SAME". If the producer is unknown, it is acceptable to state "UNKNOWN".

FIELD 4: State the full legal name, address (including country) and legal tax identification number, as defined in Field #1, of the importer. If the importer is not known, state "UNKNOWN"; if multiple importers, state "VARIOUS".

FIELD 5: Provide a full description of each good. The description should be sufficient to relate it to the invoice description and to the Harmonized System (H.S.) description of the good. If the Certificate covers a single shipment of a good, include the invoice number as shown on the commercial invoice. If not known, indicate another unique reference number, such as the shipping order number.

FIELD 6: For each good described in Field #5, identify the H.S. tariff classification to six digits. If the good is subject to a specific rule of origin in Annex 401 that requires eight digits, identify to eight digits, using the H.S. tariff classification of the country into whose territory the good is imported.

FIELD 7: For each good described in Field #5, state which criterion (A through F) is applicable. The rules of origin are contained in Chapter Four and Annex 401. Additional rules are described in Annex 703.2 (certain agricultural goods), Annex 300-B, Appendix 6 (certain textile goods) and Annex 308.1 (certain automatic data processing goods and their parts). NOTE: **In order to be entitled to preferential tariff treatment, each good must meet at least one of the criteria below.**

Preference Criteria

A The good is "wholly obtained or produced entirely" in the territory of one or more of the NAFTA countries as referenced in Article 415. **Note: The purchase of a good in the territory does not necessarily render it "wholly obtained or produced".** If the good is an agricultural good, see also criterion F and Annex 703.2. (Reference: Article 401(a) and 415)

B The good is produced entirely in the territory of one or more of the NAFTA countries and satisfies the specific rule of origin, set out in Annex 401, that applies to its tariff classification. The rule may include a tariff classification change, regional value-content requirement, or a combination thereof. The good must also satisfy all other applicable requirements of Chapter Four. If the good is an agricultural good, see also criterion F and Annex 703.2. (Reference: Article 401(b))

C The good is produced entirely in the territory of one or more of the NAFTA countries exclusively from originating materials. Under this criterion, one or more of the materials may not fall within the definition of "wholly produced or obtained", as set out in Article 415. All materials used in the production of the good must qualify as "originating" by meeting the rules of Article 401(a) through (d). If the good is an agricultural good, see also criterion F and Annex 703.2. *Reference: Article 401(c)*.

D Goods are produced in the territory of one or more of the NAFTA countries but do not meet the applicable rule of origin, set out in Annex 401, because certain non-originating materials do not undergo the required change in tariff classification. The goods do nonetheless meet the regional value-content requirement specified in Article 401 (d). This criterion is limited to the following two circumstances:

1. The good was imported into the territory of a NAFTA country in an unassembled or disassembled form but was classified as an assembled good, pursuant to H.S. General Rule of Interpretation 2(a), or

2. The good incorporated one or more non-originating materials, provided for as parts under the H.S., which could not undergo a change in tariff classification because the heading provided for both the good and its parts and was not further subdivided into subheadings, or the subheading provided for both the good and its parts and was not further subdivided.

NOTE: **This criterion does not apply to Chapters 61 through 63 of the H.S.** *(Reference: Article 401(d))*

E Certain automatic data processing goods and their parts, specified in Annex 308.1, that do not originate in the territory are considered originating upon importation into the territory of a NAFTA country from the territory of another NAFTA country when the most-favored-nation tariff rate of the good conforms to the rate established in Annex 308.1 and is common to all NAFTA countries. *(Reference: Annex 308.1)*

F The good is an originating agricultural good under preference criterion A, B, or C above and is not subject to a quantitative restriction in the importing NAFTA country because it is a "qualifying good" as defined in Annex 703.2, Section A or B (please specify). A good listed in Appendix 703.2B.7 is also exempt from quantitative restrictions and is eligible for NAFTA preferential tariff treatment if it meets the definition of "qualifying good" in Section A of Annex 703.2. **NOTE 1: This criterion does not apply to goods that wholly originate in Canada or the United States and are imported into either country. NOTE 2: A tariff rate quota is not a quantitative restriction.**

FIELD 8: For each good described in Field #5, state "YES" if you are the producer of the good. If you are not the producer of the good, state "NO" followed by (1), (2), or (3), depending on whether this certificate was based upon: (1) your knowledge of whether the good qualifies as an originating good; (2) your reliance on the producer's written representation (other than a Certificate of Origin) that the good qualifies as an originating good; or (3) a completed and signed Certificate for the good, voluntarily provided to the exporter by the producer.

FIELD 9: For each good described in field #5, where the good is subject to a regional value content (RVC) requirement, indicate "NC" if the RVC is calculated according to the net cost method; otherwise, indicate "NO". If the RVC is calculated over a period of time, further identify the beginning and ending dates (DD/MM/YY) of that period. *(Reference: Articles 402.1, 402.5)*.

FIELD 10: Identify the name of the country ("MX" or "US" for agricultural and textile goods exported to Canada; "US" or "CA" for all goods exported to Mexico; or "CA" or "MX" for all goods exported to the United States) to which the preferential rate of customs duty applies, as set out in Annex 302.2, in accordance with the Marking Rules or in each party's schedule of tariff elimination.

For all other originating goods exported to Canada, indicate appropriately "MX" or "US" if the goods originate in that NAFTA country, within the meaning of the NAFTA Rules of Origin Regulations, and any subsequent processing in the other NAFTA country does not increase the transaction value of the goods by more than seven percent; otherwise "JNT" for joint production. *(Reference: Annex 302.2)*

FIELD 11: This field must be completed, signed, and dated by the exporter. When the Certificate is completed by the producer for use by the exporter, it must be completed, signed, and dated by the producer. The date must be the date the Certificate was completed and signed.

Rules of Origin

"NAFTA eliminates all tariffs on goods originating in Canada, Mexico and the United States." This is often of such financial benefit that foreign traders attempt to defeat preferential treatment by going around the free trade area and importing through the state that has the lowest external tariff. The solution is a rigorous set of rules of origin (ROO) that define which goods are eligible:

- ROO are required because each country maintains its own external tariffs on imports from other countries. Disparities among each nation's tariffs make ROO necessary to prevent imports from third countries being shipped through one NAFTA partner into another in order to escape a higher tariff.
- NAFTA reduces tariffs only for goods made in North America.
- For duty-free treatment the good must obtain substantial North American content.
- ROO reward companies using North American parts and labor.
- ROO prevent "free riders" from benefiting through minor processing or transshipment.
- Mexico and Canada cannot be used as export platforms into the U.S. market.
- Goods containing non-regional components qualify if they are sufficiently transformed in the NAFTA region to warrant change of tariff classification.

How NAFTA ROO Work

- Each product has a ROO that applies to it.
- Rules are organized according to the Harmonized Commodity Description and Coding System (HS). The first six digits of the HS classify products using the internationally recognized commodity code.
- To determine the tariff elimination schedule for a particular product, exporters must find out the product's HS number.

Table 10.3 Examples of NAFTA Origin Rule Types

Rule Type	Description	Example
Tariff-shift	All non-NAFTA inputs must be of a different tariff class than final product. Rules state level of tariff shift required. May require non-NAFTA input be a different HS chapter, heading or item number.	Wood molding (HS 4409) made from (HS 4403) imported. Manufacturing process results in required HS heading shift.
Value-content	Set percent of value must be North American (usually coupled with a tariff-shift requirement). Some goods are subject to value-content rule only when they fail to pass tariff-shift test.	If medicaments (HS 3004), for example, fail tariff-shift rule, they must contain 50–60% North American content to get preferential treatment.

- There are two types of rules: tariff shift and value content. See Table 10.3 for an explanation of these rules.

Examples of Specific ROO

CHAPTER 44: Wood and Articles of Wood
44.01–44.21:

A change to heading 44.01 through 44.21 from any other heading, including another heading within that group.

CHAPTER 30: Pharmaceutical Products
30.04:

A change to subheading 30.04.10 through 30.04.90 from any other heading, except from heading 30.03; or a change to subheading 30.04.10 through 30.04.90 from any other subheading within heading 30.04, whether or not there is a change from any other heading, provided there is a regional value of not less than:

a. 60 percent; transaction value method
b. 50 percent; net cost method

HOT TIP

Question: What is a good?

Answer: Whatever crosses the border.

Question: What is material?

Answer: The components (stuff) that make up a good.

How to Claim NAFTA Tariff

Using the customs entry document and the certificate of origin, follow these steps:

1. Classify the good
2. Determine its HS number
3. Determine tariff staging category
4. Determine tariff difference
5. Determine preference criteria A through F
6. If you choose preference B, then apply the following rules from Chapter 4:

    a. Tariff shift?
    b. Tariff shift plus regional value content (RVC)?
    c. Regional value content?

Preference Criteria

A. The good is "wholly obtained or produced entirely" in the territory of one or more of the NAFTA countries. *Note:* The purchase of a good in one territory does not necessarily render it "wholly obtained or produced." If the good is an agricultural good, see also criterion F.

B. The good is produced entirely in the territory of one or more of the NAFTA countries and satisfies the specific rule of origin set out in Annex 401 that applies to its tariff classification. The rule may include tariff classification change, regional value content requirement, or a combination thereof.

C. The good is produced entirely in the territory of one or more of the NAFTA countries exclusively from originating materials. Under this criterion, one or more of the materials may not fall within the definition of "wholly produced or obtained." All materials used in the production of the good must qualify as "originating."

D. Goods are produced in the territory of one or more of the NAFTA countries but do not meet the applicable rule of origin because certain non-originating materials do not undergo the required change in tariff classification. The goods do nonetheless meet the regional value content requirement specified.

1. The good was imported into the territory of a NAFTA country in an unassembled or disassembled form but was classified as an assembled good.

2. The good incorporated one or more non-originating materials, provided for as parts under the HS, which could not undergo a change in tariff classification because the heading provided for both the good and its parts and was not further subdivided into subheadings, or the subheading provided for both the good and its parts and was not further subdivided.

E. Certain automatic data processing goods and their parts that do not originate in the territory are considered originating upon importation into the territory of a NAFTA country from the territory of another NAFTA country when the most-favored-nation tariff rate of the good conforms to the rate common to all NAFTA countries. [This criterion will go into effect.]

F. The good is an originating agricultural good under preference criterion A, B, or C above and is not subject to a quantitative restriction in the importing NAFTA country because it is a "qualifying good" (as defined in the NAFTA agreement).

Content Calculation

- *Tariff shift.* According to HS instructions
- *Regional value content (RVC) calculation.*

- *Transaction-value (TV) method.* Based on price paid or payable for the good.

$$RVC = \frac{TV - VNM}{TV} \times 100$$

- *Net cost (NC) method.* Based on total cost minus costs of royalties, sales promotion, and packing and shipping. (Sets limit on allowable interest.)

$$RVC = \frac{NC - VNM}{NC} \times 100$$

- Either method may be used, but the net cost method *must* be used when transaction value is not accepted under GATT customs valuation code. The net cost must also be used for certain products, such as automotive goods.
- *De minimus rule.* If a good otherwise fails eligibility, it may still be okay if non-NAFTA content is no more than 7 percent of the price or total cost of the good.

NAFTA by Industry

NAFTA goes beyond tariff reduction of general goods and specifies treatment by specific industries. The following is a cursory treatment.

Automotive Goods

NAFTA eliminates barriers to trade in North American automobiles, trucks, buses, and parts ("automotive goods") within the free trade area and eliminates investment restrictions.

Textiles and Apparel

NAFTA textiles and apparel provisions take precedence over any multi-fiber arrangement (MFA) and other arrangements between NAFTA countries and provide:

- Immediate elimination or phase-out of duties that meet rules of origin.

- In addition the United States immediately removes import quotas on Mexican goods and phases out import quotas that do not meet such rules.
- Mexico immediately eliminates tariffs on 20 percent of textile and apparel exports to the United States.
- Immediate duty-free treatment, by Mexico, of denim, underwear, sewing thread, and many household furnishings.

Textile and Apparel ROO

Specific ROO in NAFTA define when imported textile or apparel goods qualify for preferential treatment. For most products the "yarn forward" rule applies.

- *Yarn forward rule.* Goods must be made from yarn made in a NAFTA country in order to benefit from such treatment.
- *Fiber forward rule.* Goods must be produced from fiber made in a NAFTA country. The rule applies to certain goods such as cotton and synthetic fiber yarns.
- Preferential treatment is allowed for fabrics in short supply, such as silk, linen, and certain shirting fabrics.

Energy and Basic Petrochemicals

NAFTA recognizes the desirability of strengthening the important role that trade in energy and basic petrochemical goods play in North America, and the need to enhance its role by sustained and gradual liberalization.

The energy provisions incorporate and build on GATT disciplines regarding quantitative restrictions on imports and exports by providing that:

- A country may not impose minimum or maximum import or export price requirements, subject to the same exceptions that apply to quantitative restrictions.
- Each country may administer export and import licensing systems provided that the systems are operated in a manner consistent with the provisions of the agreement.

- No country may impose a tax, duty, or charge on the export of energy or basic petrochemical goods unless the same tax, duty, or charge is applied to such goods when consumed domestically.
- Any import and export restrictions on energy trade will be limited to certain specific circumstances, such as to conserve exhaustible natural resources, deal with a short supply situation, or implement a price stabilization plan.
- Imports and exports may be restricted for national security reasons.
- Mexico reserves to the Mexican state goods, activities, and investments in Mexico in the oil, gas, refining, basic petrochemicals, nuclear, and electricity sectors.
- Investment in non-basic petrochemical goods is governed by the general provisions of the agreement.

Agriculture
NAFTA sets out separate bilateral undertakings on cross-border trade in agricultural products, one between Canada and Mexico and the other between Mexico and the United States. Both include a special transitional safeguard mechanism. The rules of the U.S./Canada Free Trade Agreement of 1989 will continue to apply to agricultural trade between Canada and the United States.

Technical Standards
NAFTA is designed to create a harmonization of technical standards in its three member countries and to prohibit countries from using technical standards as a barrier to market entry.

Government Procurement
The agreement opens a significant portion of the government procurement market in each NAFTA country on a non-discriminatory basis to suppliers from other NAFTA countries for goods, services, and construction services.

Investment
NAFTA removes significant investment barriers, provides fair treatment of investors, eliminates government requirements that distort business decisions, and provides a dispute settlement mechanism for investors.

Services

NAFTA establishes a set of principles governing services trade. Virtually all services are covered with the exception of aviation and transport, maritime, and basic telecommunications services.

Telecommunications

NAFTA provides that public telecommunications networks ("public networks") and services are to be available on reasonable and nondiscriminatory terms and conditions for firms or individuals who use those networks for conducting their business. These uses include the provision of enhanced or value-added telecommunications services and intracorporate communications.

Financial Services

NAFTA established a principles-based approach to disciplining government measures regulating financial services. This section covers measures affecting financial institutions in the banking, insurance, and securities sectors as well as other financial services. These principles are:

- *Commercial presence and cross-border services.* May establish in any NAFTA country.
- *Nondiscriminatory treatment.* Must provide both national and most favored nation (MFN) treatment.
- *Procedural "transparency."* Must make procedures transparent to applicants from other NAFTA countries. Guidelines include:

    Inform interested persons of its requirements.

    Provide information on status of application.

    Make administrative determination within 120 days.

    Allow interested persons the opportunity to comment.

Intellectual Property

NAFTA embraces copyright, patent, and intellectual property laws, binding the three countries to existing international agreements, and builds upon GATT and other international treaties.

Transformation: Maquiladoras, Foreign Trade Zone (FTZ), Bonded Warehouse

To claim NAFTA tariff, goods must, in general, have 60 percent North American content. Transformation of goods to obtain this content can be achieved in three ways: a Maquiladora, a foreign trade zone (FTZ), or a bonded warehouse (the latter two are explained in Chapter 8). The Mexican Maquiladora program, created in 1966 and still in effect, creates free zones in any location in Mexico where labor may be added to a production-sharing process. It is a business form in which goods and capital equipment can be imported into Mexico duty-free. Duties on the exported product originally were imposed only on the value-added labor content; however, now all products must meet the 60 percent regional content (average), and duties no longer are assessed on a value-added basis.

Maquiladora Implications

The Mexican Maquiladora program (now referred to as IMMEX) was instituted in 1965 as a means of promoting investment in Mexico's border region (Programa de Industrialization Fronteriza). (For additional information contact www.doc.gov.) A maquiladora is a Mexican Corporation that serves a global outsourcing function that operates under a maquila program approved for it by the Mexican Secretariat of Commerce and Industrial Development (SECOFI). The maquila program entitles the company to foreign investment participation in the capital—and in management—of up to 100% without need of any special authorization. It also entitles the company to special customs treatment, allowing duty-free temporary import of machinery, equipment, parts and materials, and administrative equipment such as computers, and communications devices, subject only to posting a bond guaranteeing that such goods will not remain in Mexico permanently. All of a maquiladora's products are exported, either directly or indirectly, through sale to another maquiladora or exporter. Companies that qualify under Mexico's current Maquiladora decree gain significant tax and duty-deferral benefits. Under the current decree, maquiladoras operating under this production-sharing program can sell into the Mexican domestic market up to 70 percent of the maquiladoras' prior year's export volume. This amount increased by 5 percent per year until January 1, 2001.

On January 1, 2001, the second stage of NAFTA took effect. As of that date, all maquiladora production could be sold into the domestic market of Mexico; however, there are restrictions on the duty-relief available on non-NAFTA originating materials. Raw materials incorporated into the assembly or manufacturing of the finished good pay the lesser of:

- The total amount of Mexican duties.
- The amount of import duties paid to the United States or Canada.

Other Existing Trade Arrangements

Trade among Central and Latin American nations has skyrocketed in recent years rising from $7 billion in 1983 to $513 billion in 2004. Much of the gains can be attributed to the movement to reduce tariffs regionally. In addition to NAFTA there already exist 10 regional trade arrangements, each of which is outlined below.

The Adean Pact

The Andean Pact, which began with the Cartagena Agreement in 1969, is one of the oldest free trade agreements in existence today. The original membership of Bolivia, Chile (since withdrawn), Colombia, Ecuador, and Peru now includes Venezuela. This market of $80 million establishes a four-level common external tariff.

The Caribbean Basin Initiative (CBI)

This trade arrangement, extended from 1984 by the U.S.–Caribbean Basin Trade Partnership Act (CBTPA) of 2000, is intended to stimulate trade with Caribbean nations. CBTPA entered into force on October 1, 2000.

There are currently 19 countries that benefit from the CBI program and, therefore, may potentially benefit from CBTPA. These countries are: Antigua and Barbuda, Aruba, Bahamas, Barbados, Belize, British Virgin Islands, Costa Rica, Dominica, Grenada, Guyana, Haiti, Jamaica, Montserrat, Netherlands Antilles, Panama, St. Kitts and Nevis, St. Lucia, St. Vincent and the Grenadines, and Trinidad and Tobago. The centerpiece is that almost all goods imported from the region without regard for quotas can enter the United States free of tariffs. Contact the Office of Latin America and Caribbean (OLAC) for CBI information at: cbisupport@ita.doc.gov.

Association of Caribbean States

Launched on January 1, 1995, this market of 200 million consumers provides preferential tariffs to Antigua and Barbuda, Cuba, Mexico, Dominica, Nicaragua, Bahamas, Dominican Republic, Barbados, Paraguay, Belize, El Salvador, Grenada, St. Kitts-Nevis, St. Lucia, Guyana, St. Vincent and the Grenadines, Haiti, Surinam, Colombia, Honduras, Trinidad and Tobago, Costa Rica, and Venezuela.

Caribbean Common Market (Caricom)

This market of 7 million consumers was created on July 4, 1973, and includes Antigua and Barbuda, Bahamas, Barbados, Belize, Dominica, Grenada, Guyana, Jamaica, St. Vincent and the Grenadines, and Trinidad and Tobago.

Caricom–Bolivia Free Trade Agreement

This free trade arrangement on selected products was launched January 1, 1995, and includes the same nations as the Caricom plus Bolivia.

Caricom–Venezuela Free Trade Agreement

Again applying only to certain products, this arrangement is the same as the Caricom with the addition of Venezuela.

Central American Common Market

This customs union comprising a market of 34.5 million people began on December 13, 1960, and includes Costa Rica, El Salvador, Guatemala, Honduras, and Nicaragua.

Group of Three

This free trade area of 155.5 million people includes only Mexico, Colombia, and Nicaragua.

Latin American Integration Association (LAIA)

This is a trade preference association formed in August 1980. Its 430 million person market consists of Argentina, Bolivia, Brazil, Chile, Colombia, Ecuador, Mexico, Paraguay, Peru, Uruguay, and Venezuela.

Mercosur (Southern Cone Common Market)

Mercosur is composed of Brazil, Argentina, Paraguay, and Uruguay and was launched on March 26, 1991.

Organization of Eastern Caribbean States

This is a customs union of Antigua and Barbuda, Dominica, Grenada, Montserrat, St. Kitts-Nevis, St. Lucia, and St. Vincent and the Grenadines.

The next chapter explains how to do business in an integrated Europe.

CHAPTER 11

DOING BUSINESS IN AN INTEGRATED EUROPE

Europe has changed. Although the expansion and integration of the European Union (EU) is not complete it includes many of the newly independent states of Middle and Eastern Europe. The twenty-seven member countries are: Austria, Belgium, Bulgaria, Cyprus, Czech Republic, Denmark, Estonia, Finland, France, Germany, Greece, Hungary, Ireland, Italy, Latvia, Lithuania, Luxembourg, Malta, Netherlands, Poland, Portugal, Romania, Slovakia, Slovenia, Spain, Sweden, and United Kingdom. Candidate countries are Croatia, Macedonia, and Turkey.

It is to be noted that the Canary Islands (Spain), Azores and Madeira (Portugal), French Guyana, Guadeloupe, Martinique, and Reunion (France) are sometimes listed separately even though they are legally a part of Spain, Portugal, and France.

This enormous economic integration represents opportunity and possible fortune. The trade potential of the European Free Trade Association (EFTA) area alone is a bonanza, let alone the EU as shown in Table 11.1.

Table 11.1 Western European Trading Potential

Country	Population (Millions)	Purchasing Power Parity National Income ($ in Billions)	Per Capita Income ($)
European Union (EU)			
Germany	82.4	2,362	28,700
France	60.7	1,737	28,700
United Kingdom	60.4	1,782	29,600
Italy	58.1	1,609	27,700
Spain	40.3	937.6	23,300
Netherlands	16.4	481.1	29,500
Belgium	10.4	316.2	30,600
Luxembourg	0.474	30.74	55,600
Denmark	5.4	174.4	32,200
Greece	10.7	126.4	21,300
Portugal	10.6	188.7	17,900
Ireland	4.0	126.4	31,900
Sweden	9.0	255.4	28,400
Austria	8.2	255.9	31,300
Finland	5.2	151.2	29,000
Cyprus	0.8	20.25	27,435
Czech Republic	10.0	172.20	16,800
Estonia	1.3	19.23	14,300
Hungary	10.1	149.3	14,900
Latvia	2.3	26.53	11,500
Lithuania	3.6	45.23	12,500
Malta	0.4	7.22	18,200
Poland	38.6	463.00	12,000
Slovakia	5.4	78.89	14,500
Slovenia	2.0	39.41	19,600
Total	**457.0**	**11,651.8**	**910,735.0**
Average	**18.3**	**466.07**	**24,429**
Pending EU Applicants			
Croatia	4.5	50.33	11,200
Turkey	69.7	508.7	7,400
European Free Trade Association (EFTA)			
Switzerland	7.5	251.9	33,800
Liechtenstein	0.33	1.78	25,000
Norway	4.6	207.3	47,000
Iceland	0.3	9.4	31,400
Total	**12.74**	**1,106.8**	**137,200**
Average	**4**	**117.3**	**34,300**

Source: CIA World Fact Book, 2008 (www.cia.gov).

This chapter discusses the major elements of doing business in Europe and covers such topics as:

- The European Union (EU)
- European Free Trade Association (EFTA)
- Enlarging the EU
- How to do business in the single market
- Doing business in Russia
- Doing business in Eastern Europe

For additional information, go to www.cia.gov or www.commerce.gov; phone: 800-USA-TRAD(E) or 202-482-2000; e-mail: Gutierrez@doc.gov or webmaster@doc.gov. To find up-to-date news, go to European Union online at www.Europe.eu. Much of the data in this chapter has been sourced from the CIA, World Fact Book, 2008 (www.cia.gov).

The European Union (EU)

The EU, established a single market when they agreed to a common external tariff (CXT) in about 1968. Subsequently they harmonized most internal tariff and nontariff rules related to their so called "four freedoms": free movement of goods, services, persons, and capital.

These four freedoms amount to a principle that individual EU member states may not adopt—measures that have the effect of restricting or interfering with intra-community trade, subject to specific exceptions provided by EU law.

In practice the EU is a modern evolution of a customs union that expanded to a common market and then to a political union with the signing of the Maastricht Treaty in 1992.

Internally, the EU is attempting to lower trade barriers, adopt a common currency, and move toward convergence of living standards. Internationally, the EU aims to bolster Europe's trade position and its political and economic power. Because of the great differences in per capita income among member states (from $7,000 to $69,000) and historic national animosities, the EU faces difficulties in devising and enforcing common policies.

HISTORICAL NOTE

The European Union had its beginning in 1951 when the Treaty of Paris established the European Coal and Steel Community (ECSC) among Belgium, France, the Federal German Republic, Italy, Luxembourg, and Holland. In 1957, the European Economic Community (EEC) was formed when the members of the European Coal and Steel Community signed the Treaty of Rome. The more popular term—European Community (EC)—is the organization that resulted from the 1967 Treaty of Fusion that merged the secretariat (the "Commission") and the intergovernmental executive body (the "Council") of the older European Economic Community with those of the European Coal and Steel Community and the European Atomic Energy Community (EURATOM), which was established to develop nuclear fuel and power for civilian purposes.

European Free Trade Association

The European Free Trade Association (EFTA) is a regional grouping established in 1960 by the Stockholm Convention; headquartered in Geneva, the EFTA now comprises Iceland, Liechtenstein, Norway, and Switzerland. EFTA member countries have gradually eliminated tariffs of manufactured goods originating and traded within EFTA. Agricultural products, for the most part, are not included on the EFTA schedule for internal tariff reductions. Each member country maintains its own external tariff schedule, and each has concluded a trade agreement with the European Community that provides for the mutual elimination of tariffs for most manufactured goods except for a few sensitive products. As a result, the European Community and EFTA form what is now called the defacto European Economic Area (EEA).

Trade Potential of the Newly Independent States

The breakup of the Soviet Union offered practically virgin territory and excellent opportunities for expansion of markets.

The peaceful revolution of 1989 saw the beginning of a movement from Marxism toward market theory. But in Central and Eastern Europe, perestroika suffered in its attempt to leap forward from state enterprise to private ownership. Because there were few entrepreneurs and little private capital, the immediate mechanism adopted by these nations became a hybrid of Marxist market theory, which takes the best of the two approaches for the good of the economic growth of the regional nations.

The year 1989 was one of the most significant years of the twentieth century. It was the year the Berlin Wall crumbled, signifying the peaceful revolution of Central European nations retreating from the non-market economics. Even more significant was 1991. It was the year the Soviet Union splintered into its individual parts. It was the year the world sifted into two worlds: the industrial "haves" and the under-developed "have nots." The new free markets of Central and Eastern Europe are shown in Table 11.2.

Enlargement of the EU

The four fundamental freedoms of the EU provide the framework for limitless boundary expansion and formation of a new Europe. The Union already welcomed 15 new members. Standing in the wings to join the EU are many nations that see benefits to the economic integration. These include the European Free Trade Association (EFTA) members as well as three nations of central Europe that have already applied.

The agreement forming the European Economic Area between the EU and the EFTA countries signified the next step toward the economic integration of all Europe.

The people of Norway have rejected joining, but five former communist countries have joined the EU: Poland, Hungary the Czech Republic, Estonia, Slovenia, and Cyprus.

A "Greater Europe," stretching from the Atlantic to the Urals will develop into an organized power if it is built around a stable nucleus capable of speaking and acting as one.

Table 11.2 The New Free Market Nations of Europe

Country	Population (Millions)	Purchasing Power Parity GDP ($ in Billions)	Purchasing Power Parity Per Capita GDP
Central Europe			
Poland	38.60	463.00	12,800
Czech Republic	10.30	172.20	16,800
Slovakia	5.40	78.89	14,500
Slovenia	2.00	39.41	19,600
Hungary	10.20	149.30	14,900
Romania	22.30	171.50	7,700
Serbia/Montenegro	10.80	26.24	2,400
Croatia	4.50	50.33	11,200
Bosnia/Herzegovina	4.00	26.21	6,500
Bulgaria	7.50	61.63	8,200
Albania	3.60	17.46	4,900
Cyprus	0.75	16.80	21,500
Total	**119.95**	**1,272.97**	**Average 11,700**
Eastern Europe			
Estonia	1.3	19.23	14,300
Latvia	2.3	26.53	11,500
Lithuania	3.6	45.23	12,500
Belarus	10.3	70.50	6,800
Ukraine	47.4	299.10	6,300
Georgia	4.7	14.45	3,100
Moldova	4.5	8.60	1,900
Russia	143.4	1,408.00	9,800
Azerbaijan	7.9	30.01	3,800
Kazakhstan	15.2	118.40	7,800
Kyrgyzstan	5.1	8.50	1,700
Tajikistan	7.2	7.45	1,190
Turkmenistan	4.9	27.60	5,700
Uzbekistan	26.9	47.59	1,800
Malta	4.0	7.90	19,900
Total	**288.7**	**2,139.09**	**Average 7,206**

Source: U.S. Central Intelligence Agency, *The World Fact Book*, 2005.

Doing Business in the Single Market

The Single European Act (SEA) contains a series of amendments to the Treaty of Rome that made it easier to negotiate the directives needed to make the single market work. The key innovation in the SEA was to extend the use of majority voting in place of unanimity in the EU's main decision-making body. Without majority voting, it would have been impossible to have passed the more than 280 separate items of legislation required to eliminate internal EU frontiers and have the single market ready by the end of 1992. The measures already adopted relate to:

- The liberalization of public procurement
- The harmonization of taxation
- The liberalization of capital markets
- Standardization, thanks to a new approach to certification and testing, and recognition of the equivalence of national standards
- The abolition of technical barriers (freedom to exercise an activity and recognition of the equivalence of training qualifications) and physical barriers (elimination of border checks) to the free movement of individuals
- The creation of an environment that encourages business cooperation by harmonizing company law and approximating legislation concerning intellectual and industrial property

National Treatment

A white paper issued in 1985 consolidated the principle of mutual recognition of national laws and regulations. This eliminated the need to create a new uniform body of EU regulations. Harmonization at the EU level was necessary only where basic health, safety, or the environment were too divergent.

Customs Duties

The EU established a common commercial policy toward third countries through adoption of a common customs tariff (CCT), which applies equally to all non-EU goods entering any part of the EU for the first time. The imported product will be eligible for "free circulation" within the EU once customs duties have been paid and all customs formalities have been completed. Free circulation means that the goods will be treated in the same manner as goods of EU origin and can move within the EU without incurring further liability to customs import charges. Steps in assessing customs duties include:

- Identify the tariff classification of the goods in the CCT and the rate that applies for that classification.
- Establish the value of the goods for customs purposes.
- Apply the CCT rate to the customs value of the goods, subject to any preferential rates which may exist if the goods originate from particular countries.

Valuation

European community valuation is based upon the principles of the General Agreement on Tariffs and Trade (GATT) valuation code. The customs value is usually based on CIF (cost, insurance, and freight) and should include all payments by the buyer made as a condition of the sale of the goods. This usually means that royalties, license payments, or sales commission accruing to the exporter on resale of the goods by the importer are included in the valuation. There are six methods of ascertaining the value, and each must be applied in turn until a suitable valuation is arrived at. These alternative methods ensure that a value can be put on the goods which are, for instance, sold at an undervalue, whether because the sale is part of a barter transaction or because it is between related companies.

Customs Procedures

The EU has adopted the international harmonized system of commodity description and coding, and it applies the annex on origin rules to the International Convention on the Simplification and Harmonization of Customs Procedures. When two or more countries are involved in the manufacture of a product, origin is determined by where the substantial process or operation that is economically justified was performed. Proof of origin rests with the importer.

As of 1988, the free movement of goods meant that they were no longer subject to checks. Some 30 documents had been reduced to one—the so-called Single Administrative Document (SAD). However, on January 1, 1993, the SAD was no longer required for internal movement, but it will remain necessary for goods crossing an EU external border with a nonmember country.

Non-member Documentation

The usual documents on commercial shipments to EU countries, irrespective of value or means of transport, are the commercial invoice, bill of lading, certificate of origin (CO) when requested by the importer or required for certain items, packing list, and, depending on the nature of the goods being shipped or on the request of the importer, various special certificates (health, sanitary, etc.).

Commercial invoices should provide a clear and precise description of the product, terms of sale, and all details necessary to establish the full CIF price.

Rules of Origin (ROO)

The EU has established rules of origin (ROO) to provide within the context of its common external commercial policy a key to any differential treatment applied to imports from non-member countries. For example, the origin of goods is a necessary concept to apply preferential tariff treatment, to charge antidumping duties, or to enforce quantitative quotas.

The question of origin is relevant for extra-community trade, at importation as well as at exportation, but not for intra-EU trade that is subject to specific rules (free circulation). In intra-EU trade, the question of origin can be pertinent only in the case where measures of commercial policy (surveillance or protective measures) are decided by the EU regarding certain goods originating in the third countries and put into free circulation in one of the member states.

The ROO applicable at importation into the EU or at exportation of goods from the EU belong in two different categories: preferential and non-preferential.

Preferential Rules

The EU has some 24 different preferential trading regimes covering more than 150 countries. The major groups are as follows:

- The six EEC-EFTA agreements (Iceland, Norway, Sweden, Finland, Austria, and Switzerland), which cover both exports and imports.
- The Mediterranean Agreements covering all the Mediterranean countries (including Jordan and the Palestinian Authority), except for Libya and Turkey, which all cover imports and three of which also cover exports (Cyprus, Malta, and Israel).
- The Lome Convention and the linked arrangement for some overseas countries and territories. These two cover most of Africa south of the Sahara (except the Republic of South Africa), the Caribbean islands (formerly dependent on EU member states), and former dependencies in the Pacific—all of these are related to imports.
- The Generalized System of Preferences (GSP) for the remaining developing countries.

Note: Originating products are those obtained by one party to the agreement in question without using third-country products, and the products which have supported a sufficient processing, where the products are obtained with use of third-country products or the processing carried out must have the effect of causing the final product to be classified under a different tariff heading than the raw materials of semi-finished goods processed.

Non-preferential Rules

The no preferential rules of origin, which also have to be applied when preferential rules are not fulfilled in a preferential context of exchanges, are laid down in Regulation (EEC) No. 802/68 of June 27, 1968, the principles of which are as follows:

- Goods wholly obtained or produced in one country shall be considered as originating in that country.
- For goods produced in more than one country, origin is established in that country in which "*the last substantial process or operation* that is *economically justified* was performed, having been carried out in an *undertaking equipped for the purpose*, and *resulting in the manufacture of a new product or representing an important stage of manufacture*." These four conditions shown in italics are cumulative and to be taken in conjunction with one another.

Certificates of origin (CO) are not required on most commercial and industrial goods exported from the United States to Europe. However, Spain requires COs on all products, with the exception of motor vehicles, and other countries such as France require it on certain other goods (e.g., textile products).

VAT Harmonization

Each EU member has a standard value-added tax (VAT) that is assessed on the sale of both domestic and imported products. The VAT is a sales or consumption tax imposed on buyers upon the sale of goods, from the beginning of the production and distribution cycle to the final sale to the consumer.

The EU exporter and importer of any given item is required to file a declaration with their local value-added tax authority in the home country. The VAT authorities in the member states are to cooperate closely to ensure that frauds are not being committed. The standard rate of VAT is between 15 and 25 percent with a range of exceptions for essential goods—food, medicines, books, transport, and so on—that qualify for a lower rate. Table 11.3 shows the rates for the 27-member community. Currently, payment of VAT is made in the country where a product or service is finally sold; however, since 1996, it is paid in the

Table 11.3 VAT Rates in the 27 Member Community

	Standard	Reduced
Austria	20.0%	10.0%
Belgium	21.0%	12.0%
Bulgaria	19%	5.0%
Cyprus	15.0%	5.0%
Czech Republic	19.0%	5.0%
Denmark	25.0%	
Estonia	18.0%	0.0–5.0%
Finland	22.0%	17.0%
France	19.6%	5.5%
Germany	16.0%	7.0%
Greece	18.0%	8.0%
Hungary	25.0%	12.0%
Italy	20.0%	9.0%
Latvia	18.0%	0.0–9.0%
Lithuania	18.0%	5.0–9.0%
Luxembourg	15.0%	6.0%
Malta	18.0%	
Netherlands	19.0%	6.0%
Poland	22.0%	7.0%
Portugal	16.0%	5.0%
Romania	18.0%	6.0%
Slovakia	19.0%	10.0%
Slovenia	20.0%	8.5%
Spain	16.0%	7.0%
Sweden	25.0%	12.0%
United Kingdom	17.5%	

country of origin. In other words firms can now buy, sell, and invest in any member state without having to go through checks or formalities when crossing intra-EU borders.

Citizens may obtain goods for their own use in any EU member state and take them across borders without being subject to controls or liable for tax.

For importers from non-EU nations, the VAT should be applied on the cost, insurance, and freight (CIF) value plus the duty charged on the particular good. Thus CIF + duty (CIF × duty rate) + VAT = total cost to importers.

Note that inasmuch as the VAT must be paid on entry into the EU and again at the point of sale, the non-member exporter may (with exceptions) recover any VAT paid on entry.

Common Currency

The euro is the common currency for 15 EU countries. Known as the euro zone it includes: Austria, Belgium, Cyprus, Finland, France, Germany, Greece, Ireland, Italy, Luxembourg, Malta, the Netherlands, Portugal, Slovenia, and Spain. It is a basket of 27 currencies dominated by a 30 percent German mark share and 20 percent French franc share. All other currencies are represented but in shares ranging from as much as 12 percent to as little as 1 percent.

How the EU Standards Process Works

The EU has developed hundreds of new product standards that are an important condition of sale. In fact, standards are one of the principal pieces of the internal market program. European-wide standards are replacing divergent national product standards. The advantage is that a manufacturer will have to meet only one European-wide standard and not have to make costly changes to meet 27 different national standards.

Mutual recognition of national standards applies to non-safety aspects of unregulated products (those not covered by EU-wide directives; examples are paper and furniture). Mutual recognition applies both to intra-European trade and trade between the EU and other countries.

Markings

For products within their scope, EU approach directives require that an EU mark be affixed to the product (or its packaging, under certain circumstances) to signify that the product complies with all relevant EU legal requirements specified in appropriate directives.

Products bearing CE mark are guaranteed free circulation within the EU market. It does not eliminate the need to obtain other marks for the product that may be recognized or expected by purchasers. These include performance marks, product or process quality marks, and marks indicating environmental friendliness or recyclability.

Quality System Registration

While the EU legislation focuses on product approval, there are many instances in which the independent assessment of a manufacturer's design and/or production process is also an important factor in marketing in the EU. Process approval in Europe generally means registration by an independent third party to the relevant standard in the ISO 9000 series (quality management and quality assurance standards). ISO 9000 registration is required in EU markets, both in legal terms and as a competitive factor. Compliance with ISO 9000 standards is referenced in specific EU product safety directives as a component of the product approval process. In a growing number of sectors, European purchasers may require suppliers to attest that they have an approved quality system in place as a condition for purchase. ISO 9000 registration may also be a competitive factor in product areas where safety or liability is a concern.

Checklist: EU Standards, Testing, and Certification

- Obtain copies of applicable EU-wide directives or regulations.
- Determine if EU-wide regulations cover your product.
- Check the EU technical requirements.
- Check if European national standards apply.
- Check if any European standards are referenced.
- Check international standards.

Distribution

Great care should be taken in selecting an importing distributor in Europe because in many EU countries, statutory provisions or traditionally developed doctrines exist that restrict the freedom of contract in the distributorship area. One of such restrictions is the rule that a distributorship agreement may not be terminated or renewed, even in accordance with its terms, without payment of special compensation to the distributor unless the distributor has been found to have committed certain statutorily defined breaches. EU law is clear in that it forbids absolute territorial limits and resale price maintenance provisions in distribution contracts.

A sales subsidiary is an alternative that should be considered in lieu of an importing distributor. With the advent of the single market, a foreign exporter need not be established in each European country; rather, a sales subsidiary in one country can transship to the entire EU and may be more profitable in the long run.

Doing Business in Russia

Russia is the most politically powerful of the independent states of the former Soviet Union, and it has instituted sweeping economic reforms including broad privatization. The nation ended 2007 with its ninth straight year of growth, averaging 7 percent annually since the financial crisis of 1998. Although high oil prices and a relatively cheap ruble initially drove this growth, since 2003 consumer demand and, more recently, investment have played a significant role. Over the last six years, fixed capital investments have averaged real gains greater than 10 percent per year and personal incomes have achieved real gains more than 12 percent per year. During this time, poverty has declined steadily and the middle class has continued to expand. The nation has also improved its international financial position since the 1998 financial crisis. This is a nation with precious natural resources, a huge consumer market, and an educated workforce. With massive shortages of consumer as well as capital goods, it continues to seek many joint-venture opportunities. Investors may now buy hard currency and repatriate profits and dividends. Foreign trade activity has not only been authorized, but it is encouraged. Russia is a member of the International Monetary Fund and the World Bank. This means, in practical terms, that there is hard-currency credit available for imports. Nevertheless, many transactions still involve barter trade.

Highest Potential Imports to Russia

Russia has an almost insatiable market for data processing machines, telecommunications equipment, medical supplies, pollution control equipment, agricultural machinery, and computer software. Of course grain and other agricultural products such as animal feed, wheat, and maize are mainstays of its importing business. Goods imported from the United States receive most favored nation rates. The Russian government imposes a VAT on most goods sold in Russia, including imported goods. A VAT is levied at a standard rate of 23 percent, but the VAT on imported goods is calculated as a percentage of the sum of the customs value of the good, the imported tariff, and the excise tax. Exemptions are available for certain investors.

Exports from Russia

Russia is a nation rich in natural resources. Hydrocarbons, 40 percent of the world's natural gas, 50 percent of the world's timber, and inorganic chemicals are available as well as iron ore, metals, and an excellent machinery production capacity. Companies exporting from Russia are required to pay an average export tariff of about 20 percent on a number of goods and services sold in cash transactions, and an average of about 30 percent for those sold in non-cash (barter) transactions.

Banks

In addition to Vnesheconombank, the former state bank of the Soviet Union, many foreign banks now have offices in Moscow: Bank of America, Credit Lyonnais, Italian Commerica, Societe General, Generale Bank, and Deutsche Bank.

Export Platforms

To assist investors and joint ventures, Russia has established a major free trade zone in Kaliningrad, a Baltic seaport and established a U.S.-Russian economic development organization.

Entry Requirements

A visa is required for business travel in Russia. For visa applications contact the Russian Consulate, 1825 Phelps Place, NW, Washington, DC 20008; phone: 202-939-8907.

The next chapter discusses how to do business in Africa.

Further Readings

The ABC of Community Law, Office for Official Publications of the European Communities, Luxembourg, 1992.

Dinan, Desond, *Ever Closer Union: An Introduction to European Integration*, Desmond Dinan, Lynne Rienner Publishers, 2005.

EC 1992: A Commerce Department Analysis of European Community Directives, volume 1, U.S. Department of Commerce, International Trade Administration, May 1989.

EC 1992: A Commerce Department Analysis of European Community Directives, Volume 2, U.S. Department of Commerce, International Trade Administration, September 1989.

EC 1992: A Commerce Department Analysis of European Community Directives, Volume 3, U.S. Department of Commerce, International Trade Administration, March 1990.

"EC Single Market Opens to Business," *Business America*, U.S. Department of Commerce, March 8, 1993.

Europe in Ten Lessons, Commission of the European Communities, Luxembourg, 1992.

The European Community 1992 and Beyond, Commission of the European Communities, Luxembourg, 1992.

European Community and Europe: A Legal Guide to Business Development, California Chamber of Commerce and California Trade and Commerce Agency, 1993.

The European Community as a Publisher, 1992–93, Office for Official Publications of the European Communities, Luxembourg, 1992.

The European Financial Common Market, Commission of the European Communities, Luxembourg, 1992.

European Trade Fairs: A Key to the World for U.S. Exporters, U.S. Department of Commerce, International Trade Administration, February 1993.

European Union, Commission of the European Communities, Luxembourg, 1992.

Freidman, Thomas L. *The World Is Flat: A Brief History of the Twenty-First Century*, Farrar, Straus and Giroux, 2004.

From Single Market to European Union, Commission of the European Communities, Luxembourg, 1992.

Hagigh, Sara E., and Mary Saunders, "Europe 1992: Preparing for the Europe of Tomorrow," *Business America*, February 24, 1992, pp. 6–8 and 30–33.

International Trade Resources Guide, California Chamber of Commerce and California Trade and Commerce Agency, 1994.

Nelson, Brent F., and Alexander Stubb Nelson, *The European Union: Readings on the Theory and Practice of European Integration*, Lynne Rienner Publishers, 2003.

Nelson, Carl A., *International Business: A Manager's Guide to Strategy in the Age of Globalism*, Thomson Business Press, 1999.

Nelson, Carl A., *Protocol for Profit: A Manager's Guide for Competing Worldwide*, Thomson Business Press, 2000.

Saunders, Mary, "Obtaining EC-Wide Certification for Industrial Products," *Business America*, March 8, 1993, pp. 28–31.

A Single Market for Goods, Commission of the European Communities, Luxembourg, 1992.

The Single Market in Action, Commission of the European Communities, Luxembourg, 1992.

Trading in the European Union, Business link, www.businesslink.gov.uk., 2008.

U.S. Department of Commerce, ITA Document, "Chemicals and European Community Directives," October 1, 1991.

U.S. Department of Commerce, ITA Document, "EC Labor Policy—An Integral Part of 1992," October 1, 1991.

U.S. Department of Commerce, ITA Document, "EC Product Standards under the Internal Market Program," February 10, 1993.

U.S. Department of Commerce, ITA Document, "The European Community and Environmental Policy and Regulations," April 1, 1991.

Van Gudenaren, John, *Uniting Europe: An Introduction to the European Union*, Rowman and Littlefield, 2004.

CHAPTER 12

DOING BUSINESS IN AFRICA

According to United Nations' figures, Africa, once the backwater of international trade, has recently surpassed Latin America in the global race for investments and economic growth. Africa is a changing continent!

With more than 50 sovereign nations, the continent of Africa is the second-largest trading area in the world. It has an estimated population of over 900 million people. According to UNESCO, more than 2,000 languages are spoken in Africa, representing an equally vast number of different cultures. However, most business continues to take place in the urban areas and there, for the sake of business, the various cultures become fused. Much of the data in this chapter has been sourced from the CIA, *World Fact Book*, 2008 (www.cia.gov).

African Trading Potential

Always rich in natural resources (diamonds, cobalt, copper, gold, manganese, and uranium), the nations of Africa are just coming into their own as international traders. They are accomplishing this by moving into new industries and taking advantage of new competencies.

Do keep in mind that most African nations were once European colonies; therefore, throughout the continent there are strong remnants of those cultures interlaced with the new. There are lingering sensitivities about colonization, so do be careful to avoid those discussions in conversation. In general, international politics and the positive achievements of the country you are visiting are good topics. Table 12.1 shows the trading potential of the African continent.

Table 12.1 African Trading Potential

		Purchasing Power Parity	
Country	Population (Millions)	National Income ($ in Billions)	Per Capita National Income ($)
North Africa			
Algeria	32.9	233.2	7,200
Egypt	78.9	303.5	3,900
Libya	5.9	65.8	11,400
Morocco	33.2	138.3	4,200
Tunisia	10.2	83.5	8,300
Total	**161.1**	**824.3**	**Average 7,000**
Central Africa			
Central African Republic	3.5	5.5	1,640
Cameroon	15.5	29.6	2,000
Chad	7.6	7.5	1,000
Congo, Republic	2.7	3.9	1,500
Gabon	1.2	7.7	6,400
Burundi	5.7	4.1	740
Dem. Rep. of Congo (Zaire)	50.5	34.9	710
Rwanda	8.1	5.5	690
Total	**98.8**	**97.7**	**Average 1,835**
East Africa			
Ethiopia	59.6	32.9	560
Kenya	28.8	43.8	1,550
Somalia	7.1	4	600
Sudan	34.5	31.2	830
Uganda	22.8	22.7	1,020
Total	**152.8**	**134.6**	**Average 912**

(*Continued*)

Table 12.1 (Continued)

Country	Population (Millions)	Purchasing Power Parity National Income ($ in Billions)	Per Capita National Income ($)
West Africa			
Benin	6.3	7.6	1,300
Gambia	1.3	1.3	2,500
Ghana	22.4	54.4	2,500
Guinea	7.5	8.8	1,180
Liberia	2.9	2.8	1,000
Mali	10.4	8.0	790
Mauritania	2.6	4.7	1,890
Niger	9.9	9.4	970
Nigeria	114.0	106.3	960
Senegal	10.0	15.6	1,600
Sierra Leone	5.3	2.7	530
Togo	5.1	8.2	1,670
Total	**192.9**	**207.7**	**Average 1,245**
Southern Africa			
Angola	11.20	11.00	1,000
Botswana	1.50	5.25	3,600
Lesotho	2.10	5.10	2,400
Mozambique	19.10	16.80	900
Namibia	1.60	6.60	4,100
South Africa	43.50	290.60	6,800
Swaziland	0.99	4.00	4,200
Tanzania	31.20	22.10	730
Zambia	9.60	8.30	880
Zimbabwe	11.00	26.20	2,400
Total	**131.78**	**395.95**	**Average 2,701**
Continent totals	**714.40**	**1,359.10**	**Average 2,171**

Source: CIA, *World Fact Book*, 2008 (www.cia.gov).

HOT TIP

All countries except Liberia, Eritrea, Gabon, Nigeria, Mauritania, and Sudan are eligible for the General System of Preferences (GSP).

American Partnership for Economic Growth

The Partnership for Economic Growth and Opportunity in Africa is an American initiative to recognize the achievements of many countries in sub-Saharan Africa (SSA) that are pursuing economic and political reform. Through this partnership, the United States seeks to provide support for accelerated growth and development by offering countries the opportunity to participate in an assistance program at one of three different levels.

Level 1 Participation

The first level offers the following:

Enhanced Market Access. There are two kinds of enhanced market access: (1) Less-developed countries that are General System of Preferences (GSP)-eligible would continue to receive basic GSP benefits, that is, duty-free access to U.S. markets for about 4,000 product groups; (2) least-developed countries that are GSP-eligible would receive enhanced GSP, which is basic GSP plus approximately 1,800 additional products.

Investment Support. The Overseas Private Investment Corporation (OPIC) issues guarantees for a proposed $150 million fund investing in the region, sponsored by private sector participants. In addition, OPIC works to secure partial guarantees for special infrastructure investment funds, with aggregate capital of up to $500 million, concentrating on economic infrastructure projects such as telecommunications, power, transportation, and financial services.

Support for Regional Integration. Up to $25 million annually can be provided under USAID's Initiative for Southern Africa (ISA) for private sector and trade-related activities in areas of regional concern, including investment policy harmonization, regional business ties, financial sector development, privatization, and facilitating cooperation between the private sector and regional governments.

Support for American–African Business Relations. Up to $1 million annually from USAID to help catalyze relations between U.S. and African firms.

Level 2 Participation

To provide additional support to those countries pursuing accelerated growth-through-reform programs, the administration offers, at the discretion of the president, the following package of opportunities:

Further Enhanced Market Access. Expansion of the GSP program by inclusion of some product groups that are currently statutorily excluded or products that have traditionally been excluded.

Debt Reduction. Support an approach that leads to the extinction of concessional bilateral debt for the poorest countries, and urge the World Bank and International Monetary Fund (IMF) boards to provide maximum relief under the Enhanced Heavily Indebted Poor Countries (HIPC) debt initiative for HIPC-eligible countries in support of their growth-promotion efforts. The administration will seek comparable action from other creditor countries.

United States–Africa Economic Cooperation Forum. A cabinet/minister-level forum to meet once a year in order to raise the level and caliber of dialogue between Africa's strongest reformers and the United States, and to highlight successes and obstacles.

Bilateral Technical Assistance to Promote Reforms. Up to $5 million annually from USAID to finance short-term technical assistance to help African governments liberalize trade and promote exports; to bring their legal regimes into compliance with WTO standards pursuant to joining the WTO; and to make financial and fiscal reforms. The U.S. Department of Agriculture will provide technical assistance to promote agribusiness linkages.

Support for Agricultural Market Liberalization. Up to $15 million annually under the new multiyear Africa Food Security Initiative to support agricultural market liberalization, export development, and agribusiness investment.

Trade Promotion. The Trade Development Agency (TDA) can increase the number of reverse trade missions focusing on growth-oriented countries.

Reprogramming Commodity Assistance. To support countries experiencing budget shortfalls in the course of their growth-through-reform programs, and to encourage more effective spending on human resource development and agricultural policy reform, the administration can take steps to focus PL-480 Title I assistance more on growth-oriented countries in SSA and can explore the possibilities of increasing funding for Title III assistance from within PL-480.

' *Support for Economic Policy Reform.* Up to $10 million annually from USAID to finance specific growth-oriented programs are made available.

Level 3 Participation

In the future, and as appropriate, the United States will be open to pursuing free trade agreements with strong-performing, growth-oriented SSA countries.

Useful Nation-by-Nation Business Information

This section is organized into five regions: North Africa, Central Africa, East Africa, West Africa, and South Africa. These groupings lend themselves to condensed statements about business and economic conditions that are useful for the foreign business person. Much of the information in the following section has been sourced from the CIA, World Fact Book, 2008 (www.cia.gov), and *Protocol for Profit: A Manager's Guide to Competing Worldwide* with the permission of International Thompson Learning Business Press.

North Africa

In this region, which includes Algeria, Egypt, Libya, Morocco, and Tunisia, you can expect business to cease five times a day for Islamic prayers. Visitors of all religions are encouraged to face Mecca out of respect. The ninth month of the Islamic calendar is called Ramadan, and during this period all work stops before noon. Thursday or Friday is the Muslim day of rest. It is common in all these states to eat with the right hand and to avoid consuming pork and alcohol.

Algeria

This is the second largest country in Africa. Oil and natural gas form the backbone of the Algerian economy. Hydrocarbons account for nearly all export receipts. The current government has made continued efforts to admit private enterprise to the hydrocarbon industry and has instituted reforms, including privatization of some public sector companies.

Egypt

In 2005, Prime Minister Ahmed Nazif's government reduced personal and corporate tax rates, reduced energy subsidies, and privatized several enterprises. The stock market boomed, and GDP grew about 5 percent per year in 2005–2006, and topped 7 percent in 2007. Despite these achievements, the government has failed to raise living standards for the average Egyptian, and has had to continue providing subsidies for basic necessities. The subsidies have contributed to a sizeable budget deficit—roughly 7.5 percent of the GDP in 2007—and represent a significant drain on the economy. Foreign direct investment has increased significantly in the past two years, but the NAZIF government will need to continue its aggressive pursuit of reforms in order to sustain the spike in investment and growth and to begin to improve economic conditions for the broader population. Egypt's export sectors—particularly natural gas—have bright prospects. The main airports are at Heliopolis, near Cairo, and at Alexandria. Egypt's marine ports are Port Said and Suez, and a free industrial zone is located in northern Sinai, all of which are serviced by inland waterways. The telecommunications system is undergoing intensive upgrading.

Libya

Libya faces a long road ahead in liberalizing the socialist-oriented economy, but initial steps—including applying for WTO membership, reducing some subsidies, and announcing plans for privatization—are laying the groundwork for a transition to a more market-based economy. The non-oil manufacturing and construction sectors, which account for more than 20 percent of the GDP, have expanded from processing mostly agricultural products to include the production of petrochemicals, iron, steel, and aluminum. Climatic conditions and poor soils severely limit agricultural output, and Libya imports about 75 percent of its food. Libya's primary agricultural water source remains the Great Manmade River Project, but significant resources are being invested in desalinization research to meet growing water demands. The per capita GDP of about $6,700 is the highest in Africa. The non-oil manufacturing and construction sectors have expanded from processing mostly agricultural products to include petrochemicals, iron, steel, and aluminum.

Morocco
Continued dependence on foreign energy and Morocco's inability to develop small- and medium-sized enterprises also contributed to the slowdown. In 2005, Morocco launched the National Initiative for Human Development (INDH), a $2 billion social development plan to address poverty and unemployment and to improve the living conditions of the country's urban slums. Moroccan authorities are implementing reform efforts to open the economy to international investors. In 2000, Morocco entered an Association Agreement with the European Union and, in 2006, entered a Free Trade Agreement (FTA) with the United States. Long-term challenges include improving education and job prospects for Morocco's youth, and closing the income gap between the rich and the poor. The most important ports in terms of cargo volumes are Casablanca, Mohammedia, Jor Lasfa, and Safi. Morocco, with a per capita GDP of $4,250, has a good telecommunications system and several international airports. Morocco is an associate member of the European Union.

Tunisia
This economy came back strongly in the latter half of the twentieth century as a result of good harvests, continued export growth, and higher domestic investment. The government appears committed to implementing its structural adjustment program supported by the International Monetary Fund and to servicing its foreign debt. Tunisia has gradually removed barriers to trade with the European Union.

Central Africa

This grouping of nations includes Burundi, Cameroon, Central African Republic, Chad, the Republic of Congo, Gabon, the Democratic Republic of the Congo (Zaire), and Rwanda.

Burundi

Burundi is a landlocked, resource-poor country with an underdeveloped manufacturing sector. The economy is predominantly agricultural with more than 90 percent of the population dependent on subsistence agriculture. Economic growth depends on coffee and tea exports, which account for 90 percent of foreign exchange earnings. The ability to pay for imports, therefore, rests primarily on weather conditions and international coffee and tea prices. Burundi grew about 5 percent annually in 2006, but the GDP growth probably fell to under 4 percent in 2007. Political stability and the end of the civil war have improved aid flows and economic activity has increased, but underlying weaknesses—a high poverty rate, poor education rates, a weak legal system, and low administrative capacity—risk undermining planned economic reforms.

Cameroon

Because of its offshore oil resources, Cameroon has one of the highest incomes per capita in tropical Africa. With support from the IMF and World Bank, the Cameroon government has begun to introduce reforms designed to spur business investment, increase efficiency in agriculture, and recapitalize the nation's banks.

Central African Republic

Subsistence agriculture, including forestry, is the backbone of the Central African Republic economy. Agricultural products accounts for about 50 percent of the GDP and 60 percent of export earnings. The diamond industry accounts for about 30 percent. Multilateral and bilateral development assistance, particularly from France, plays a major role in providing capital for new investment.

Chad

Industry is based almost entirely on the processing of agricultural products, including cotton, sugar cane, and cattle. Chad is highly dependent on foreign aid. Oil companies are exploring areas north of Lake Chad and in the Doba basin in the south.

Congo, Republic of

The current administration presides over an uneasy internal peace and faces difficult economic challenges of stimulating recovery and reducing poverty. Although the Congo's economy is a mixture of village agriculture and handicrafts, it has a beginning industrial sector based largely on oil and supporting services. Oil has supplanted forestry as the mainstay of the economy, providing about two-thirds of government revenues and exports. The government, responding to pressure from business people and the electorate, is reducing bureaucracy and government regulation.

Democratic Republic of the Congo (Zaire)

The economy of the Democratic Republic of the Congo—a nation endowed with vast potential wealth—is slowly recovering from two decades of decline. Conflict, which began in August 1998, dramatically reduced national output and government revenue, increased external debt, and resulted in the deaths of more than 3.5 million people from violence, famine, and disease. Foreign businesses curtailed operations due to uncertainty about the outcome of the conflict, lack of infrastructure, and the difficult operating environment. Conditions began to improve in late 2002 with the withdrawal of a large portion of the invading foreign troops. Although short-term prospects for improvement are dim, improved political stability would boost the country's long-term potential to effectively exploit its vast wealth of mineral and agricultural resources.

Gabon

Located along the equator, Gabon is rich in natural resources and is one of the most secure and stable countries on the continent. The economy, previously dependent on timber and manganese is now dominated by the oil sector that accounts for about 50 percent of the GDP. The high oil prices of the early 1980s contributed to a substantial increase in per capita national income, stimulated domestic demand, reinforced migration from rural to urban areas, and raised the level of real wages to among the highest in sub-Saharan Africa.

Rwanda

Rwanda is a poor rural country with about 90 percent of the population engaged in (mainly subsistence) agriculture. It is the most densely populated country in Africa and is landlocked. Primary foreign exchange earners are coffee and tea. The 1994 genocide decimated Rwanda's fragile economic base, severely impoverished the population, particularly women, and eroded the country's ability to attract private and external investment. However, Rwanda has made substantial progress in stabilizing and rehabilitating its economy to pre-1994 levels, although poverty levels are higher now. The GDP has rebounded and inflation has been curbed.

East Africa

East Africa includes the nations of Burundi, Ethiopia, Kenya, Rwanda, Somalia, Sudan, Tanzania, and Uganda.

Ethiopia

Ethiopia's poverty-stricken economy is based on agriculture, accounting for almost half of the GDP, 60 percent of exports, and 80 percent of total employment. Coffee is critical to its economy. The manufacturing sector is heavily dependent on inputs from the agricultural sector. Over 90 percent of large-scale industry, but less than 10 percent of agriculture, is state run; the government is considering selling off a portion of state-owned plants. Since 1992, because of some easing of civil strife and aid from the outside world, the economy substantially improved.

Kenya

Kenya has one of the highest annual population growth rates in the world, and this presents a serious problem for the country's economy. GDP growth in the near term has kept slightly ahead of population—annually averaging 2.2 percent. There are international airports at Nairobi, Mombassa, and Kisumu, as well as several export processing zones. Telecommunications are considered among the best in Africa.

Somalia

Despite the lack of effective national governance, Somalia has maintained a healthy informal economy, largely based on livestock, remittance/money transfer companies, and telecommunications. Agriculture is the most important sector, with livestock normally accounting for about 40 percent of the GDP and about 65 percent of export earnings.

Nomads and semi-pastoralists, who are dependent upon livestock for their livelihood, make up a large portion of the population. Livestock, hides, fish, charcoal, and bananas are Somalia's principal exports, while sugar, sorghum, corn, qat, and machined goods are the principal imports. Telecommunication firms provide wireless services in most major cities and offer the lowest international call rates on the continent. Mogadishu's main market offers a variety of goods from food to the newest electronic gadgets.

Sudan

Sudan's economy is booming on the back of increases in oil production, high oil prices, and large inflows of foreign direct investment. GDP growth registered more than 10 percent per year in 2006 and 2007. From 1997 to date, Sudan has been working with the IMF to implement macroeconomic reforms, including a managed float of the exchange rate. In January 2007, the government introduced a new currency, the Sudanese pound, at an initial exchange rate of $1.00 equals 2 Sudanese pounds.

Uganda

Uganda has substantial natural resources, including fertile soils, regular rainfall, and sizable mineral deposits of copper and cobalt. In recent years, this economy has turned in a solid performance based on continued investment in the rehabilitation of its infrastructure, improved incentives for production and exports, and gradually improving domestic security. Agriculture is the most important sector of the economy, employing over 80 percent of the workforce. Coffee is the major export crop and accounts for the bulk of export revenues.

West Africa

This grouping of countries includes Benin, Cameroon, Gambia, Ghana, Guinea, Liberia, Mali, Mauritania, Niger, Nigeria, Senegal, Sierra Leone, and Togo.

Benin

With a stable democracy in place, the government has undertaken to improve its poorly developed infrastructure and make sweeping market-oriented reforms. Agriculture accounts for about 35 percent of the GDP, employs about 60 percent of the labor force, and generates a major share of foreign exchange earnings. Port facilities and the international airport near Cortonou are being upgraded to serve as a hub for Benin's many landlocked neighbors.

Gambia

This country's official name is *The* Gambia. Although politically stable, it has no important mineral or other natural resources and has a limited agricultural base. About 75 percent of the population is engaged in crop production and livestock raising, which contribute 30 percent to the GDP. Small-scale manufacturing activity—processing peanuts, fish, and hides—accounts for less than 10 percent of GDP. Tourism is a growing industry. Gambia imports one-third of its food, all fuel, and most manufactured goods. Exports are concentrated on peanut products (about 75 percent of total value).

Ghana

Supported by substantial international assistance, Ghana has been implementing a steady economic rebuilding program, including moves toward privatization and relaxation of government controls. Ghana is heavily dependent on cocoa, gold, and timber exports and is encouraging foreign trade and investment. Ghana opened a stock exchange in 1990. Sound macro-economic management along with high prices for gold and cocoa helped sustain GDP growth in 2007.

Guinea

Guinea possesses many natural resources and considerable potential for agricultural development. Thanks to its rich mineral and other natural resources, it is now one of the few African nations where the standard of living is on the rise.

Liberia

Civil war and government mismanagement destroyed much of Liberia's economy, especially the infrastructure in and around the capital, Monrovia. Richly endowed with water, mineral resources, forests, and a climate favorable to agriculture, Liberia had been a producer and exporter of basic products, primarily raw timber and rubber. Local manufacturing, mainly foreign owned, had been small in scope. President Johnson Sirleaf, a Harvard-trained banker and administrator, has taken steps to reduce corruption, build support from international donors, and encourage private investment. Embargos on timber and diamond exports have been lifted, opening new sources of revenue for the government. The reconstruction of infrastructure and the raising of incomes in this ravaged economy will largely depend on generous financial and technical assistance from donor countries and foreign investment in key sectors, such as infrastructure and power generation. Richly endowed with water, mineral resources, forests, and a climate favorable to agriculture, Liberia is known for having little or no restrictions (almost no inspection requirements or safety standards) for registering merchant ships.

Mali

Landlocked Mali is the largest country in West Africa, but among the poorest countries in the world, with about 70 percent of its land area desert or semi-desert. Economic activity is largely confined to the riverine area irrigated by the Niger. About 10 percent of the population live as nomads, and some 80 percent of the labor force is engaged in agriculture and fishing. Industrial activity is concentrated on processing farm commodities. In consultation with international lending agencies, the government has adopted a structural adjustment program, aiming at GDP annual growth of 4.6 percent, inflation of no more than 2.5 percent on average, and a substantial reduction in the external current account deficit.

Mauritania

A majority of the population depends on agriculture and livestock for livelihood, even though most of the nomads and many subsistence farmers were forced into the cities by recurrent droughts. Mauritania has extensive deposits of iron ore, which account for almost 50 percent of total exports. The nation's coastal waters are among the richest fishing areas in the world. The country's first deep-water port opened near Nouakchott in 1986. The government has an economic reform program in consultation with the World Bank, the IMF, and major donor countries.

Niger

Niger is one of fourteen landlocked countries in Africa and the world's sixth largest uranium producer. The economy depends heavily on exploitation of these large uranium deposits. About 90 percent of the population is engaged in farming and stock raising, activities that generate almost half the national income. France is a major customer, while Germany, Japan, and Spain also make regular purchases.

Nigeria

Prior to adopting democratic elections and becoming a civil society, crime and scams were a problem in Nigeria—it was the world's major drug-smuggling and money-laundering center. Although Nigeria is Africa's leading oil-producing country, it remains very poor. Lagos has set ambitious targets for expanding oil production capacity and is offering foreign companies more attractive investment incentives. In the last year the government has begun showing the political will to implement the market-oriented reforms urged by the IMF, such as to modernize the banking system, to curb inflation by blocking excessive wage demands, and to resolve regional disputes over the distribution of earnings from the oil industry.

Senegal

This is a country ready to do international business. It has been stable since independence, and the government has relaxed trade and investment restrictions. The agricultural sector accounts for about 12 percent of the GDP and provides employment for about 80 percent of the labor force. About 40 percent of the total cultivated land is used to grow peanuts, an important export crop. Another principal economic resource is fishing, which brings in about 23 percent of total foreign exchange earnings. Mining is dominated by the extraction of phosphate, but production has faltered because of reduced worldwide demand for fertilizers in recent years. Tourism has become increasingly important to the economy. There is an international airport and a free trade zone at Dakar, the capital, as well as the second largest maritime port in West Africa. Senegal enjoys most-favored-nation trading status with the United States under the GSP and reduced rates with the European Union under the Lome Convention.

Sierra Leone

This country is ready to do business; however, the economic and social infrastructure is not well developed. Subsistence agriculture dominates the economy, generating about one-third of the GDP and employing about two-thirds of the working population. Manufacturing, which accounts for roughly 10 percent of the GDP, consists mainly of the processing of raw materials and of light manufacturing for the domestic market. Diamond mining provides an important source of hard currency. The economy suffers from high unemployment, rising inflation, large trade deficits, and a growing dependency on foreign assistance.

Togo

The economy is heavily dependent on subsistence agriculture, which accounts for about 33 percent of the GDP and provides employment for 78 percent of the labor force. Primary agricultural exports are cocoa, coffee, and cotton, which together account for about 30 percent of total export earnings. Togo is self-sufficient in basic foodstuffs when harvests are normal. In the industrial sector phosphate mining is by far the most important activity, with phosphate exports accounting for about 40 percent of total foreign exchange earnings. Togo serves as a regional commercial and trade center. The government, with IMF and World Bank support, is implementing a number of economic reform measures to encourage foreign investment and bring revenues in line with expenditures.

Southern Africa

This group of countries includes Angola, Botswana, Lesotho, Mozambique, Namibia, South Africa, Swaziland, Tanzania, Zambia, and Zimbabwe.

Angola

Angola's high growth rate is driven by its oil sector, with record oil prices and rising petroleum production. Oil production and its supporting activities contribute about 85 percent of the GDP. Increased oil production supported growth averaging more than 15 percent per year from 2004 to 2007. A postwar reconstruction boom and resettlement of displaced persons has led to high rates of growth in construction and agriculture as well. Much of the country's infrastructure is still damaged or undeveloped from the 27-year-long civil war. Subsistence agriculture provides the main livelihood for 80 to 90 percent of the population, but accounts for less than 15 percent of the GDP. Oil production is vital to the economy, contributing about 60 percent to GDP. For the long run, Angola has the advantage of rich natural resources in addition to oil—notably gold, diamonds, and arable land.

Botswana

Botswana has transformed itself from one of the poorest countries in the world to a middle-income country with a per capita GDP of more than $11,000 in 2006. The economy has historically been based on cattle raising and crops. Agriculture today provides a livelihood for more than 80 percent of the population but produces only about 50 percent of food needs. The mining industry, mostly on the strength of diamonds, has gone from generating 25 percent of the GDP in 1980 to 50 percent today. No other sector has experienced such growth, especially not agriculture, which is plagued by erratic rainfall and poor soil.

Lesotho

Small, landlocked, mountainous, and completely surrounded by South Africa, Lesotho has no important natural resources other than water. Its economy is based on agriculture, light manufacturing, and remittances from laborers employed in South Africa. The great majority of households gain their livelihoods from subsistence farming and migrant labor. Manufacturing depends largely on farm products to support the milling, canning, leather, and jute industries; other industries include textile, clothing, and construction (in particular, a major water improvement project which will permit the sale of water to South Africa).

Mozambique
Mozambique has sizable agricultural, hydropower, and transportation resources. The economy depends heavily on foreign assistance to keep afloat. Continuation of civil strife dims chances for foreign investment.

Namibia
Namibia is the fourth-largest exporter of nonfuel minerals in Africa and the world's fifth-largest producer of uranium. Alluvial diamond deposits are among the richest in the world, making Namibia a primary source for gem-quality diamonds. Namibia also produces large quantities of lead, zinc, tin, silver, and tungsten. More than half the population depends on agriculture (largely subsistence agriculture) for its livelihood.

South Africa
The nation of South Africa is without question the economic powerhouse of Africa with a gross domestic product of about $290 billion. Political reform and political stability have turned South Africa into a hot market. Many of the white one-seventh of the South African population enjoy incomes, material comforts, and health and educational standards equal to those of Western Europe. In contrast, most of the remaining population suffers from the poverty patterns of the third world, including unemployment and lack of job skills. The main strength of the economy lies in its rich mineral resources, which provide two-thirds of exports. Economic developments in the future will be driven partly by the changing relations among the various ethnic groups. Local economists estimate that the economy must grow by between 5 and 6 percent in real terms to absorb the more than 300,000 workers entering the labor force annually. There are international airports at Johannesburg and Cape Town and marine ports at all the major coastal cities. Telecommunications as well as road and rail services are extensive.

Swaziland

The economy is based on subsistence agriculture, which occupies most of the labor force and contributes nearly 25 percent to the GDP. Manufacturing, which includes a number of agroprocessing factories, accounts for another quarter of the GDP. Exports of sugar and forestry products are the main earners of hard currency. Surrounded by South Africa except for a short border with Mozambique, Swaziland is heavily dependent on South Africa, from which it receives 75 percent of its imports and to which it sends about half of its exports.

Tanzania

Tanzania is one of the poorest countries in the world. The economy depends heavily on agriculture, which accounts for more than 40 percent of the GDP, provides 85 percent of exports, and employs 80 percent of the work force. An economic recovery program announced in the mid-1980s has generated notable increases in agricultural production. The World Bank, the International Monetary Fund, and bilateral donors have provided funds to rehabilitate Tanzania's deteriorated economic infrastructure. Subsequent growth features a pickup in industrial production and a substantial increase in output of minerals led by gold. Inland waterways and two railways connect the country's several air and maritime ports.

Zambia

Zambia's economy has experienced modest growth in recent years, with real GDP growth 2005 through 2007 between 5 and 6 percent per year. Some of the world's largest copper mines are located in this country; however, economic difficulties stem from a chronically depressed level of copper production. A high inflation rate has also added to Zambia's economic woes in recent years.

Zimbabwe

Agriculture employs three-fourths of the labor force and supplies almost 40 percent of exports. The manufacturing sector, based on agriculture and mining, produces a variety of goods and contributes 35 percent to the GDP. Mining accounts for only 5 percent of both the GDP and employment, but supplies of minerals and metals account for about 40 percent of exports. The Reserve Bank of Zimbabwe routinely prints money to fund the budget deficit, causing the official annual inflation rate to rise from 32 percent in 1998, to 26,000 percent in November 2007.

Trade Blocs and Special Treaties

Through its well-developed infrastructure and deepwater ports, South Africa handles much of the trade for the whole southern African region. In order to counter the economic dominance of South Africa in the southern African region, the countries to the north of South Africa have organized themselves into various economic groupings.

Southern African Customs Union (SACU). Formed in 1970, the SACU enables Botswana, Swaziland, Lesotho, and Namibia to share in the customs revenue from their trade that passes through South African ports.

Southern African Development Conference (SADC). Member states of the SADC include those of the SACU, as well as Angola and its oil-rich enclave of Cabinda, Mozambique on the east coast and the countries of south-central Africa, Zimbabwe, Zambia, and Malawi.

Treaty for Enhanced East African Cooperation. In the eastern region of Africa the countries of Kenya, Uganda, and Tanzania have agreed to allow for the free flow of goods and people.

Economic Community of Central African States. Members of the Economic Community of Central African States are Cameroon, the Central African Republic, Chad, Equatorial Guinea, oil-rich Congo and Gabon, and the vast country of Zaire.

Economic Community of West African States (ECOWAS). The ECOWAS is a solid geographical bloc of 16 states from Nigeria in the east to Mauritania in the west. The countries of Mauritania, Mali, and Niger are located in the southern stretch of the Sahara Desert, while the remaining countries are splayed out along the coast line. As a result of their respective colonial histories, these countries are divided into French- and English-speaking states. The francophone countries include the republics of Benin, Burkina Faso, Togo, the Ivory Coast (Côte d'Ivoire), Guinea, and Senegal, while the remaining states of Nigeria, Ghana, Liberia, Sierra Leone, and the Gambia have English as their official language. The republic of Guinea Bissau is a Portuguese-speaking country to the south of Senegal.

Funding Sources

This section is not an exhaustive list of financial institutions and programs but serves as an excellent guide to sources for African investment.

Export-Import Bank of the United States (EXIM Bank)

The Export-Import Bank of the United States (EXIM Bank) provides U.S. exporters with the financing tools they need to successfully compete for business in Africa. EXIM Bank's products and initiatives help U.S. exporters in all regions of Africa, including high-risk and emerging markets.

Through the use of EXIM Bank's products, international buyers may qualify to obtain advantageous terms of credit from a U.S. exporter for short-term transactions. Transactions requiring medium- or long-term financing may qualify for an EXIM Bank commercial loan guarantee, allowing lenders to offer you competitive term financing. To learn more, go to www.exim.gov/products/special/africa/index.cfm.

Under this program, EXIM Bank is able to help small- and medium-sized companies in many African markets purchase needed U.S. goods and services to participate in the global economy.

The Africa program will assist businesses in obtaining financing for the purchase of U.S.-made spare parts, raw materials, and agricultural commodities. The short-term export credit insurance will generally be made available in the private sector through irrevocable letters of credit from creditworthy banks in the respective countries. Coverage will be provided primarily under EXIM Bank's short-term "bank letter of credit policy."

Calvert New Africa Fund

The fund has no sector-specific requirements; participating countries must have liquid capital exchange. Areas of investment include tourism, cottage industries, minerals, and technology (75 percent in South Africa). The minimum investment is $2,000. The only restriction is that the fund can invest a maximum of 5 percent of holdings in one company. Contact: Manager, Calvert New World Fund, Inc.; 103 West Main Street, 4th Floor; Durham, NC 27707; phone: 800-548-7786 or 919-688-0620/8092; fax: 919-688-9095.

Commonwealth Africa Investment Fund (COMAFIN)

This private equity fund provides risk capital for equity investments. The fund channels investment to privatized/privatizing companies, new ventures, and small- and medium-sized private sector businesses in Africa's 19 commonwealth nations. The fund size is between $62.5 million and $70 million (CDC investment, $25 million). The focus is on resource-based projects, particularly agribusiness, minerals, manufacturing, power, telecommunications, services (including tourism), and infrastructure and property development. Special emphasis is on ventures that encourage the growth of communication and trade in commonwealth countries. Contact in Zimbabwe: Phone: 011-263-70-68-59; fax: 011-263-4-70-55-03. Contact in London: Phone: 011-44-171-828-44-88; fax: 011-44-171-828-65-05.

Morgan Stanley Africa Investment Fund

This non-diversified, closed-ended fund invests in African government debt securities and in equity securities of firms organized in Africa or firms with Africa as their principal trading partner. The fund targets countries with functioning stock markets such as Botswana, Côte d'Ivoire, Egypt, Ghana, Kenya, Mauritius, Namibia, Swaziland, South Africa, and Zimbabwe. The fund size is $323.6 million. Contact: Morgan Stanley Asset Management, Inc., 1221 Avenue of the Americas, New York, NY 10020; phone: 800-221-6726.

Development Finance Company of Uganda

This company is managed by the Commonwealth Development Corporation. The $3.4 million fund is invested in 11 Ugandan companies, including a fish processing plant and the country's first rose exporting business. Contact: Development Finance Company of Uganda Limited, PO Box 2767, Crusader House, Portal Avenue, Kampala, Uganda; phone: 011-256-41-25-61-25.

New South Africa Fund

This is a non-diversified, closed-ended fund that invests primarily in South African issues and to a lesser extent in issues of other countries in southern Africa. The fund targets industries across the board in South Africa, Botswana, Lesotho, Mauritius, Namibia, Swaziland, and Zimbabwe. The fund size is $67.8 million. Contact: Bear Stearns Funds Management, 245 Park Avenue, 15th Floor, New York, NY 10167; phone: 212-272-3550; fax: 212-272-3098.

Southern Africa Fund, Inc.

This is a non-diversified, closed-end fund that invests in individual stocks of various South African companies. The fund targets industries across the board in Angola, Botswana, Lesotho, Malawi, Mozambique, Namibia, South Africa, Swaziland, Zambia, and Zimbabwe. The fund size is $90 million. Contact: Alliance Capital Management Information Line, 1345 Avenue of the Americas, New York, NY 10105; phone: 800-247-4154.

Mauritius Venture Capital Fund (MVCF)

This fund invests in early stage and start-up projects to expansions, buy-outs and buy-ins, and privatizations in the form of equity or quasi-equity amounts ranging from $100,000 to $1 million. Contact: Mauritius Equity Investment Management Limited, 6th Floor, Sir William Newton Street, Port Louis, Mauritius; phone: 011-230-211-4949; fax: 011-230-211-9393; e-mail: 101663.764@compuserve.com.

Enterprise Fund—South Africa

This fund provides development capital to medium-scale enterprises as equity and quasi-equity investment. It will support small- and medium-sized businesses in connection with the transfer of ownership and management of businesses to previously disadvantaged sectors of the economy. The fund size is $27 million. Contact: Capital Fund, PO Box 11177, 55 Fax Street, Johannesburg 2001, South Africa; phone: 011-27-11498-21-52; fax: 011-27-11-498-21-38.

Tanzania Venture Capital Fund (TVCF)

The fund and its associated company, Equity Investment Management, Ltd., now invest in 16 diverse projects ranging from cut flowers export to a regularly scheduled charter private airline. TVCF capital totals $7,610,000 with disbursements and commitments totaling $4.1 million. Contact: Tanzania Venture Capital Fund (TVCF), Equity Management Ltd., Plot 1404/45, Ghana Avenue, PO Box 8020, Dar es Salaam, Tanzania; phone: 011-255-51-444/51-348-83; fax: 011-255-51-444-440.

Cauris Investment

This is a regional venture capital fund for countries of the Union Economique et Monetaire Ouest Africa (UEMOOA) or the West African Economic and Monetary Union. It targets small- and medium-sized, majority-owned African companies in the areas of food, manufacturing, or services with potential for superior earnings. It provides such businesses with debt, equity, or lease financing. Contact: Advisor to the Director of Financial Institutions and Industries Department, Banque Ouest Africane de Developpement, BP1172 Lome, Togo; phone: 011-228-21-42-44; fax: 011-228-21-72-69.

Enterprise Fund

Sponsored by the European Union for small- and medium-sized businesses, this is a $4 million fund that supplies up to $100,000 per company.

Contact: Manager, Venture Fund Management Company, Ltd., 5th Floor Tower Block, Box 2617, SSNIT Pension House, Liberia Road, Accra, Ghana; phone: 011-233-21-66-61-65; fax: 011-233-21-66-40-55.

Ghana Venture Capital Fund (GVCF)

GVCF targets equity and loan investments of up to $500,000 with an equity stake of 10 to 40 percent. A credit return of at least 20 percent per year net of inflation is desired. All companies must be based in Ghana. Contact: Manager, Venture Fund Management Company, Ltd., 5th Floor Tower Block, Box 2617, SSNIT Pension House, Liberia Road, Accra, Ghana; phone: 011-233-21-66-61-65; fax: 011-233-21-40-55.

Africinvest

This start-up venture capital firm targets small- and medium-sized businesses in Senegal with equity investments of 5 to 20 percent. Contact: Beal et Compagnie Internationale, BP 2969, Dakar, Senegal; phone: 011-221-214-474; fax: 011-221-214-897/222-095.

Société Financiàre—Senivest

Sponsored by CBAO Bank in Dakar, SENIVEST targets small- to medium-sized businesses operating in Senegal with an asset range of CFA100 billion to CFA1,000 million with potential for rapid growth. The director general is a member of the West African Enterprise Network. Contact: SENIVEST, 3, Place de l'Independence, BP 129 Dakar, Senegal; phone: 011-221-231-000.

Bankers Association for Finance Trade (BAFT)

BAFT is an association of banks that promotes U.S. exports, international trade, and international investment. BAFT's Access to Export Capital (AXCAP) program catalogs banks and other institutions that are involved in trade finance and the services they offer. AXCAP also has a national inventory of services of government export credit agencies like EXIMBank, OPIC, and SBA. Contact: Executive Director,

Bankers Association for Finance Trade, 1120 Connecticut Avenue, NW, 5th floor, Washington, DC 20036; phone: 202-663-7575; fax: 202-663-5538; e-mail: baft@aba.com.

Commonwealth Development Corporation (CDC)

CDC invests in venture capital funds in Ghana, Tanzania, and Uganda. It has venture capital funds operating in eight sub-Saharan African countries. Contact: Commonwealth Development Corporation, One Bessborough Gardens, Pimlico, London, W1V2JQ, United Kingdom; phone: 011-44-171-828-4488.

Key Contacts and Web Sites

Let there be no doubt that Africa is changing, and one of the ways we know this is the availability and openness of information. Here are just some of the ways to gain information about African markets.

African Development Bank (ADB) Information

U.S. companies may contact the U.S. commercial liaison officer with the African Development Bank for further assistance. Contact: phone: 225-21-46-16; fax: 225-22-24-37; Web site: www.afdb.org/. *Mailing address:* American Embassy—Abidjan, U.S. Department of State, Washington, DC 20520-2010. *Street address:* Commercial Liaison to African Development Bank, U.S. and Foreign Commercial Service, Ambassade des Etats-Unis d'Amerique, 5 Rue Jesse Owens, 01 BP 1712 Abijan 01, Côte d'Ivoire.

Common Market of Eastern and Southern Africa (COMESA) Information

Members include Angola, Burundi, Comoros, Democratic Republic of the Congo, Eritrea, Ethiopia, Kenya, Madagascar, Malawi, Mauritius, Namibia, Rwanda, Seychelles, Sudan, Swaziland, Tanzania, Uganda,

Zambia, and Zimbabwe. Contact: COMESA Secretariat, Ben Bella Road, P.O. Box 30051, Lusaka, Zambia; phone: 260-1-229725; fax: 260-1-225107; e-mail: comesa@comesa.int.

Greater Horn Information Exchange Information

Members include Sudan, Eritrea, Ethiopia, Somalia, Kenya, Tanzania, Burundi, Rwanda, and Uganda. Contact: Web site: http://l98.76.84.1/HORN/.

Multilateral Investment Guaranty Agency (MIGA) Investment Promotion Network

Affiliated with the World Bank, MIGA promotes foreign investment in emerging markets, information sharing, and marketing opportunities. Contact: Web site: www.ipanet.net.

South African Development Community (SADC) Information

Members include Angola, Botswana, Lesotho, Malawi, Mozambique, Namibia, South Africa, Swaziland, Tanzania, Zambia, and Zimbabwe. Web site: www.sadcexpo.org.

United Nations—Africa Economic Recovery

Web site: www.un.org/ecosocdev/geninfo/afrec/.

The Business Person's Guide to Africa

This is a one-stop guide to the economic, political, and cultural information that is necessary for conducting business in 13 very important African countries. The countries are Algeria, Botswana, Côte d'Ivoire, Ghana, Kenya, Morocco, Nigeria, Senegal, South Africa, Tanzania, Tunisia, Uganda, and Zimbabwe.

Contact the National Minority Business Council, Inc., 25 West 45th Street, Suite 301, New York, NY 10036, Attention: International Trade

Department; phone: 877-ASK-NMBC or 212-997-4753; Web site: www.nmbc.org; e-mail: nmbc@msn.com.

The next chapter is about doing business in China and India, the two most populous nations in the world.

CHAPTER 13

DOING BUSINESS IN CHINA AND INDIA

Why bundle China with India in this book? Because these two nations have 25 percent of the world's total population and represent the largest potential area of production as well as a major market for your goods. And they are growing at a rapid pace, which means that they are excellent places to do business. China and India are the most populous nations (each with a billion people), and the whole area has potential for regional economic integration. Much of the data in this chapter has been sourced from the CIA, *World Fact Book*, 2008 (www.cia.gov).

People's Republic of China (PRC)

World trade has made the People's Republic of China (PRC) the fastest growing economy in the world. In 2004, China became the largest merchandise trader in Asia, and the third-largest exporter and importer in world merchandise trade.

Foreign trade as a percentage of the GNP has been as much as 38 percent.

China is a nation moving toward a sociocapitalistic market system. State-owned enterprises, banking, taxation, social security, and foreign trade are all in a state of reform.

In the past, trade with China was conducted by the former Ministry of Foreign Trade within the overall plans and guidelines established by the relevant communist economic policy-making bodies such as the State Economic and Financial Commission, the State Planning Commission, and the State Energy Commission.

China's foreign trade structure has undergone significant change and is still fluid. In recent times there has been a significant shift to private enterprise. A large number (about 6,000) of foreign trading corporations (FTCs) have been granted trading rights. About 300 specialized FTCs remain under the direct control of the Ministry of Foreign Trade and Economic Cooperation (MOFTEC), which still formulates centralized plans for a small portion of state-critical products.

Development Zones and Free Trade Zones

Over the years of reform the government has promoted foreign trade by establishing special economic zones (SEZs) in about 20 coastal provinces and free trade zones (FTZs) in most coastal cities. In addition to offering low wage rates, these zones provide preferential treatment including tax holidays, import/export duty exemption, low-income tax rates, and other incentives to induce technology- and export-oriented foreign investment.

Negotiating a Contract

Negotiations with China tend to be more technical, more detailed, and more time-consuming than negotiations with other countries. For Western, time-conscious people, the pace of Chinese negotiations is extremely frustrating. The Chinese approach to negotiating is characterized by patience and attention to the greatest detail. The Chinese are excellent negotiators who are well aware of the ploys and tactics used by negotiators all over the world, and they use these with varying degrees of subtlety. Chinese business people place emphasis on getting to know their trading partners and maintaining relationships with "old friends."

Payment

Chinese sellers prefer to be denominated in their own currency—renminbi (RMB). Most sales and purchase transactions in the China trade typically call for payment by irrevocable letters of credit (L/Cs) against presentation of a sight draft and shipping documents. Chinese end users must be able to acquire foreign currency for imports. That can be done three ways: (1) the government allocates hard currency for a specific deal, (2) the importer can use retained foreign currency from previous deals, or (3) a Chinese importer can request assistance from an FTC, which would buy the goods using its own foreign currency then sell the product to the end user in RMB.

Value-Added Tax (VAT)

Exporters are subject to China's value-added tax (VAT). That, together with the new consumption tax, replaces the 1958 consolidated industrial and commercial tax. Customs duty is first calculated, then consumption tax (if applicable) is determined and, last, the VAT is then computed.

Hong Kong China

Hong Kong is a "special administrative region" of China. Long noted for its huge re-export trade and as entrepôt to the world, the Chinese government has stated that it will not change the arrangement for 50 years. More than 38,000 trading companies are registered on the tiny island, all of which are eager to do business with outsiders. These companies are typically small and tend to specialize in importing, exporting, or re-exporting. Many companies that wish to foray into the China market begin by establishing operations in Hong Kong.

The best way to make contact is to try www.Hongkong.com or write or phone the Chinese consulate nearest your city. Address your inquiry to the foreign trade officer and ask to be put in touch with the appropriate office in China. Another way is to call 202-482-3583 and ask for the fax: "Everything you want to know about exporting to China," or call the Pac Rim Flash fax 202-482-3875.

You may order the excellent publication *The China Business Guide* (current year) by calling 202-512-1800 with order number 003-009-00637-6. The cost is about $5.

The Republic of China

Trading with the Republic of China (ROC), commonly known as Taiwan, has become easier and more convenient thanks to dedicated efforts of government, private enterprise, and trade-related organizations. Rules have been simplified, infrastructure improved, and trade services enhanced. Tariffs are based on the harmonized system with an average nominal rate of 8.64 percent and the average effective rate of 3.62 percent.

The best way to make contact is through CETRA or TAITRA, the premier trade-promotion agencies of the ROC. CETRA is a nonprofit organization, sponsored by domestic associations and exporters, has a staff of over 700 in its Taipei headquarters, as well as additional personnel in offices located in major cities around the world. It offers a wide range of information and service to both domestic and foreign firms. CETRA's address is Cetra Tower 4-7 Fl., 333 Keelung Road, Sec.1, Taipei, Taiwan, 110, Republic of China; phone: 886-2-2725-5200; fax: 886-2-2757-6653; Web site: www.cetra.org.tw. Other valuable contacts are www.taiwantrade.com and The Taiwan External Trade Development Council (TAITRA) is a non-profit trade promotion organization that enhances trade opportunities for world-wide trading. Contact: wwww.taitra.org.tw or e-mail taitra@taitra.or.

India

India, whose population is over 1 billion people, is the world's largest democracy. It has a labor force of about 500 million of which 60 percent is employed in agriculture or agriculture-related industries that contribute only about 22 percent of the GDP.

India is also a country driven by religious beliefs that are dominated by Hindus (83 percent), followed by Muslims (only 11 percent of India's population but the world's third-largest Muslim population of about 115 million), Sikhs (2 percent), and Christians (2 percent). Hindi is the language spoken by 30 percent of the population, but its people speak 24 other languages including English as one of the 14 official languages. Its economy has been a mixture of traditional village farming, modern agriculture, and handicrafts, but an economic revolution has brought a myriad of modern industries and support services.

Starting in 1991, India has gradually opened up its markets through economic reforms by reducing government controls on foreign trade and investment. Privatization of public-owned industries and some sectors to private and foreign players has continued amid political debate.

Recent government reforms have thrown open the economy and begun a liberalization to reduce controls on production, trade, and investment. The country's arms (outreach) are extended to foreign investment, particularly infrastructure sectors. India has a growing number of international airports. The railway system is the largest in Asia and the fourth largest in the world. India also has an excellent national highway system connecting all major cities and maritime ports, and there are export processing zones at Kandia, Mumbai (Bombay), Calcutta, Falta, Cochin, New Okha, and Visakhapatnam. Measured by purchasing power parity (PPP), the economy of India is the fourth largest in the world and it is the second fastest growing major economy in the world, with a GDP growth rate, as of the first quarter of 2006, of 9.1 percent.

India's large English-speaking middle class has contributed to the country's growth. Outsourcing has become a major base of tech companies for future targeted research and development, including the likes of Google, IBM, and Microsoft. All of this has helped the services sector to increase its share of the economy to approximately 50 percent.

India is also a major exporter of financial, research, and technology services. India's most important trading partners are the United States, China, the United Kingdom, Singapore, Hong Kong, the United Arab Emirates, Switzerland, and Belgium.

The following are things you should know when doing business in India:

- An understanding of the religions of this nation is a must before doing business.

- India is a land of castes, and you would do well to study them before traveling there.
- The British left their conservative influence.
- Titles and age are important factors of life in India.
- Do make appointments and be punctual.
- The handshake is an acceptable greeting, but you should expect and may use the *namaste* greeting as well. This is formed by placing the palms together with fingers pointed up near the chin and nodding the head.
- When greeting a woman avoid touching—not even a handshake, unless she offers her hand. Use the *namaste*.
- Expect to speak English when doing business.
- Dress conservatively. Most men wear business suits. A woman can wear suits with moderate-length skirts or even pantsuits.
- Indian women often wear a sari to special affairs; visiting women may wear them, too.
- Expect Indians to be a flexible, tolerant, and conversant people, so be careful you are not drawn into conversations about religion and politics.
- Expect Indian negotiators to be sharp at the bargaining table.
- Don't overtip—10 percent is fine in better restaurants that haven't added a service charge to the bill.
- Tip taxi drivers 10 percent by first rounding off the fare.
- Hindus are vegetarians who believe that the cow is sacred.
- Muslims eat no pork nor do they drink alcohol.
- Sikhs eat no meat and can be identified by their turbans.
- Jains do not eat meat, honey, or most vegetables. These people practice nonviolence.
- Muslims as well as Hindus generally keep their women hidden away in the kitchen, although this is less pronounced among Hindus.
- Use your right hand to accept or pass food.
- Do talk about sport, travel, art, literature, and Indian culture.
- Expect a swirl of bicycles, motorcycles, and cars. Be careful crossing streets.

- Don't talk about poverty, homelessness, or similar subjects. Avoid talking about politics.
- Never talk to a woman walking alone.

For additional information about trading with India go to www.tradeindia.com or www.indiatrade.com.

The next chapter discusses how to do business with countries in the Middle East.

CHAPTER 14

DOING BUSINESS IN THE MIDDLE EAST

Fourteen nations make up the region called the Middle East. They are Cyprus, Gaza Strip, Iran, Iraq, Israel, Jordan, Kuwait, Lebanon, Oman, Qatar, Saudi Arabia, Syria, Turkey, and the West Bank. Table 14.1 shows the major statistics of these countries. Much of the data in this chapter has been sourced from the CIA, *World Fact Book*, 2008 (www.cia.gov).

In the Middle East, except for Israel and much of Turkey, which is less orthodox, you can expect to cease business five times a day for Islamic prayers. Visitors who are not of that religion need not face Mecca, but should do so out of respect. The ninth month of the Islamic calendar is called Ramadan, and during this period all work stops before noon. Thursday or Friday is the Muslim day of rest.

It is common in all these states to eat with the right hand and not to eat pork or drink alcohol.

Nation-by-Nation Information

When developing business to business with countries in this region it is wise to conduct a review of economic information, a synopsis

Table 14.1 Middle East Trading Potential

Country	Population (Millions)	Purchasing Power Parity	
		National Income ($ in Billions)	Per Capita Income ($)
Cyprus	0.75	16.80	21,500
Gaza Strip	1.40	0.77	600
Iran	68.70	561.60	8,300
Iraq	26.70	94.10	3,400
Israel	6.40	154.50	24,600
Jordan	5.90	26.80	4,700
Kuwait	2.40	44.77	19,200
Lebanon	3.80	23.69	6,200
Oman	3.10	39.60	13,200
Qatar	0.88	23.60	27,400
Saudi Arabia	27.10	338.00	12,800
Syria	18.80	72.30	3,900
Turkey	70.40	572.00	8,200
West Bank	2.40	1.80	1,100
Totals	**238.73**	**1,970.33**	**Average 11,078**

Source: CIA, *World Fact Book*, 2008 (www.cia.gov).

of which is offered below. CIA, *World Fact Book*, 2006 (www.cia.gov) is the source for this information.

Cyprus

The Republic of Cyprus has a market economy dominated by the service sector, which accounts for 76 percent of GDP. Tourism and financial services are the most important sectors; erratic growth rates over the past decade reflect the economy's reliance on tourism, which often fluctuates with political instability in the region and economic conditions in Western Europe. Nevertheless, the economy grew a healthy 3.7 percent per year in 2004, 2005, and 2006, well above the European Union (EU) average. Cyprus joined the European exchange rate mechanism (ERM2) in May 2005 and adopted the euro in January 2008. The

Turkish Cypriot economy has roughly one-third of the per capita GDP of the south, and economic growth tends to be volatile, given north Cyprus's relative isolation, bloated public sector, reliance on the Turkish lira, and small market size. The Turkish Cypriot economy grew by 10.6 percent in 2006–2007, fueled by growth in the construction and education sectors, as well as increased employment of Turkish Cypriots in the Republic of Cyprus.

Gaza Strip

High population density, limited land access, and strict internal and external controls have kept economic conditions in the Gaza Strip—the smaller of the two areas under the Palestinian Authority (PA)—even more degraded than in the West Bank. The beginning of the second intifada in September 2000 sparked an economic downturn, largely the result of Israeli closure policies; these policies, which were imposed in response to security interests in Israel, disrupted labor and commodity relationships with the Gaza Strip. Israeli withdrawal from the Gaza Strip in September 2005 offered some medium-term opportunities for economic growth, especially given the removal of restrictions on internal movement. After Hamas violently took over the territory in June 2007, widespread private sector layoffs and shortages of most goods have resulted.

Iran

Iran is a nation tired of revolution and war and trying to rebuild. There is a growing need for foreign business and hard currency, which has brought about a change of focus toward more strengthening of the country's economic situation and less religious fervor. This has opened the door for more business with industrialized nations previously excluded by fierce anti-Western rhetoric. Iran's economy is a mixture of central planning, state ownership of oil and other large enterprises, village agriculture, and small-scale private trading and service ventures. Significant informal market activity flourishes and shortages are common. High oil prices in recent years have enabled Iran to amass nearly

$70 billion in foreign exchange reserves. Yet this increased revenue has not eased economic hardships, which include double-digit unemployment and inflation. The economy has seen only moderate growth.

Iraq

Iraq's economy is dominated by the oil sector, which has traditionally provided about 95 percent of foreign exchange earnings. Although looting, insurgent attacks, and sabotage have undermined economy rebuilding efforts, economic activity is beginning to pick up in areas recently secured by the U.S. military surge. Oil exports are approximately equal to the levels seen before Operation Iraqi Freedom, and total government revenues have benefited from high oil prices. Despite political uncertainty, Iraq is making some progress in building the institutions needed to implement economic policy and has negotiated a debt reduction agreement with the Paris Club and a new Stand-By Arrangement with the IMF. The International Compact with Iraq was established in May 2007 to integrate Iraq into the regional and global economy, and the Iraqi government is seeking to pass laws to strengthen its economy. This legislation includes a hydrocarbon law to establish a modern legal framework to allow Iraq to develop its resources and a revenue sharing law to equitably divide oil revenues within the nation, although both are still bogged down in discussions. The Central Bank has been successful in controlling inflation through appreciation of the dinar against the U.S. dollar. Reducing corruption and implementing structural reforms, such as bank restructuring and developing the private sector, will be key to Iraq's economic success.

Israel

Israel has a market economy with substantial government participation. It depends on imports of crude oil and natural resources. It has intensively developed its agricultural and industrial sectors over the past 20 years. Diamonds, magnesium, high-technology equipment, and agricultural products (fruits and vegetables) are leading exports. Israel usually posts balance-of-payments deficits, which are covered by large transfer payments from abroad and by foreign loans. To earn needed foreign exchange, Israel has been targeting high-technology niches in international markets. Roughly half of the government's external debt is owed to the United States, its major source of economic and military aid. Israel's GDP, after contracting slightly in 2001 and 2002 due to the Palestinian conflict and troubles in the high-technology sector, has grown by about 5 percent per year since 2003. The economy grew an estimated 5.4 percent in 2007, the fastest pace since 2000. The Ben Gurion International Airport near Tel Aviv is the main conduit for air cargo. There are free trade zones located at Haifa and Eilat.

Jordan

The Persian Gulf crisis that began in August 1990 aggravated Jordan's already serious economic problems. Economic recovery depends on substantial foreign investment and aid, debt relief, and economic reform. Thus, the government has restructured its tax and intellectual property rights laws and loosened investment restrictions. Through increased trade liberalization, ambitious investment plans, and closer business relations with neighboring countries and Europe, Jordan is clearing the way for greater foreign commerce activity. Jordan's five-year plan calls for lowering trade barriers and large investments in transportation, communications, and natural resources. There are international airports at Amman, Aqaba, and Zisya. The highway system is one of the best in the Middle East and is linked to neighboring countries. There are free trade zones in Zarka and Aqaba.

Kuwait

Kuwait is a small and rich country with a relatively open economy and self-reported crude oil reserves of about 96 billion barrels—10 percent of world reserves. Petroleum accounts for nearly half of the GDP, 95 percent of export revenues, and 80 percent of government income. Kuwait's climate limits agricultural development. Consequently, with the exception of fish, it depends almost wholly on food imports. About 75 percent of potable water must be distilled or imported. Kuwait continues its discussions with foreign oil companies to develop fields in the northern part of the country.

Lebanon

Business in Lebanon is recovering after a long period of disruption. Lebanon's 1975 civil war cut national output by half, and all but ended Lebanon's position as a Middle Eastern entrepôt and banking hub. A peace agreement in October 1990 enabled the central government to begin restoring control in Beirut (the Paris of the Middle East), collect taxes, and regain access to key port and government facilities. The Israeli–Hizballah conflict in July–August 2006 caused an estimated $3.6 billion in infrastructure damage, and prompted international donors to pledge nearly $1 billion in recovery and reconstruction assistance. Donors met again in January 2007 and pledged over $7.5 billion to Lebanon for development projects and budget support, conditioned on progress on Beirut's fiscal reform and privatization program. Internal Lebanese political tension continues to hamper economic activity, particularly in the tourism and retail sectors.

Oman

Oman has a middle-income economy with notable oil and gas resources, a substantial trade surplus, and low inflation. Work on a liquefied natural gas (LNG) facility contributes to slightly higher oil and gas exports. Oman continues to liberalize its markets, and joined the World Trade Organization (WTO) in November 2000. In 2005, Oman signed agreements with several foreign investors to boost oil reserves, build and operate a power plant, and develop a second mobile phone network in the country.

Qatar

Oil and gas account for more than 60 percent of Qatar's GDP, roughly 85 percent of export earnings, and 70 percent of government revenues. Oil and gas have given Qatar a per capita GDP of about 80 percent of that of the leading Western European industrial countries. In recent years, Qatar has consistently posted trade surpluses largely because of high oil prices and increased natural gas exports, becoming one of the world's fastest-growing and highest per capita income countries.

Saudi Arabia

Saudi Arabia has an oil-based economy with strong government controls over major economic activities. Saudi Arabia possesses 20 percent of the world's proven petroleum reserves, ranks as the largest exporter of petroleum, and plays a leading role in the Organization of the Petroleum Exporting Countries (OPEC). Roughly 5.5 million foreign workers play an important role in the Saudi economy, particularly in the oil and service sectors. The government is encouraging private sector growth to lessen the kingdom's dependence on oil and to increase employment opportunities for the swelling Saudi population. It has begun to permit private sector and foreign investor participation in the power generation and telecom sectors. As part of its effort to attract foreign investment and diversify the economy, Saudi Arabia acceded to the WTO in 2005 after many years of negotiations. The government has announced plans to establish six "economic cities" in different regions of the country to promote development and diversification.

Syria

The Syrian economy grew by an estimated 3.3 percent in real terms in 2007 led by the petroleum and agricultural sectors, which together account for about one-half of the GDP. Higher crude oil prices countered declining oil production and led to higher budgetary and export receipts. Damascus has implemented modest economic reforms in the past few years, including cutting lending interest rates, opening private banks, consolidating all of the multiple exchange rates, raising prices on some subsidized items most notably gasoline and cement, and establishing the Damascus Stock Exchange, which is set to begin operations in 2009. President Assad signed legislative decrees to encourage corporate ownership reform, and to allow the Central Bank to issue

Treasury bills and bonds for government debt. Nevertheless, the economy remains highly controlled by the government. Long-run economic constraints include declining oil production, high unemployment and inflation, rising budget deficits, and increasing pressure on water supplies caused by heavy use in agriculture, rapid population growth, industrial expansion, and water pollution. The Government spurred economic development loosening controls on domestic and foreign investment while maintaining strict political controls. The international airport is in Damascus and the airport at Aleppo have been upgraded. There are free trade zones at Aleppo, Damascus, Latakia, and Tartous. Telecommunications are in the process of receiving significant upgrades.

Turkey

The Republic of Turkey founded in 1923 in the aftermath of World War I and the fall of the Ottoman Empire rests at the nexus of Europe and Asia. The country was founded as a secular parliamentary democracy adhering to the principle of the separation of church and state. From its inception Turkey has looked west, becoming a member of various European and world bodies seeking acceptance as a full member of the European Union. Because of its geographic location and the assimilation of diverse cultures over its long history, its people are equally at ease with European, Middle Eastern, and Asian visitors. Its 2007 census counted 71 million.

The United States has designated Turkey as one of the world's "big emerging markets" (BEMs). Manufacturing (27 percent), agriculture (15 percent), and transportation and telecommunications (12 percent) are the leading sectors in Turkey's GDP. As member of the European Custom Union, Turkey is seeking elimination of trade barriers and greater commercial investments. Global companies are exploring investment and joint venture opportunities in power generation and distribution, telecommunications, automotive, and tourism sectors. Further legislation to facilitate foreign investments, repatriation of profits, and concessions to investors is high on the government's priority list.

Agriculture remains Turkey's most important economic sector. The government has launched a multibillion dollar development plan in the southeast region of the country. It will include building a dozen dams on the Tigris and Euphrates Rivers to generate power and irrigate large tracts of farmland.

Istanbul, formerly Constantinople and Byzantium, rests on both the continents of Europe and Asia on the banks of the Bosphorus. The city is a vast commercial center with an established stock exchange and a population of 9.2 million people. Ankara is the modern capital city with a population of 3.7 million people. It is one hour by air from Istanbul. World-class hotels, modern international airports serviced by all major international airlines, and a network of superhighways make Turkey business- and tourism-friendly.

West Bank

The West Bank—the larger of the two areas under the Palestinian Authority (PA)—has experienced a general decline in economic growth and degradation in economic conditions made worse since the second intifada began in September 2000. The downturn has been largely the result of the Israeli closure policies—the imposition of border closures in response to security incidents in Israel—that disrupted labor and commodity market relationships. International aid of $1.14 billion to the West Bank and Gaza Strip in 2004 prevented the complete collapse of the economy and allowed some reforms in the government's financial operations.

Business Protocol

When doing business in the countries of the Middle East, you should pay particular attention to the business culture and protocols. Here are some tips:

- Appointments for private sector business are essential; however, this is less important in the public sector. Make appointments and try to be there 10 to 15 minutes early to give the impression that you care.

- Dress conservatively. Men should wear long-sleeved shirts and pants (a tie is not necessary). Women should wear a scarf on their heads and a full-length skirt (or a long-sleeved shirt and pants underneath a dark, loose-fitting, below-the-knee overcoat). Most Iranian women, especially followers of Homeyni, wear a "chador" (a long black dress).
- Women should not wear makeup.
- Shake hands for welcoming and greetings. Hugging and kissing is done only between friends. Instead of actually kissing, cheeks are touched during the greeting embrace.
- Don't shake hands with the opposite sex. Don't show affection in public for a member of the opposite sex.
- Exchange business cards on first meeting. Have business cards printed in Arabic.
- Use these common words: "Selam" for hello, and "merci" or "mutshakeram" for thank you.
- Private sector hours vary and depend entirely on the owner.
- The workweek is Saturday through Thursday. Businesses are closed every Thursday (normally for a half day) and all day Friday.
- Accept tea when it is offered; it is a customary rite of hospitality.
- Business is often discussed over meals in restaurants.
- It is not traditional to exchange gifts in business relations, but they are not refused. It is not a good idea to give presents to government officers—they become offended. Private sector persons can accept and exchange gifts.
- Take a small gift when you're invited to dinner (candy or flowers).
- Once within the home, traditional clothing is often discarded in exchange for Western clothes.
- Take off your shoes when entering a carpeted area.
- Avoid conversation about politics and war.
- It is okay to use first names, but in the beginning call people by their full name, including job titles when you're talking with officials.
- Working hours for government institutions are typically 8 A.M. to 3 P.M. with a one-hour lunch. Working hours for private companies are typically 9 A.M. to 2 P.M., lunch is 2 P.M. to 4 P.M., and work resumes from 4 P.M. to 8 P.M.

- Don't go near presidential palaces. Guards have been known to shoot first and ask questions later.
- Don't enter any mosque unless you have been invited to do so.
- Carry your passport with you at all times.
- Don't photograph soldiers or military installations—it's against the law.
- Don't arrive late for a flight—airport security is the tightest in the world.
- Shaking the head side to side means, "I don't understand." Shaking the head upwards and saying "tut" means no.
- Protocol is important.
- Ice breakers include the three Fs—football (soccer), food, and family.

For more information about business to business in the Middle East go to www.export.gov/middleeast.

The next chapter is about doing business in Asian Pacific Basin.

CHAPTER 15

DOING BUSINESS IN THE ASIAN PACIFIC BASIN

This chapter concentrates on Asia Pacific, including Japan and the other Pacific Basin countries. China is treated separately (see Chapter 13). Additional information is available at 800-USA-TRAD(E) (872-8723), the PACRIM hotline 202-482-3875, or www.commerce. gov. Much of the data in this chapter has been sourced from the CIA, *World Fact Book*, 2008 (www.cia.gov).

Background

By far, this trading region is the largest in the world. Asia covers over 17 million miles and has a population of over 3 billion people. In the east it includes Australia and New Zealand as well as Japan, which is the richest.

The Pacific Basin is the fastest-growing region of the world but is also the most widely dispersed (Figure 15.1). As a coherent trade area, it is weakened by its geography but as Table 15.1 shows, the economic

Figure 15.1 Dispersement of Potential Asian Bloc

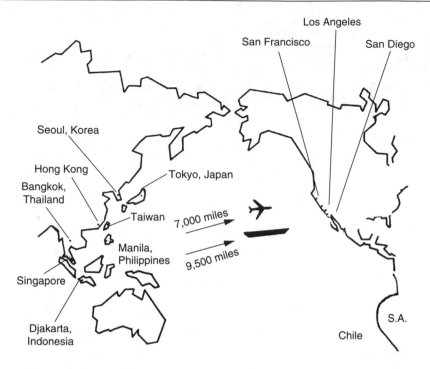

potential is formidable. Nevertheless, there are economic gaps, for instance, Indonesia's per capita GDP is about $935 billion with a per capita of $3,000, while Singapore's is about $136 billion with a per capita of $30,000 (CIA, 2006).

The Four Tigers—Hong Kong, South Korea, Singapore, and Taiwan—are best known for their extraordinary economic progress during the second half of the twentieth century. Of course, Japan stands alone as the major trading nation of Asia, but since 1960, for example, South Korea's economy has grown by about 1,500 percent and its per capita income has risen nearly eightfold.

The entire Pacific Basin region, which already accounts for 40 percent of world trade is now poised to grow at rates that were previously attributed only to the Four Tigers.

Table 15.1 Asia-Pacific Trading Potential

Country	Population (Millions)	Purchasing Power Parity	
		National Income ($ in Billions)	National Per Capita Income ($)
Australia	20.3	640.1	31,900
Brunei	0.4	6.8	23,600
Cambodia	13.9	36.8	2,600
Indonesia	245.5	935	3,800
Japan	127.5	4,018.0	31,500
Laos	6.3	13.4	2,100
Malaysia	24.4	290.2	12,100
New Zealand	4.0	101.8	25,200
Papua New Guinea	4.7	11.1	2,400
Philippines	89.5	451.3	5,100
Singapore	4.5	136.6	30,900
North Korea	23.1	40.0	1,700
South Korea	48.8	965.3	20,400
Thailand	64.6	560.7	8,300
Vietnam	84.4	258.6	3,100
Total	**755.6**	**8,465.7**	**Average 13,646.6**

Source: CIA, *World Fact Book*, 2006 (www.cia.gov).

Nation-by-Nation Information

Australia

Australia has an enviable Western-style capitalist economy with a per capita GDP on par with the four dominant Western European economies. Rising output in the domestic economy, robust business and consumer confidence, and rising exports of raw materials and agricultural products are fueling the economy. Australia's emphasis on reforms, low inflation, and growing ties with China are other key factors behind the economy's strength. Conservative fiscal policies have kept Australia's budget in surplus since 2002 due to strong revenue growth.

Brunei

Brunei's small, well-to-do economy encompasses a mixture of foreign and domestic entrepreneurship, government regulation, welfare measures, and village tradition. Crude oil and natural gas production account for nearly half of GDP and more than 90 percent of government revenues. Per capita GDP is far above most other less-developed countries, and substantial income from overseas investment supplements income from domestic production. Plans for the future include upgrading the labor force, reducing unemployment, strengthening the banking and tourist sectors, and, in general, further widening the economic base beyond oil and gas.

Indonesia

Indonesia, a vast polyglot nation, has undergone significant economic reforms. Indonesia's debt-to-GDP ratio has been declining steadily, its foreign exchange reserves are at an all-time high of over $50 billion, and its stock market has been one of the three best performers in the world in 2006 and 2007, as global investors sought out higher returns in emerging markets. The government has introduced significant reforms in the financial sector, including tax and customs reforms, the introduction of Treasury bills, and improved capital market supervision. Indonesia's new investment law, passed in March 2007, seeks to address some of the concerns of foreign and domestic investors. Indonesia still struggles with poverty and unemployment, inadequate infrastructure, corruption, a complex regulatory environment, and unequal resource distribution among regions.

Japan

Japan, a nation of dynamic people, has a population of about 127 million, a GDP of about $4 trillion, and a per capita GNP of over $31,500. That makes Japan a prime target for international market expansion.

Government and industry cooperation, a strong work ethic, mastery of high technology, and a comparatively small defense allocation

(1 percent of GDP) helped Japan advance with extraordinary rapidity to the rank of second most technologically powerful economy in the world after the United States and the third-largest economy in the world after the United States and China, measured on a purchasing power parity (PPP) basis. One notable characteristic of the economy is how manufacturers, suppliers, and distributors work together in closely knit groups called *keiretsu*.

The average Japanese tariff is low—about 3.4 percent—but on certain items, such as foodstuffs and leather goods, tariffs and quotas are quite trade restrictive. Duties are assessed on the CIF value at ad valorem or specific rates, and in a few instances are charged on a combination of both.

The key to marketing success in Japan is commitment and persistence. You must ensure that your product is of the highest quality with excellent after-sales service. Without these two qualities a product that might sell satisfactorily in other countries may not do well in Japan.

The services of the Japan External Trade Organization (JETRO) are, generally speaking, free of charge and should be the first stop for any firm contemplating doing business in or with Japan. Japan has established this nonprofit, government-supported organization dedicated to promoting mutually beneficial trade between businesses of other nations. JETRO is headquartered in Tokyo but maintains a network of 30 offices in Japan as well as 77 overseas offices in 57 countries. For the New York office, call 212-997-0400 or fax 212-997-0464. For the Houston office, phone 713-0759-9595; for Los Angeles, phone 213-624-8855; for San Francisco, phone 415-392-1333 and fax 415-788-6927; for Atlanta, phone 404-681-0600, for Chicago, phone 312-832- 6000. Or you can contact the U.S. Web site at www.jetro.org.

The U.S. Department of Commerce has set up a special Japan Export Information Center. To contact, call 202-377-2425 or the Japan Export Promotion Hotline fax 202-377-0469.

Malaysia

Malaysia, a middle-income country that transformed itself since 1971 from a producer of raw materials into an emerging multi-sector economy. Growth was almost exclusively driven by exports—particularly of electronics. As an oil and gas exporter, Malaysia has profited from higher world energy prices, although the cost of government subsidies for domestic gasoline and diesel fuel has risen and offset some of the benefit. Malaysia "unpegged" the ringgit from the U.S. dollar in 2005, but so far there has been little movement in the exchange rate. The economy remains dependent on continued growth in the United States, China, and Japan, which are top export destinations and key sources of foreign investment.

New Zealand

Over the past 20 years the government has transformed New Zealand from an agrarian economy dependent on concessionary British market access to a more industrialized, free-market economy that can compete globally. This dynamic growth has boosted real incomes, broadened and deepened the technological capabilities of the industrial sector, and contained inflationary pressures. Per capita income has risen for six consecutive years and was more than $27,800 in 2007 in purchasing power parity terms. New Zealand is heavily dependent on trade—particularly in agricultural products—to drive growth. Exports are equal to about 22 percent of the GDP. Thus far the economy has been resilient, and the labor government promises that expenditures on health, education, and pensions will increase proportionately to output.

North Korea

North Korea, one of the world's most centrally planned and least open economies, faces desperate economic conditions. Industrial capital stock is nearly beyond repair as a result of years of under-investment and shortages of spare parts. Industrial and power output have declined in parallel.

Papua New Guinea

Papua New Guinea is richly endowed with natural resources, but exploitation has been hampered by rugged terrain and the high cost of developing an infrastructure. Agriculture provides a subsistence livelihood for 85 percent of the population. Mineral deposits, including oil, copper, and gold, account for nearly two-thirds of export earnings.

The Philippines

The Philippines was less severely affected by the Asian financial crisis of 1998 than its neighbors, aided in part by its high level of annual remittances from overseas workers and no sustained run-up in asset prices or foreign borrowing prior to the crisis. From a 0.6 percent decline in 1998, the GDP expanded by 7 percent in 2007. Nonetheless, it will take a higher, sustained growth path to make appreciable progress in the alleviation of poverty given the Philippines' high annual population growth rate and unequal distribution of income.

Singapore

Singapore, a highly developed and successful free-market economy, enjoys a remarkably open and corruption-free environment, stable prices, and a per capita GDP equal to that of the four largest Western European countries. The economy depends heavily on exports, particularly in electronics and manufacturing. It was hard hit in 2001–2003 by the global recession and by the slump in the technology sector. The government hopes to establish a new growth path that will be less vulnerable to the external business cycle and will continue efforts to establish Singapore as Southeast Asia's financial and high-tech hub. Fiscal stimulus, low interest rates, a surge in exports, and internal flexibility led to vigorous growth in 2004–2007, with real GDP averaging 7 percent.

South Korea

Since the early 1960s, South Korea has achieved an incredible record of growth and integration into the high-tech modern world economy. Four decades ago, the GDP per capita was comparable with levels in the poorer countries of Africa and Asia. In 2004, South Korea joined the trillion dollar club of world economies. Today its GDP per capita is equal to the lesser economies of the European Union. This success was achieved by a system of close government and business ties, including directed credit, import restrictions, sponsorship of specific industries, and a strong labor effort.

Thailand

With a well-developed infrastructure, a free-enterprise economy, and pro-investment policies, Thailand appears to have fully recovered from the Asian financial crisis of 1998. The Thai economy grew by 4.5 percent in 2007 and has pursued preferential trade agreements with a variety of partners in an effort to boost exports and to maintain high growth. In 2004, Thailand and the United States negotiated a free trade agreement.

Regional Integration

The idea of a single Asian Pacific Basin trade bloc similar to NAFTA and the European Union is forming. The Asian bloc could become the largest trade area with a total population of over 3 billion compared to the European Union with about 350 million and NAFTA with a population of about 700 million. The Association of South East Asian Nations (ASEAN), formed in 1975, has considered expanding to become the Asia-Pacific Economic Cooperation (APEC) trade bloc or possibly the East Asia Economic Caucus (EAEC) that is similar to APEC but would exclude Canada, New Zealand, Australia, and the United States. Until an Asian regional trading area is in fact formed, business practices continue to be conducted on a nation-by-nation basis.

Asia-Pacific Economic Cooperation (APEC)

At the Asia-Pacific Economic Cooperation (APEC) summit held in September 1999, 18 Pacific Rim nations agreed to remove trade and investment barriers by the year 2010 for industrialized countries and

10 years later for developing economies. APEC is made up of Australia; Brunei Darussalam; Canada; Chile; People's Republic of China; Hong Kong, China; Indonesia; Japan; Republic of Korea; Malaysia; Mexico; New Zealand; Papua New Guinea; Peru; The Republic of the Philippines; The Russian Federation; Singapore; Chinese Taipei; Thailand; United States of America; Viet Nam.

Further Readings and Additional Information

Destination Japan: A Business Guide for the 90's (2 ed.) and China and Hong Kong business publications can be ordered from the U.S. Government Printing Office. Contact the Web site at http://bookstore.gpo.gov/.

Africa, Near East, and South Asia documents: http://bookstore.gpo.gov/.

The next chapter offers 20 tips to help you gain export/import success and big profits.

CHAPTER 16

20 KEYS TO IMPORT/EXPORT SUCCESS

Success in the international market place is measured in profits and market share. It is also measured in the satisfaction you feel in reaching new horizons and visiting places that previously were only dreams. You and your firm can be successful if you act on these 20 critical keys.

1. The most important key to success is commitment by you, the decision maker, to enter the global market.

You'll reap tax advantages, sales volume advantages, the excitement of the international experience, and lots of profit.

Change your game and get into the global competition. Get to work and earn a share of the more than $7 trillion that's out there waiting for enthusiastic entrepreneurial Americans.

2. Get beyond cultural obstacles.

Accept the fact that the rest of the world isn't like the United States. People in other countries like their way of doing things. Get used to the idea that cultural differences exist, but be assured that the differences can be understood and learned. At a minimum, the differences can be appreciated and respected. Remember that there are more similarities among peoples of the world than there are differences.

For example, the Japanese like cars, and they don't dislike American cars. The problem is that American car manufacturers haven't figured out how to satisfy the Japanese car consumer who is used to a different style and, above all, different service considerations. The world is becoming more and more internationalized.

3. Plan, plan, plan, but do not treat international trade as a stand-alone process.

Plan for success. Assuming that your initial market research effort reveals some demand for your product, either as it is or with minor redesign, develop a strategic plan for your business. From the beginning, *write* the plan. What is your competitive advantage? What are your geographical and product line priorities? How are you going to penetrate the market?

4. The market, the market, the market.

An early investigation of the market is the key that leads to success. Get an estimate of the demand for the products that you already manufacture. The best information will come from your own industry—here and overseas. Talk to those who have experience. Don't overlook available statistics and library resources. Lay out a map of the world and apply some logic. If you plan to export, divide the world into export regions and prioritize the regions based on broad assumptions of their need for your product and their ability to pay. Based on your common understanding of the various countries, regions, languages, environments, and cultures, select one or more target countries for start-up. Be sure to consider the political and financial stability of the country. Use the same logic for imports. Examine a map of the United States or your region and divide the map into target segments. Do not try to sell to all of the United States, the entire world, or even one entire foreign country immediately, but remember that nothing happens until you sell something.

5. Information is critical.

Research is critical to the success of your market plan. Begin with a list of the kinds of information you will need to support your analysis. What do you need to know about the regions of the United States (imports) or the foreign country (exports) you have selected? What level of detail will you require? Next, organize a list of the potential sources of your research. Classify your sources and begin the process of doing a logical sort of the material. You can gain the most accurate and meaningful information by traveling to the potential market.

6. What are your market goals?

Develop a well-researched, solidly reasoned market plan; it should include a background review, an analysis of the market environment, and a description of your goals in terms of your company.

7. Where there are competitors, there is a market.

Take a close look at the competition. It will be to your benefit to discover that there is competition. Why? Because where there is competition, there is a market.

8. Be persistent—don't give up.

Don't become discouraged if you find that your product is ahead of its time in the international marketplace. Don't give up on exporting. WD-40 and Coca-Cola created a global market for their products. Search for products that have an overseas market and are similar to yours.

9. Adapt the product to the market.

Learn what products your customers like and how they like the products, whether you are importing an article for American tastes or exporting a product for a foreign market. Be ready to adapt your product to the market. Redesign your product and compete.

10. Budget for success.

Include international goals in your financial plan. Treat import/export start-up as you would any other entrepreneurial venture. Budget from the beginning and keep good books. Watch your costs and cash flow. Like any new business, expect short-term losses, but plan for long-term gains.

11. Manage for success.
Develop the tactical plans that implement your overall strategic plan, such as a personnel plan, an advertising policy, a market entry, and a sales approach. Motivate your personnel by emphasizing teamwork.

12. Be patient in developing international trade.
International trade takes a little longer than domestic trade. After all, there are oceans in between, and the transportation systems are slower. Every transaction will require financing. International financing and banking methods are sophisticated and generally excellent, but negotiations and transactions across borders take more time than does domestic business.

13. The best long-term investment is a well-planned trip.
Things go right when the boss checks everything. And, in international business that means international travel. After you have developed your strategic plan, visit the overseas sources or markets you have chosen. There is nothing like getting first-hand information. You will find it interesting, rewarding, and essential to meet the people with whom you will be doing business. Even after you have established a successful sales and distribution network, it is necessary that you or representatives of your company visit at least twice a year.

14. Walk on two legs.
Carefully choose a good international banker, freight forwarder, and customs house broker. Talk with them to learn the language of international business—pricing, quotations, shipping, and getting paid. Establish a good relationship, and then stick with it. Deal with a bank that has personnel who are experienced in the international marketplace.

15. Proper communication gets sales results.

Provide customer service the international way by communicating often, clearly, and simply. Keep your overseas business partners on the team by being particularly sensitive to communications, letters, faxes, and phone calls. Above all, develop a Web site and use the Internet.

16. Expert counsel saves money.

Minimize your inevitable mistakes by asking for help. Banks, customs house brokers, freight forwarders, and the U.S. Department of Commerce are sources of free information. And most private consultants ask reasonable fees.

17. Selection of distributors is critical.

Your objective is to get your product in front of your buyer—the decision-making unit (DMU). The wrong distributor can stifle your market efforts and tie you up legally.

18. Stick to a marketing strategy.

Don't chase orders. Of course, fill the over-the-counter orders, but be proactive rather than reactive. Establish an effective marketing effort according to your market plan.

19. International partners and customers should be treated the same as domestic counterparts.

It may surprise some people that foreigner's debt ratios are often less than half of the U.S. bad debt ratios. The reason is that in the United States credit is a way of life. In overseas markets, credit is still something to be earned as a result of having a record of prompt payment. Use common sense in extending credit to overseas customers, but don't use tougher standards than you use for your U.S. clients.

20. Don't fret about the international business cycle.

Don't worry about booms or busts; just do it. International trade is exciting and profitable because there are so many side benefits. Think of traveling to such exotic places as Hong Kong or Vienna and writing off the trip as an expense to the company.

Okay, you've found the sources, developed the markets, written the business plan, and have the entrepreneurial spirit to make your own import/export business a success. The time to get into the import/export market—and make lots of money—is now! Good luck.

HOMELAND SECURITY

See the Homeland Security organization chart on the following page.

Figure A.1 Homeland Security Organization Chart

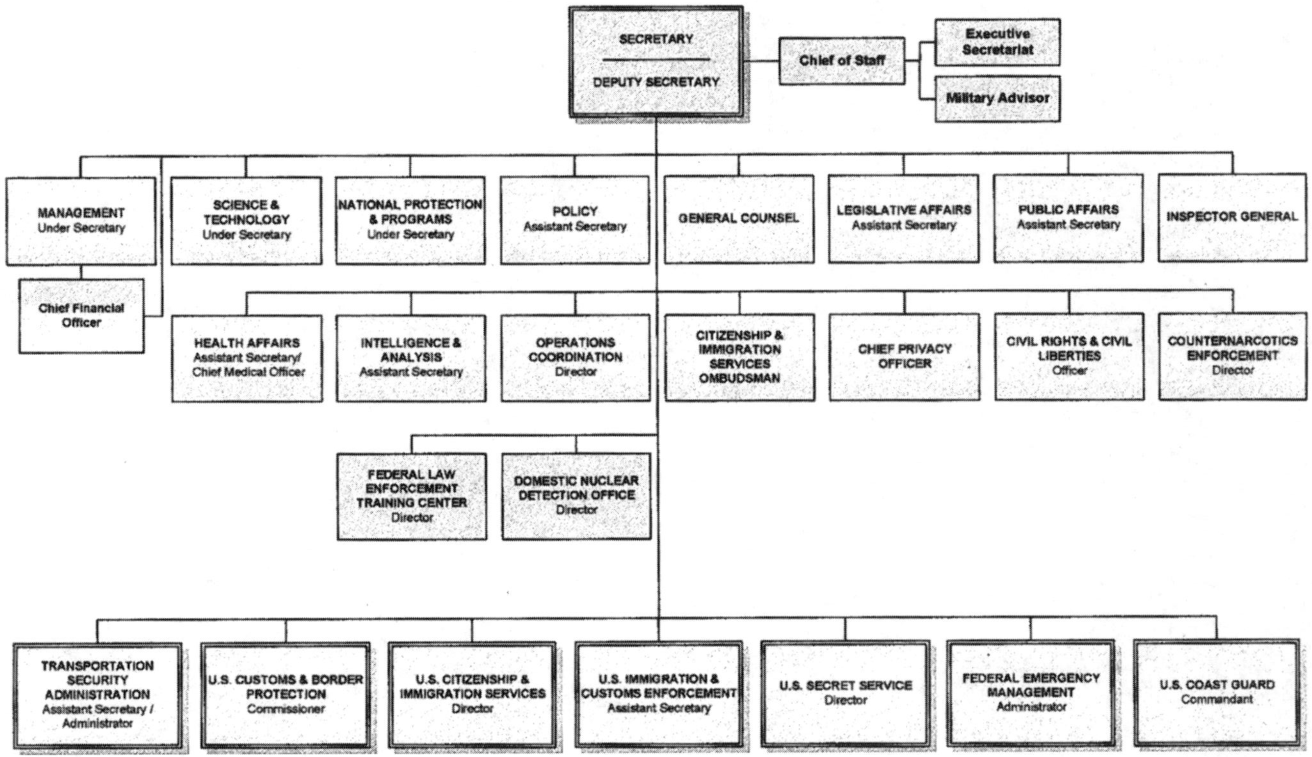

Executive Secretariat

Military Advisor

Chief of Staff

SECRETARY
DEPUTY SECRETARY

MANAGEMENT
Under Secretary

Chief Financial Officer

SCIENCE & TECHNOLOGY
Under Secretary

NATIONAL PROTECTION & PROGRAMS
Under Secretary

POLICY
Assistant Secretary

GENERAL COUNSEL

LEGISLATIVE AFFAIRS
Assistant Secretary

PUBLIC AFFAIRS
Assistant Secretary

INSPECTOR GENERAL

HEALTH AFFAIRS
Assistant Secretary/
Chief Medical Officer

INTELLIGENCE & ANALYSIS
Assistant Secretary

OPERATIONS COORDINATION
Director

CITIZENSHIP & IMMIGRATION SERVICES OMBUDSMAN

CHIEF PRIVACY OFFICER

CIVIL RIGHTS & CIVIL LIBERTIES
Officer

COUNTERNARCOTICS ENFORCEMENT
Director

FEDERAL LAW ENFORCEMENT TRAINING CENTER
Director

DOMESTIC NUCLEAR DETECTION OFFICE
Director

TRANSPORTATION SECURITY ADMINISTRATION
Assistant Secretary /
Administrator

U.S. CUSTOMS & BORDER PROTECTION
Commissioner

U.S. CITIZENSHIP & IMMIGRATION SERVICES
Director

U.S. IMMIGRATION & CUSTOMS ENFORCEMENT
Assistant Secretary

U.S. SECRET SERVICE
Director

FEDERAL EMERGENCY MANAGEMENT
Administrator

U.S. COAST GUARD
Commandant

ATA CARNET COUNTRIES AND THEIR CUSTOMS TERRITORIES (2008)

For updates and additional information on the countries listed, please go to www.atacarnet.com/CountriesandTerritoriesAccepting ATACarnets.aspx.

Algeria (DZ)
Andorra (AD)
Australia (AU)
Austria (AT)

Balearic Isles
Belarus (BY)
Belgium (BE)
Botswana (BW)
Bulgaria (BG)

Canada (CA)
Canary Islands
Ceuta
Chile (CL)
China (CN)
Corsica
Côte d'Ivoire (CI)

Croatia (HR)
Cyprus (CY)
Czech Republic (CZ)

Denmark (DK)

Estonia (EE)
European Union (EU)

Finland (FI)
France (FR)
French Guiana (GF)

Guam
Germany (DE)
Gibraltar (GI)
Greece (GR)
Guadeloupe (GP)
(Bailiwick of) Guernsey

Hong Kong (HK)
Hungary (HU)

Iceland (IS)
India (IN)
Iran (IR)*
Ireland (IE)
Isle of Man
Israel (IL)
Italy (IT)

Japan (JP)
Jersey

Korea (South) (KR)

Latvia (LV)
Lebanon (LB)
Lesotho (LS)
Liechtenstein
Lithuania (LT)
Luxembourg (LU)

Macao
Macedonia (MK)
Malaysia (MY)
Malta (MT)
Martinique (MQ)
Mauritius (MU)
Mayotte
Melilla
Miquelon
Monaco (MC)
Mongolia (MN)
Morocco (MA)

Namibia (NA)
Netherlands (NL)
New Caledonia (NC)

New Zealand (NZ)
Norway (NO)

Pakistan (PK)
Poland (PL)
Portugal (PT)
Puerto Rico

Reunion Island (RE)
Romania (RO)
Russia (RU)

Saipan
Senegal (SN)
Serbia (CS)
Singapore (SG)
Slovakia (SK)
Slovenia (SI)
South Africa (ZAR)
Spain (ES)
Sri Lanka (LK)
St. Barthelemy
St. Martin, French part
St. Pierre
Swaziland (SZ)
Sweden (SE)
Switzerland (CH)

Tahiti (French Polynesia – PF)
Taiwan (TW)[†]
Tasmania
Thailand (TH)
Tunisia (TN)
Turkey (TR)

Ukraine (UA)
United Kingdom (GB)
United States of America (US)

Wallis and Futuna Islands

*Iran is accepting carnets. However, U.S. restrictions do not allow a U.S.-issued carnet for Iran.
[†]Taiwan requires a separate carnet called a TECRO.

COMMONLY USED TRADE TERMS

International trade, like other specialized fields, has developed its own distinctive vocabulary that can mystify lay people. Many businesspeople stumble over the commonly used terms and acronyms that guide, regulate, and facilitate trade. Lack of precision in the language impedes communication, causes misunderstandings, and delays transactions. Undoubtedly, it loses sales for global companies.

This glossary of terms frequently used in global trade was sourced from the U.S. Information Agency; U.S. Departments of Commerce, State, and Treasury; the U.S. International Trade Commission; the Office of the U.S. Trade Representative; the World Trade Organization; and the UNCTAD Secretariats in Geneva. It also includes other terms researched by the author that are particularly applicable to the scope of this book.

acceptance   A bill of exchange accepted by the drawee, as evidenced by the drawee's signature on the face of the bill. The drawee commits to pay the bill at maturity. (The payee of the bill must be sure that the drawee has the means and the will to do this.)

acceptance draft   A sight draft document against acceptance. See *sight draft* and *documents against acceptance*.

acceptance letter of credit   A letter of credit (L/C) available by acceptance calling for a *time draft* (or *usance draft* in international parlance). Drawn on an intermediate accepting bank, acceptance L/Cs are popular where both buyer and seller need interim finance to facilitate cash flow.

ad valorem   According-to-value. See *duty*.

advance payment   The buyer delivers cash to the seller before the seller releases the goods. Some sellers ask for such partial payment to show good faith on the part of the buyer and also to enhance their cash flow related to the sale of a particular custom-made item. May not mean exactly the same thing as *payment in advance*.

advising bank   The bank, usually in the country of the exporter, that notifies the exporter of the availability of the *letter of credit*. The advising bank is responsible for authenticating and forwarding the L/C but makes no commitment to pay unless it agrees to act as confirming bank. See also *negotiating bank*.

advisory capacity   A term indicating that a shipper's agent or representative is not empowered to make definitive decisions or adjustments without approval of the group or individual represented. Compare *without reserve*.

affreightment (contract of)   An agreement between a steamship line (or similar carrier) and an importer or exporter in which cargo space is reserved on a vessel for a specified time and at a specified price. The importer/exporter is obligated to make payment whether or not the shipment is made.

after date   A phrase indicating that payment on a draft or other negotiable instrument is due a specified number of days after presentation of the draft to the drawee or payee. Compare *after date* and *at sight*.

after sight   A phrase indicating that the date of maturity of a draft or other negotiable instrument is fixed by the date on which it was drawn a specified number of days after presentation of the draft to the drawee or payee. Compare with *at sight* and *after date*.

agent   See *representative*.

air waybill   The carrying agreement between shipper and air carrier which is obtained from the airline used to ship the goods. Technically, it is a nonnegotiable instrument of air transportation which serves as a receipt for the shipper, indicating that the carrier has accepted the goods listed and obligates itself to carry the consignment to the airport of destination according to specified conditions. Compare *inland bill of lading, ocean bill of lading*, and *through bill of lading*.

all-risks clause   An insurance provision which provides additional coverage to an open cargo policy usually for an additional premium. Contrary to its name, the clause does not protect against all risks. The more common perils it does cover are theft, pilferage, nondelivery, fresh water damage, contact with other cargo breakage, and leakage. Loss of market and losses caused by delay are not covered.

alongside   A phrase referring to the side of a ship. Goods to be delivered alongside are to be placed on the dock or lighter within reach of the transport ship's tackle so that they can be loaded aboard the ship.

amendment—letter of credit   A change in the terms, amount, or expiration date of a letter of credit usually in the interest of the beneficiary. (Exporters should check Art. 9.d.iii of UCP 500 very carefully, especially regarding adverse amendments.)

applicant   Party (usually an importer) applying to the issuing bank to issue the letter of credit.

arbitrage   The process of buying foreign exchange, stocks, bonds, and other commodities in one market and immediately selling them in another market at higher prices.

assignment of proceeds   Document signed by the beneficiary under a letter of credit assigning the rights to proceeds from an L/C drawing to a third party. From the perspective of the assignee, an assignment differs radically from a transferable letter of credit. The latter conveys a right to the transferee to present documents under an L/C; the former does not.

ATA   A French abbreviation signifying temporary admission.

ATA carnet   A customs document that enables the holder to carry or send goods temporarily into certain foreign countries without paying duties or posting bonds.

at sight   A phrase indicating that payment on a draft or other negotiable instrument is due upon presentation or demand. Compare *after sight* and *after date*.

authority to pay   A document comparable to a revocable letter of credit but under whose terms the authority to pay the seller stems from the buyer rather than from a bank.

baby letter of credit   Second of two letters of credit in a back-to-back L/C arrangement.

back-to-back letter of credit   A baby letter of credit in which the issuing bank is secured by a master L/C. The applicant of the baby L/C will be the beneficiary of the master, and the terms of the two L/Cs will be such that documents presented under the baby can obtain payment under the master. Back-to-backs are popular among intermediaries wanting to protect their position between the buyer and manufacturer.

balance of trade   The balance between a country's exports and imports.

bank affiliate trade association   A trade association partially or wholly owned by a banking institution.

banker's acceptance   A draft bearing the acceptance of a drawee bank thus qualifying for financing in the liquid U.S. dollar banker's acceptance market. (A useful vehicle for fixed-term, fixed-rate financing, especially for banks without access to low-cost U.S. dollar funds.)

banker's bank   A bank that is established by mutual consent by independent and unaffiliated banks to provide a clearinghouse for financial transactions.

bank holding company (BHC)   Any company that directly or indirectly owns or controls, with power to vote, more than 5 percent of voting shares of each of one or more other banks.

barratry   Negligence or fraud on the part of a ship's officers or crew resulting in loss to the owners. See *open cargo policy*.

barter   Trade in which merchandise is exchanged directly for other merchandise without use of money. Barter is an important means of trade with countries using currency that is not readily convertible.

beneficiary   The person in whose favor a letter of credit is issued or a draft is drawn, usually an exporter.

bill of exchange   A written, unconditional demand, signed by the drawer and addressed to the drawee, to pay a sum of money at sight or at some future date (*x* days after sight or *x* days after bill of lading date) to the order of the payee or to the bearer. Frequently known as a draft or as a bill. See *draft*.

bill of lading   A document that provides the terms of the contract between the shipper and the transportation company to move freight between stated points at a specified charge. A receipt for goods delivered to a carrier for shipment, a contract of carriage, and a document of title issued by a carrier to the shipper. This transport document is the primary evidence of shipment of goods and the exporter's key to prompt payment. See also *charter party bill of lading*.

blanket policy   See *open cargo policy*.

blocked currency   Exchange that cannot be freely converted into other currencies. Cash deposit that cannot be transferred to another country because of local regulations or a shortage of foreign exchange.

bonded warehouse   A building authorized by customs authorities under bond or guarantee of compliance with revenue laws for the storage of goods without payment of duties until removal.

booking   An arrangement with a steamship company for the acceptance and carriage of freight.

broker   See *export broker*.

Brussels Tariff Nomenclature   See *Customs Cooperation Council Nomenclature*.

buying agent   An agent who buys in a country for foreign importers, especially for such large foreign users as mines, railroads, governments, and public utilities. Synonymous with *purchasing agent*.

C&F   Cost and freight. See *CFR*.

C&I   Cost and insurance. A pricing term indicating that certain costs are included in the quoted price.

carnet   A customs document allowing special categories of goods to cross international borders without payment of duties.

carrier   A transportation line that hauls cargo.

cash against documents (CAD)   Payment for goods in which a commission house or other intermediary transfers title documents to the buyer upon payment in cash.

cash in advance (CIA)   Payment for goods in which the price is paid in full before shipment is made. This method is usually used only for small purchases or when the goods are built.

cash with order (CWO)   Payment for goods in which the buyer pays when ordering and in which the transaction is binding on both parties.

certificate of free sale   A certificate, required by some foreign governments, stating that the goods for export, if products under the jurisdiction of the U.S. Federal Food and Drug Administration, are acceptable for sale in the United States; that is, that the products are sold freely without restriction. The FDA will issue shippers a letter of comment to satisfy foreign requests or regulations.

certificate of inspection   A document in which certification is made as to the good condition of the merchandise immediately prior to shipment. The buyer usually designates the inspecting organization, usually an independent inspection firm or government body.

certificate of manufacture   A statement by a producer, sometimes notarized, which certifies that manufacture has been completed and that the goods are at the disposal of the buyer.

certificate of origin   Certificate stating origin of goods, usually signed by the embassy in the country of the exporter which represents the country of the importer.

CFR   Cost and freight. Incoterm indicating that the sale price includes all costs of shipment and freight up to the port of destination. The buyer must insure the cargo from the port of loading because if the cargo is lost, the buyer will bear the consequence. See also *Incoterms 2000.*

chamber of commerce   An association of businesspeople whose purpose is to promote commercial and industrial interests in the community.

charter party   A written contract, usually on a special form, between the owner of a vessel and a charterer who rents use of the vessel or a part of its freight space. The contract generally includes the freight rates and the ports involved in the transportation.

charter party bill of lading   A bill of lading subject to a charter party arrangement. Note also that charter party bills of lading are not acceptable under letters of credit unless allowed explicitly (see UCP 500 Art. 25.a.).

CIF   Cost, insurance, and freight. Incoterm indicating that costs are included in the quoted sale price. Includes all costs of shipment and insurance and freight up to the port of destination. The seller must insure the cargo as far as the port of delivery, because if the cargo is lost, the seller will bear the consequence. See *Incoterms 2000.*

CIF&C   Cost, insurance, freight, and commission. A pricing term indicating that commission costs are included in the price.

CIF&E   Cost, insurance, freight, and exchange (currency). A pricing term indicating that currency exchange costs are included in the price.

clean bill of lading   A bill of lading signed by the transportation company indicating that the shipment has been received in good condition with no irregularities in the packing or general condition of all or any part of the shipment. See *foul bill of lading.*

clean draft   A draft to which no documents have been attached.

collecting bank   Bank in the importer's country involved in processing a collection.

collection   The procedure involved in a bank's collecting money for a seller against a draft drawn on a buyer abroad, usually through a correspondent bank.

collection papers   All documents (invoices, bills of lading, etc.) submitted to a buyer for the purpose of receiving payment for a shipment. Also the documents submitted, usually with a draft or against a letter of credit, for payment of an export shipment.

combined transport bill of lading   A bill of lading used when more than one carrier is involved in a shipment, for example when a consignment travels by rail and by sea. Sometimes referred to as a *multimodal bill of lading*.

commercial attaché   The commercial expert on the diplomatic staff of a country's embassy or large consulate in a foreign country.

commercial invoice   Seller's itemized list of goods shipped with descriptions, details, prices, and costs addressed to the buyer. The invoice should represent a complete record of the business transaction between the exporter and the foreign importer with regard to the goods sold. It is also a document of content and, therefore, must fully identify the overseas shipment as well as serve as the basis for the preparation of all other documents covering the shipment. In addition, some countries may require further documentation such as quality certificates, certificates of origin, certificates of free sale, and customs invoices.

commercial letter of credit   Common parlance in the United States for a documentary letter of credit, or DC, as it is known elsewhere. See *letter of credit*.

commission agent   See *purchasing agent* and *foreign sales representative*.

commission representative   See *foreign sales representative*.

commodity credit corporation   A government corporation controlled by a country's department or ministry of agriculture to provide financing and stability to the marketing and exporting of agricultural commodities.

common carrier An individual, partnership, or corporation that transports persons or goods for compensation.

compensation A form of countertrade in which the seller agrees to take full or partial payment in goods or services generated from the sale.

conference line. A member of a steamship conference. See *steamship conference*.

confirmation The act of a bank to add its commitment to that of the issuing bank to pay the beneficiary for compliant documents. Under Art. 9.b. of UCP 500, confirming banks must be requested or authorized by the issuing bank to "add their confirmation" to the letter of credit. Note that the act of confirmation does not relieve the issuing bank of its obligation to the beneficiary.

confirmed letter of credit Issued by a bank abroad whose validity and terms are confirmed to the beneficiary in the home bank. A letter of credit bearing the confirmation, or commitment to pay, of a second bank, most often in the country of the exporter. Confirmations are the exporter's insurance against nonpayment by the issuing bank for most reasons other than a discrepancy.

confirming bank Bank adding its commitment to pay for compliant documents to that of the issuing bank, usually at the request of same. Confirming banks are very often correspondents of issuing banks. L/C beneficiaries should understand clearly how soon the confirming bank will pay after presentation of conforming export documents.

consignee The person, firm, or representative to whom a seller or shipper sends merchandise and who, upon presentation of the necessary documents, is recognized as the owner of the merchandise for the purpose of the payment of customs duties. This term is also applied to one to whom goods are shipped, usually at the shipper's risk, when an outright sale has not been made. See *consignment*.

consignee marks See *marks*.

consignment Payment method in which the buyer pays for goods after selling them. The exporter retains title to the goods until they are sold (as well as 100 percent risk of nonpayment by the buyer). Also a term pertaining to merchandise shipped to a consignee abroad when an actual purchase has not been made, under an agreement by which the consignee is obligated to sell the goods for the account of the consignor, and to remit proceeds as goods are gold.

consolidator's bill of lading   Bill of lading issued by consolidator (forwarder) to a shipper as a receipt for goods to be consolidated with other cargoes prior to shipment.

consul   A government official residing in a foreign country who is charged with the representation of the interests of his or her country and its nationals.

consular declaration   A formal statement, made to the consul of a foreign country, describing goods to be shipped.

consular invoice   A detailed statement regarding the character of goods shipped, duly certified by the consul of the importing country at the port of shipment.

consulate   The official premises of a foreign government representative.

contingency insurance   Insurance taken out by the exporter complementary to insurance bought by the consignee abroad.

control of goods   Of vital interest to all parties involved in trade, control of goods is exercised through the transport document. It determines whether the buyer will be able to clear an inbound shipment without the transport document (and thus without paying for the documents held at the bank).

correspondent bank   A bank overseas with which a local bank has a relationship. Relationships between banks are just one factor that determine appetite for confirmation and thus have relevance to importers and exporters.

counterpurchase   One of the most common forms of countertrade in which the seller receives cash but contractually agrees to buy local products or services as a percentage of cash received and over an agreed period of time.

countertrade   International trade in which the seller is required to accept goods or other instruments of trade in partial or whole payment for its products.

countervailing duty   An extra duty imposed by importing country to offset export grants, bounties, or subsidies paid to foreign suppliers in certain countries by the government of those countries as an incentive to export.

country of origin   The country where a product is made, as determined by the amount of work done on the product in the country and attested by a certificate of origin.

credit risk insurance   A form of insurance that covers the seller against loss resulting from nonpayment of the buyer.

customs   The duties levied by a country on imports and exports. The term also applies to the procedures and organization involved in such collection.

customs broker   A firm representing the importer in dealings with customs, responsible for obtaining and submitting documents for clearing merchandise through customs, arranging inland transport, and paying related charges.

Customs Cooperation Council Nomenclature (CCCN)   The customs tariff used by many countries worldwide, including most European nations. It is also known as the Brussels Tariff Nomenclature. Compare *Standard Industrial Classification, Standard International Trade Classification*, and *tariff schedule*.

D/A   See *documents against acceptance*.

D/P   See *documents against payment*.

date draft   A draft drawn to mature in a specified number of days after the date it is issued, with or without regard to the date of acceptance.

DC   Popular abbreviation outside the Americas for documentary letter of credit. The equivalent in the United States is L/C, or more properly the commercial L/C.

deferred payment L/C   A letter of credit available by deferred payment calling for a time draft (or usance draft in international parlance) drawn on the issuing bank. Popular in cases of supplier credit.

delivery point   See *specific delivery point.*

demurrage   Storage fee for inbound merchandise held beyond the free time allowed by the shipping company. Excess time taken for loading or unloading a vessel as a result of a shipper. Charges are assessed by the shipping company.

department of commerce   An agency of government whose purpose it is to promote commercial industrial interests in the country.

devaluation   The official lowering of the value of one country's currency in terms of one or more foreign currencies. Thus, if the U.S. dollar is devaluated in relation to the French franc, one dollar will buy fewer francs than before.

discount (financial)   A deduction from the face value of commercial paper in consideration of cash by the seller before a specified date.

discrepancy   An instance in which documents presented do not conform to the L/C. Article 13.a. of UCP 500 state that "banks must examine all documents stipulated in the credit with reasonable care." In fact banks exercise extreme care, and international standard banking practice dictates that exporters must exercise detailed vigilance in preparing documents under letters of credit if they are not to be frustrated by delays in obtaining payment.

discrepancy—letter of credit   When documents presented do not conform to the terms of the letter of credit, it is referred to as a "discrepancy."

dishonor   Refusal on the part of the drawee to accept a draft or pay upon maturity.

dispatch   An amount paid by a vessel's operator to a charterer if loading or unloading is completed in less time than stipulated in the charter party.

distributor   A firm that sells directly for a manufacturer, usually on an exclusive contract for a specified territory, and who maintains an inventory on hand.

dock receipt   A receipt issued by an ocean carrier or its agent acknowledging that the shipment has been delivered or received at the dock or warehouse of the carrier.

documentary collection   An order written by the seller to the bank to deliver documents against payment, or *documents against acceptance*, to the buyer. The seller's bank will act on the instruction of the seller in a principal agent relationship and remit the documents to a branch, or a correspondent, in the country of the buyer, with instructions for collection. A key factor in the effectiveness of such collections is the control of goods exercised through the transport document.

documentary credit   See *commercial letter of credit.*

documentary draft   A draft to which documents are attached.

documentation documents   See *shipper's documents.*

documents against acceptance (D/A)   A type of payment for goods in which the documents transferring title to the goods are withheld until the buyer has accepted the draft issued against him or her.

documents against payment (D/P)   A type of payment for goods in which the documents transferring title to the goods are withheld until the buyer has paid the value of a draft issued against him or her.

Domestic International Sales Corporation (DISC)   The DISC incentive was created by the Revenue Act of 1971 and provides for deferral of federal income tax on 50 percent of the export earnings allocated to the DISC with the balance treated as dividends to the parent company. Since its enactment, the DISC had been the subject of an ongoing dispute between the United States and certain other signatories of the General Agreement on Tariffs and Trade (GATT). Other nations contended that the DISC amounted to an illegal export subsidy because it allows indefinite deferral of direct taxes on income from exports earned in the United States. Under new rules put into effect on January 1, 1985, to receive a tax benefit that is designed to equal the tax deferral provided by the DISC, exporters must establish an office abroad.

domicile The place where a draft or an acceptance is made payable.

draft The same as a bill of exchange. A written order for a certain sum of money to be transferred on a certain date from the person who owes the money or agrees to make the payment (the drawee) to the creditor to whom the money is owed (the drawer of the draft). See *date draft*, *documentary draft*, *sight draft*, and *time draft*. Also colloquial American terminology for a documentary collection. Internationally this may refer to the bill of exchange.

drawback (import) The repayment, up to 99 percent of customs duties paid on merchandise which later is exported as part of a finished product, is known as a drawback. It refers also to a refund of a domestic tax which has been paid upon exportation of imported merchandise.

drawee One on whom a draft is drawn and who owes the stated amount. See *draft*.

drawer One who draws a draft and receives payment. See *draft*.

dumping Exporting merchandise into a country (e.g., the United States) at prices below the prices in the domestic market.

duty The tax imposed by a government on merchandise imported from another country.

EDI Electronic data interchange. The exchange between computers of trade documentation. EDI can take two forms, financial and documentary, and suffers from a curse common in the world of computers, at least two message format standards. They are ANSI (popular in the United States) and EDIFACT (popular elsewhere).

EMC See *export management company*.

ETC See *export trading company*.

eurodollars   U.S. dollars on deposit in any branch of any bank located outside the United States. Likewise, euroyen are Japanese yen on deposit in banks outside Japan and may be outside of Europe too. Any eurocurrency is a foreign currency deposit and should be treated with care if offered as a form of payment. For example, a U.S. exporter offering U.S. dollars to be delivered in some countries may face a challenge to convert these eurodollars to U.S. dollars.

evergreen clause   A provision in the letter of credit for the expiration date to extend without requiring an amendment.

EX (point of origin)   A pricing term (EXF = ex factory; EXW = ex warehouse, etc.) under which the seller agrees to place the goods at the buyer's disposal at the agreed place, with costs from that point being paid by the buyer.

exchange   A pricing term indicating that costs are included in the price.

exchange permit   A governmental permit sometimes required of an importer to convert its own country's currency into foreign currency with which to pay a seller in another country.

exchange rate   The price of one currency expressed in terms of another. Exchange rates may be quoted spot, for delivery within two working days, or forward, for delivery at some future time. Exchange rates are apt to fluctuate. Any international trader with an eye for profit will be aware of the currency circumstances affecting a partner.

exchange regulations/restrictions   Restrictions imposed by an importing country to protect its foreign exchange reserves. See *exchange permit*.

excise tax   A domestic tax assessed on the manufacture, sale, or use of a commodity within a country. Usually refundable if the product is exported.

EXIMBank   Export-Import Bank of the United States.

expiration date   The final date upon which the presentation of documents and drawing of drafts under a letter of credit may be made.

export   To send goods to a foreign country or overseas territory.

export broker   One who brings together the exporter and importer for a fee and then withdraws from the transaction.

export declaration   A formal statement made to the collector of customs at a port of exit declaring full particulars about goods being exported.

export license   A governmental permit required to export certain products to certain destinations.

export management company (EMC)   A firm that acts as a local export sales agent for several noncompeting manufacturers.

export merchant   A producer or merchant who sells directly to a foreign purchaser without going through an intermediate such as an export broker.

export trading company (ETC)   Firm formed under the Export Trading Company Act of 1982 that buys domestic products for sale overseas taking title to the goods (which an export-management company usually does not do).

factor   A finance company willing to purchase a receivable at a discount, either with recourse to the seller or without. In exchange for immediate payment, the seller will transfer title to the receivable to the factor. This is a convenient but expensive alternative to other methods of converting receivables to cash.

factoring   A method used by businesses including trading companies to obtain cash for discounted accounts receivables or other assets.

FAS   Free alongside ship. Incoterm indicating that the sale price includes cost of transport to the port of embarkation, but not the costs of loading, export clearance, ocean freight, or insurance. The buyer must insure the cargo as far as the port of delivery, because if the cargo is lost, the buyer will bear the consequence. See *Incoterms 2000*.

FCIA   See *Foreign Credit Insurance Association*.

FI   Free in. A pricing term indicating that the charterer of a vessel is responsible for the cost of loading goods into the vessel.

FIO   Free in and out. A pricing term indicating that the charterer of a vessel is responsible for the cost of loading and unloading goods from the vessel.

floating policy   See *open cargo policy*.

FO   Free out. A pricing term indicating that the charterer of a vessel is responsible for the cost of loading goods from the vessel.

FOB   Free on board. Incoterm indicating that the sale price includes the cost of transport to and loading at the port of embarkation, but not the costs of export clearance, ocean freight, or insurance. The buyer must insure the cargo as far as the port of delivery, because if the cargo is lost, the buyer will bear the consequence. See *Incoterms 2000*.

force majeure   The title of a standard clause in marine contracts exempting the parties for nonfulfillment of their obligations as a result of conditions beyond their control, such as earthquakes, floods, or war.

Foreign Credit Insurance Association (FCIA)   An association of about 50 insurance companies that operate in conjunction with the EXIMBank to provide comprehensive insurance for exporters against nonpayment. The FCIA underwrites the commercial credit risks. EXIMBank covers the political risk and any excessive commercial risks.

foreign currency account   An account maintained by a bank in foreign currency and payable in that currency.

foreign distribution   See *distributor*.

foreign exchange   A currency or credit instruments of a foreign country. Also, transactions involving purchase and/or sale of currencies.

foreign freight forwarder   See *freight forwarder*.

foreign sales agent   An individual or firm that serves as the foreign representative of a domestic supplier and seeks sales abroad for the supplier.

foreign sales corporation (FSC)   An American territorial tax scheme whereby a corporation within a U.S. possession, such as the Virgin

Islands, or within a qualifying jurisdiction, such as Barbados, may exempt 15 to 30 percent of export profits from U.S. corporate tax. To qualify for special tax treatment, an FSC must be a foreign corporation, maintain a summary of its permanent books of account at the foreign office, and have at least one director resident outside of the United States. A portion of the foreign sales corporation's income (generally corresponding to the tax-deferred income of the DISC) would be exempt from U.S. tax at both the FSC and the U.S. corporate parent levels. This exemption is achieved by allowing a domestic corporation that is an FSC shareholder a 100 percent deduction for a portion of dividends received from an FSC attributable to economic activity actually conducted outside the U.S. customs territory. Interest, dividends, royalties, or other investment income of an FSC would be subject to U.S. tax.

foreign sales representative   A representative or agent residing in a foreign country who acts as a salesperson for a U.S. manufacturer, usually for a commission. Sometimes referred to as a sales agent or commission agent. See also *representative*.

foreign trade zone (FTZ)   U.S. term for a site sanctioned by the authorities in which imported goods are exempted from duties until withdrawn for domestic sale or use. Can be used for commercial warehousing, assembly plants, and reexport.

forfeit   The sale of a term debt against a discounted cash payment in which the seller forfeits the right to future payments by the debtor. A popular method for exporters of capital equipment to dispose of long-term overseas debt.

forwarder's bill of lading   Bill of lading issued by a forwarder to a shipper; a receipt for merchandise to be shipped.

foul bill of lading   A receipt for goods issued by a carrier bearing a notation that the outward containers or goods have been damaged. See also *clean bill of lading*.

FPA   Free of particular average. The title of a clause used in marine insurance indicating that partial loss or damage to a foreign shipment is not covered. (Note: Loss resulting from certain conditions, such as the sinking or burning of a ship, may be specifically exempted from the effect of the clause.)

fraud   The misrepresentation of information. All too common in international trade, especially transactional deals relating to commodities and a perfect reason why any sensible importer, exporter, or middleman will develop a relationship with a competent trade bank.

free port   An area generally encompassing a port and its surrounding locality into which goods may enter duty-free or are subject to only minimal revenue tariffs.

free sale   See *certificate of free sale*.

free trade zone   A term used by all countries (except the United States) for a site sanctioned by the authorities in which imported goods are exempted from duties until they are withdrawn for domestic sale or use. Can be used for commercial warehousing, assembly plants, and reexport. See *foreign trade zone*.

freight forwarder   A company that books shipment of goods, often as an agent for an airline. Usually, many small shipments are combined to take advantage of bulk discounts. Forwarders also may provide other services, such as trucking, warehousing, and document preparation.

General Agreement on Tariffs and Trade (GATT)   A Geneva-based organization that governed world trade until the formation of the World Trade Organization (WTO) in 1995. Formed by 23 countries at a conference in Geneva in 1947 to increase trade by lowering duties and quotas. GATT is a multilateral trade treaty among governments, embodying rights and obligations. The detailed rules set out in the agreement constitute a code that the parties to the agreement have agreed upon to govern their trading relationships.

general license (export)   Government authorization to export without specific documentary approval.

gross weight   Total weight of goods, packing, and container, ready for shipment.

guarantee letter   Commitment popular outside the United States guaranteeing payment in the event of nonperformance by the applicant. See also *standby letter of credit.*

handling charges   The forwarder's fee to a shipper client.

harmonized code   Harmonized Commodity Description and Coding System. An international classification system that assigns identification numbers to specific products. The code ensures that all parties use a consistent classification for purposes of documentation, statistical control, and duty assessment.

horizontal trade association   A trade association that exports a range of similar or identical products supplied by number of manufacturers or other producers. An association of agricultural cooperatives is a prime example.

ICC   See *International Chamber of Commerce.*

import   To bring merchandise into a country from another country or overseas territory.

import license   A governmental document that permits the importation of a product or material into a country where such licenses are necessary.

in bond   A term applied to the status of merchandise admitted provisionally into a country without payment of duties. See *bonded warehouse.*

inconvertibility   The inability to exchange the currency of one country for the currency of another.

Incoterms 2000   Terms of sale indicating costs and responsibilities included in the price under a sales contract (i.e., EXW FOB, CFR, CIF, DDP). Defined under ICC Publication No. 460, these are worldwide standardized terms that transcend borders and should be clearly understood by all parties negotiating an international sales contract.

inherent vice   An insurance term indicating defects or characteristics of a product that could lead to deterioration without outside influence. See *all-risks clause.*

inland bill of lading   A bill of lading used in transporting goods overland to the exporter's international carrier. Although a through bill of lading can sometimes be used, it is usually necessary to prepare both an inland bill of lading and an ocean bill of lading for export shipments. See also *air waybill, ocean bill of lading,* and *through bill of lading.*

inland carrier   A transportation line that handles export or import cargo between the port and inland points.

insurance certificate   A certificate furnished, usually in duplicate, whenever the seller provides ocean marine insurance. The certificates are negotiable documents and must be endorsed before being submitted to the bank. The seller can arrange to obtain an open cargo policy that the freight forwarder maintains.

International Chamber of Commerce (ICC)   A nongovernmental organization serving worldwide business. Members in 123 countries represent tens of thousands of business organizations and companies and promote world trade and investment based on free and fair competition. ICC Publishing SA, based in Paris, produces many publications, some of which are de facto standards in global commerce, such as Uniforms Customs and Practices for Documentary Credits (UCP 500), Uniform Rules for Collections (URC 522), and Incoterms 2000 (ICC 460).

international freight forwarder   See *freight forwarder.*

invoice   See *commercial invoice.*

irrevocable   An adjective attached to an L/C to denote an instrument that cannot be amended or canceled without the agreement of all parties (including the beneficiary). The adjective is popular and redundant: Under Article 6 of UCP 500, credits shall be deemed to be irrevocable unless otherwise indicated. In most circumstances, revocable L/Cs are worthless and, as a consequence, are very rare.

joint venture   A commercial or industrial arrangement in which principals of one company share control and ownership principals of other.

latest shipment date   Last day on which goods may be shipped (as evidenced by "on board" date on a bill of lading or the flight date on air waybill).

legal weight   The weight of the goods plus immediate wrappings which go along with the goods such as the contents of a tin can together with its can. See also *net weight*.

letter of credit (L/C)   An undertaking written by the issuing bank to pay the beneficiary a stated sum of money, within a certain time, against the presentation of conforming documents. Other parties to a letter of credit may be the advising bank, the confirming bank, the negotiating bank, the paying bank and the reimbursing bank, but the main contract of payment is between the issuing bank and the beneficiary. Since the issuing bank is very often located in a separate country from the beneficiary, the beneficiary relies on the advising bank, locally, for notification of the arrival of the L/C and to authenticate it. Conforming documents may consist of various export documents, as in a documentary letter of credit, or a simple statement by the beneficiary, as in a standby letter of credit.

license   See *export license*, *import license*, and *validated license*.

licensing   The grant or technical assistance service and or the use of product rights, such as a trademark in return for royalty payments.

lighter   An open or covered barge towed by a tugboat and used mainly in harbors and inland waterways.

lighterage   The loading or unloading of a ship by means of a barge, or lighter, that because of shallow water, prevents the ship from coming to shore.

marine bill of lading   B/L for shipment by sea.

marine insurance   An insurance that will compensate the owner of goods transported on the seas in the event of loss which cannot be legally recovered from the carrier. Also covers air shipments.

marks   A set of letters, numbers, and/or geometric symbols, generally followed by the name of the port of destination, placed on packages for export for identification purposes.

master letter of credit   First of two *letters of credit* in a *back-to-back L/C* arrangement.

maturity date   The date upon which a draft or acceptance becomes due for payment.

MEA   Manufacturer's export agent. See *export management company*.

most-favored-nation status   Designation of a country's status in relation to a trading partner. All countries having this designation receive equal treatment with respect to customs and tariffs.

multimodal bill of lading   A bill of lading used when more than one mode of transport is involved in a shipment; for example, when a consignment travels by rail and by sea. Sometimes referred to as a combined transport bill of lading.

named point   See *specific delivery point*.

negotiable bill of lading   Bill of lading consigned to the order of, and endorsed in blank by, the shipper. Whoever carries a negotiable bill of lading in their hand carries the document of title to the goods. That is why banks often call for a "hill set" of bills of lading under their L/Cs. See also *straight bill of lading*.

negotiating bank   The bank that checks the exporter's documents under the letter of credit and advances cash to the exporter, at a small discount, in the expectation of reimbursement by the issuing bank.

net weight   Weight of the goods alone without any immediate wrapping; for example, the weight of the contents of a tin can without the weight of the can. See *legal weight*.

nomenclature of the Customs Cooperation Council   See *Customs Cooperation Council Nomenclature*.

ocean bill of lading   A bill of lading indicating that the exporter consigns a shipment to an international carrier for transportation to a specified foreign market. Unlike an inland bill of lading, the ocean bill of lading also serves as a collection document. If it is a "straight B/L," the foreign buyer can obtain the shipment from the carrier by simply showing proof of identity. If a "negotiable B/L" is used, the buyer must first pay for the goods, post a bond, or meet other conditions agreeable to the seller. See also *air waybill, inland bill of lading,* and *through bill of lading.*

offset   A variation of countertrade in which the seller is required to assist in or arrange for the marketing of locally produced goods.

onboard bill of lading   A bill of lading in which a carrier acknowledges that goods have been placed onboard a certain vessel.

open account   A trade arrangement in which goods are shipped to a foreign buyer without guarantee of payment. The obvious risk this method poses to the supplier makes it essential that the buyer's integrity be unquestionable.

open cargo policy   Synonymous with "floating policy." An insurance policy that binds the insurer automatically to protect with insurance all shipments made by the insured from the moment the shipment leaves the initial shipping point until delivered at the destination. The insuring conditions include clauses naming such risks insured against as perils of the sea, fire, jettison, forcible theft, and barratry. See *all-risks clause, barratry,* and *perils of the sea.*

opening bank   Common terminology among bankers for issuing bank in the letter of credit process.

open insurance policy   A marine insurance policy that applies to all shipments made by an exporter over a period of time rather than to one shipment only.

OPIC   Overseas Private Investment Corporation. A wholly owned government corporation designed to promote private investment in developing countries by promoting political risk investment and some financing assistance.

"order" bill of lading   A negotiable bill of lading made out to the order of the shipper.

packing credit   Common international parlance, especially in Asia, for pre-export finance provided against a letter of credit.

packing list   A list prepared by the seller itemizing goods shipped, quantities, sizes, weights and packing marks. Very common in trade finance, the packing list should be prepared so as to be consistent with other documents especially tinder a letter of credit.

parcel post receipt   The postal authorities' signed acknowledgment of delivery to them of a shipment made by parcel post.

paying bank   The bank nominated in the letter of credit to pay out against conforming documents, without recourse. Exporters interested in their cash flow should understand whether the paying bank is in their own country or the country of their customer, the importer.

payment in advance   The buyer delivers cash to the seller before the seller releases the goods. Can be referred to as cash in advance or CAD and may not mean exactly the same as advance payment.

perils of the sea   A marine insurance term used to designate heavy weather, straining, lightning, collision, and sea water damage.

phytosanitary inspection certificate   A certificate, issued to satisfy import regulations of foreign countries, indicating that a shipment has been inspected and is free from harmful pests and plant diseases.

piggybacking   The assigning of export marketing and distribution functions by one manufacturer to another.

port marks   See *marks*.

pre-export finance   Terminology of U.S. bankers for a loan to an exporter to finance the accumulation of materials, the manufacture, assembly, production, packaging, and transport of physical goods to fulfill an export order. Commonly guaranteed by EXIMBank or SBA Working Capital Guarantee programs.

presentation period   Time allowed after issue of transport document to present documents under an L/C.

presenting bank   Bank in a documentary collection process presenting export documents to the drawee for payment. The exporter and the presenting bank behave in a principal/agent relationship, and it is therefore wise for the uncertain exporter to ensure that the collection is presented by some bank other than the importer's bank.

procuring agent   See *purchasing agent*.

pro forma invoice   A provisional invoice written by the seller which serves as a quotation to the buyer. Following negotiations, the exporter issues this document which confirms product details, prices, shipping, and payment terms. This is the starting point for further documentation.

purchasing agent   An agent who purchases goods in his or her own country on behalf of large foreign buyers such as government agencies and large private concerns.

quota   The total quantity of a product or commodity that may be imported into a country. Usually quotas protect a domestic market. In the United States, sugar, wheat, cotton, tobacco, textiles, and apparel are governed by quotas.

quotation   An offer to sell goods at a stated price and under stated terms.

rate of exchange   The basis upon which money of one country will be exchanged for that of another. Rates of exchange are established and quoted for foreign currencies on the basis of the demand, supply, and stability of the individual currencies. See *exchange*.

received for shipment bill of lading   Bill of lading indicating goods received for shipment (but not "onboard"). Unacceptable B/L unless specifically allowed by the letter of credit or unless it is marked "onboard" with a date and signature.

recourse   Payment with recourse means that the paying party retains the right to the funds in the event that reimbursement (from another party) is not forthcoming. An important concept in trade finance.

red clause letter of credit   An L/C allowing the beneficiary to draw down an advance payment prior to shipment, usually against presentation of a simple receipt. So called because traditionally it was written in red ink, the purpose of this clause is to finance the seller during the preparation of the export order. The applicant will be liable for any drawings even if goods are never shipped. This is one reason why importers should expect red clause L/Cs to be collateralized differently from plain import L/Cs.

reimbursing bank   The bank empowered by the issuing bank (i.e., with a bank balance) to charge the account of the issuing bank and to pay to the bank collecting funds under a letter of credit.

remitting bank   Exporter's bank in a documentary collection process taking export documents and sending them to a correspondent in the country of the importer (the drawee in the collection process).

representative   An individual or firm that acts on behalf of a supplier. The word "representative" is preferred to the word "agent" in writing since agent, in an exact legal sense, connotes more binding powers and responsibilities than representative. See also *foreign sales representative*.

revocable   An adjective attached to an L/C indicating that it can be altered or canceled after the buyer has opened the L/C through his or her bank. Compare to *irrevocable*.

revolving letter of credit   L/C that reinstates automatically. It may revolve in relation to time or value, the latter being cumulative or noncumulative.

royalty payment   The share of the product or profit paid by a licensee to a licensor. See *licensing*.

SA   societé anonyme. French expression for a corporation.

S/D   See *sight draft*.

sales agent   See *foreign sales representative*.

sales representative   See *foreign sales representative*.

sanitary certificate   A certificate that attests to the purity or absence of disease or pests in a shipment of food products, plants, seeds, and live animals.

shipper's documents   Commercial invoices, bills of lading, insurance certificates, consular invoices, and related documents.

shipper's letter of credit   An L/C issued by the exporter to the freight forwarder. It covers key details of the transaction, shipping terms, and other applicable instructions that the freight forwarder must follow.

ship's manifest   A true list in writing of the individual shipments comprising the cargo of a vessel, signed by the captain.

SIC   See *Standard Industrial Classification*.

sight draft (S/D)   A draft drawn so as to be payable upon presentation to the drawee or at a fixed or determinable date thereafter. See *documents against acceptance* and *documents against payment*.

SITC   See *Standard International Trade Classification*.

specific delivery point   A point in sales quotations which designates specifically where and within what geographical locale the goods will be delivered at the expense and responsibility of the seller; for example, FAS (named vessel) at (named port of export).

spot exchange   The purchase or sale of foreign currency, usually against an equivalent amount of local currency, for immediate delivery (e.g., within two working days after the agreement).

Standard Industrial Classification (SIC)   A numeric system developed by the U.S. government for the classification of commercial services and industrial products. SIC also classifies establishments by type of activity.

Standard International Trade Classification (SITC)   A numeric system developed by the United Nations to classify commodities used in international trade and in reporting trade statistics.

standby letter of credit   An L/C popular in the United States that guarantees payment in the event of nonperformance by the applicant. Similar in method to commercial letters of credit and subject to UCP 500 but different in three significant aspects: (1) beneficiary's statement or claim of default suffices to draw (in contrast to a pile of detailed export documents under commercial L/C), (2) discrepancy rate is between low and zero, (3) expect banks to collateralize standby L/Cs somewhat differently from commercial L/Cs (i.e., 100 percent).

state-controlled trading company   In a country with a state trading monopoly, a trading entity empowered by the country's government to conduct export business.

steamship conference   A group of vessel operators joined together for the purpose of establishing freight rates. A shipper may receive reduced rates if the shipper enters into a contract to ship on vessels of conference members only.

steamship guarantee   A guarantee issued by a bank to a steamship line against financial loss arising from the release of a consignment without the appropriate transport document. Popular because goods frequently arrive at the port of discharge before documents are available to clear them.

stocking distibutor   A distributor that maintains an inventory of goods of a manufacturer.

straight bill of lading   A B/L consigned directly to a party who holds title to the goods. Straight B/Ls are discomforting to bankers if the consignee party is not the bank. A straight B/L cannot be endorsed to another party. See also *negotiable bill of lading*.

swap arrangements   A form of countertrade in which the seller sells on credit and then transfers the credit to a third party.

SWIFT   Society for Worldwide Interbank Financial Telecommunication. A cooperative owned by a consortium of banks designed to carry formatted messages between them in a secure environment. The messages all relate to financial transactions between banks and their customers.

switch arrangements   A form of countertrade in which the seller sells on credit and then transfers the credit to a third party.

tare weight   The weight of packing and containers without the goods to be shipped.

tariff schedule   A schedule or system of duties imposed by a government on goods imported or exported; the rate of duty imposed in a tariff.

tenor   The time fixed or allowed for payment, as in "the tenor of a draft."

TEU   Twenty-foot equivalent unit. A measurement of cargo based on a standard ocean shipment container, which is 20 feet in length.

through bill of lading   A single bill of lading covering both the domestic and international carriage of an export shipment. An air waybill, for instance, is essentially a through bill of lading used for air shipments. Ocean shipments, on the other hand, usually require two separate documents—an inland bill of lading for domestic carriage and an ocean bill of lading for international carriage. Through bills of lading, therefore, cannot be used for ocean carriage. See also *air waybill, inland bill of lading,* and *ocean bill of lading.*

time draft   A draft drawn so as to mature at a certain fixed time after presentation or acceptance.

trade acceptance   A time draft in which the drawee signs the word "accepted" across the face and thus commits to pay the holder upon maturity. The instrument will be as valuable as the creditworthiness of the accepting party allows.

trade development program (TDP)   A program designed to promote economic development in the third world and the sale of U.S. goods and services to these developing countries. It operates as part of the International Development Cooperative Agency.

trade mission   A mission to a foreign country organized to promote trade through the establishment of contracts and exposure to the commercial environment. Trade missions are frequently organized by federal, state, or local agencies.

tramp steamer   A ship not operating on regular routes or schedules.

transport document   A bill of lading, an air waybill, a truck receipt, any other document acting as a receipt for goods and a contract of carriage. Of all these transport documents, only a bill of lading is a document of title.

transshipment   Shipment of merchandise to destination abroad on more than one vessel. Liability may pass from one carrier to the next, or it may be covered by a through bill of lading issued by the first carrier.

trust receipt   Release of merchandise by a bank to a buyer in which the bank retains title to the merchandise. The buyer, who obtains the goods for manufacturing or sales purposes, is obligated to maintain the goods (or the proceeds from their sale) distinct from the remainder of his or her assets and to hold them ready for repossession by the bank.

turnkey   A method of construction whereby the contractor assumes total responsibility from design through completion.

UCP 500   Uniform Customs and Practice for Documentary Credits, Publication No. 500 of the International Chamber of Commerce. The indisputable authority on letters of credits recognized internationally, UCP 500 serves as the self-regulation of the L/C industry and renders L/Cs a more reliable form of payment. Importers and exporters are advised to be particularly careful of any L/C that does not clearly state (usually in the final paragraph) that it is subect to UCP 500.

unconfirmed letter of credit   A letter of credit that does not carry any confirmation by a second bank, usually located in the country of the beneficiary. Exporters intent on collecting payment under such L/Cs should hold a view as to risk of nonpayment for various reasons.

URC 522   Uniform Rules for Collections, Publication No. 522 of the International Chamber of Commerce. An internationally recognized code for the handling of collections, clean or documentary.

usance   Banker's terminology, in use more commonly overseas than in the United States, indicating time allowed for payment of a bill of exchange (contrast with sight above).

usance draft   More often referred to in the United States as a time draft. See also *documents against acceptance*.

usance letter of credit   Sometimes referred to in the United States as a time L/C.

validated license   A government document authorizing the export of commodities within limitations set forth in the document.

vertical ETC   An export trading company that integrates a range of functions taking products from suppliers to consumers.

visa   A signature of formal approval on an entree document. Obtained from a consulate.

WA   With average. A marine insurance term meaning that a shipment is protected from partial damage whenever the damage exceeds a given percentage.

warehouse receipt   A receipt issued by a warehouse listing goods received for storage.

wharfage   Charge assessed by the carrier for the handling of incoming or outgoing ocean cargo.

without reserve   A term indicating that a shipper's agent or representative is empowered to make definitive decisions and adjustments abroad without approval of the group individual represented. Compare *advisory capacity*.

Internet Glossary

Don't be intimidated by Web jargon. Here, in simple English, are explanations of some basic terms you will encounter as you wander on the Web.

applet   A small program or application, usually written in java (see *java*) language. Applets run on your browser and power most of the fancier features, from animations to calculators.

bandwidth   Measures the amount of information that can be transmitted over a connection. The lower the bandwidth, the slower the downloading of material, especially pictures. (Slang: A person with low bandwidth is slow on the uptake.) A very high bandwidth connection is known as a *broadband connection*.

blog   A Web log, which is usually shortened to *blog*, is a type of Web site where entries are made (such as in a journal or diary), displayed in a reverse chronological order. Blogs often provide commentary or news on a particular subject, such as food, politics, or local news; some function as more personal online diaries. A typical blog combines text, images, and links to other blogs, Web pages, and other media related to a topic. Most blogs are primarily textual although many focus on photographs (photoblog), videos (vlog), or audio (podcasting).

bookmark   A direct link to an often-visited site that you've saved on your browser for easy access.

bot   Short for *robot*. Performs a function on the Web automatically or electronically. A site that seeks out the cheapest prices for clothes is a shopping bot.

browser   Program that allows you to interact with the World Wide Web. Examples include Netscape Navigator and Microsoft Explorer.

cache   High-speed memory that your computer sets aside to store frequently accessed data.

chat room   A variation on the message board. A site for live, online conversation. Occasionally useful but usually rife with misinformation and inane chatter.

cookie   The programming code from a Web site you visit that is stored on your computer. Visit the site later, and the cookie is sent back to the Web site to remind it of your preferences.

cyberspace   A general term for the Internet and anything else online. Attach "cyber" to a business description, and you've got a hot stock.

domain name   Unique name that identifies a Web site (see *URL*).

download   To go online and bring a file from where you are into your own computer. The opposite of *upload*.

hacker   The robbers of the Internet highway. Some are crooks, others just annoying pranksters. They use their computers to gain unauthorized access to networks and protected Web servers.

hits   How many visits a Web site gets, no matter how brief they are. Leading portal Yahoo! has 37 million hits a month.

home page   A Web site's main or central page, or, alternatively, the page that appears on your browser when you log on.

HTML   Stands for *hypertext markup language*, the programming language for most Web pages.

hyperlink   Or just plain *link* (to another site). Usually appears underlined and in a different color. Click on one, and you're transported to another Web page.

ISP   Stands for *Internet service provider*. Organizations that charge monthly fees for providing Internet access. Examples include AOL and Earthlink.

java   A programming language from Sun Microsystems that is used to create applets.

message board   A place where people can post, read, and respond to messages written by other users.

plug-in   Add-on program that enhances the capabilities of your Web browser, such as the ability to hear live audio feeds and see live video clips; for instance, RealPlayer and Shockwave.

server   Computer that controls a network of computers or powers a Web site. Lots of Web traffic slows servers down, even for those that have a fast Internet connection.

snail mail   Mail delivered by the U.S. Postal Service.

spam   Unwanted e-mail advertisements or solicitations. Too much electronic spam can clog your e-mail in-box and slow everything down to a crawl.

streaming   Audio or video that plays on your computer while being transmitted over the Web. Example: live tickers or radio broadcasts.

surf   Overused Web term that describes the action of moving from one Web site to another to another to another.

URL   Stands for *universal resource locator*, the Internet address you enter into your browser window. Most begin with "http://www." and end with ".com" (commercial sites), ".gov" (government sites), and ".edu" (educational sites).

virus   A program usually hidden in a file or e-mail that infects your computer by altering or deleting files.

INDEX

ABOUT THE AUTHOR

Dr. Carl Nelson has more than 45 years of global experience in government and private business and has authored seven books in the field of international business and trade.

As a former U.S. Navy captain, business executive, and specialist in international trade, Dr. Nelson has traveled the world. He lived for two years in Japan and one year in South Vietnam, and he is intimately knowledgeable of Europe, Hawaii, South Korea, Hong Kong, Australia, New Zealand, Philippines, India, and the Indian Ocean area. His experience includes third world economic development under the U.S. Agency for International Development (USAID) and California/Mexico NAFTA and Maquiladora operations.

As a professional writer, Dr. Nelson has published fiction and non-fiction books, many short stories, articles, and technical papers. His nonfiction works include *Global Success*, *Managing Globally*, *Exporting*, *Protocol for Profit*, *International Business*, and *Winning the Trade Game*. His novel *The Advisor (Cô-Vân)* was published in 1999 by Turner and was the 1989 winner of the best fiction award at the first Southern California Writer's Conference. His second novel, *Secret Players*, was awarded best political thriller by the San Diego Book Awards Association, and a third novel, *Madam President and the Admiral*, was a finalist for the National Best Book Award and has been nominated for a Pulitzer.

He is professor of international business at the California International Business University (CIBU), San Diego, where he teaches graduate-level courses.

Dr. Nelson is a graduate of the U.S. Naval Academy at Annapolis, Maryland, and earned his Doctorate in Business Administration (DBA), Finance (emphasis on international finance and trade) from the Aliant/United States International University (USIU) in San Diego, California. He is also a graduate of the Naval War College and holds a Master of Science degree in management (economics/systems analysis) from the Naval Post Graduate School in Monterey, California. In 1989 he was recognized by USIU with its outstanding alumni award, and in 2003 he was recognized with the Distinguished Global Educator award from CIBU.

Dr. Nelson is listed in the *2006 Who's Who in America, 2006 Who's Who in American Education, 2007 Who's Who in the World*, and *1984 Who's Who in California*.